Library of Philosophy

LP25: Influence

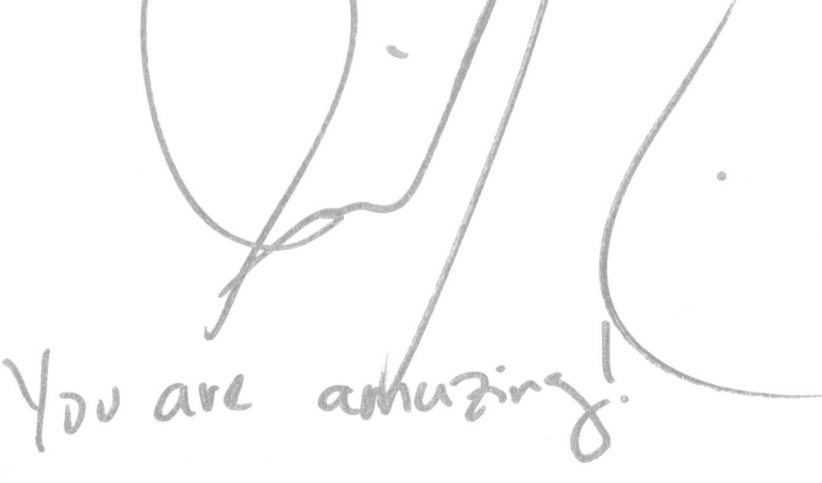

You are amazing!

Copyright © 2012 by J. M. Richardson

RICHARDSON

This book is dedicated to my loving family and to you, my reader pursuing success.

LP25: Influence

Preface

The Journey

About the Book and the Author's Intention

The language in this book began in my sophomore year at the Georgia Institute of Technology as an undergraduate student. I believe that Georgia Tech instills within its students a remarkable competence in solving complex problems. Georgia Tech is also great at enkindling a spirit to innovate on campus. While many students from Georgia Tech are successful by most measures, it is my hope that the brilliant colleagues I encounter could assert their unique ideas through understanding the psychology of others and themselves. The truth about your communication: its manner stems from a subconscious place that reflects how you perceive yourself and your own capabilities. Lacking communication skills usually indicates a deep-seeded doubt in one's own sense of self-worth or self-importance. My intention is that this book will create an opportunity to help individuals take their ideas from solution to implementation.

As the author of this book, I have experienced many ups and downs both personally and vicariously. Most of the stories transcribed in this book are the result of candid conversations with those down on their luck and those who have traveled to the heights of the wheel of fortune. The philosophy in this book is predicated on the teachings of a broad panoply of literature. Influences from religions, concepts from various philosophers, biographies of the wealthy, and the lessons of the criminalized are all put into perspective in this Library of Philosophy 25 Week Curriculum. Compiling this collection has helped in the development of my character and increased my determination to achieve my own place in the world. It is therefore my wish that this book will aid you as you begin your journey.

While the sources contributing to this book may be vast, much of what you will read is not an introduction to something new. It will, however, be presented in a way that may be more useful to you in your daily routines. One thing to keep in mind is that ideas that are genuinely true have never been false. They may have been perceived to be false at certain times, but they were never truly false. Using this metric for the content in this book, I have tried to identify and explain things that are true.

Realize that it is not enough to simply know what you want in life, or have what you need to accomplish it. Knowing yourself precedes any of these things. Knowing yourself offers you the opportunity to prepare for life's hurdles. How you see yourself, and the value that you bring to the world will ultimately establish what you will fully become and your contentment. This kind of journey requires much time, but achieving great success requires time, patience, and the ability to recognize the right opportunities. Once you complete this book, you will find it difficult to take your life experiences for granted. There may be portions of the book that seem too blunt or too esoteric, but it is my hope to expose you to all kinds of ways of thinking so that when you actually encounter them, you will be prepared. For the purpose of this book, power, control, manipulation, empowerment, skill, and impartation are all synonyms of each other. This means that you should not focus on the connotation that chosen words have in this book, but rather the meaning of the statement of which they are a part. Before continuing this book, take notice that each word is used for its denoted meaning and not meant to advocate any particular philosophy.

This book is meant to assist you in your journey. In order for this book to be effective, there are five distinct parts and five sections in each part. Within each section there are many points with quoted testimonies from other pieces of literature. Ensuing the testimonies will be metaphors and explanations. Interspersed throughout the text are quizzes.

These quizzes are meant to be of a reflective quality and to aid in internalizing the content of each section. They can be utilized within the physical space provided, or copied and customized by way of size or category for your usage. To gain the most from the content in this book, it is highly encouraged that you customize each of the quizzes to your unique circumstances.

Part One, "Dreams of the Goal", discourses on framing. It is important to define the lens through which you look at your life and the lives of others. The more you understand about your lenses, the more you can predict yourself and others. It will help you determine your consequent actions for a given circumstance. This part begins by defining leadership and the act of leading. It ends by taking a moment to consider what the future may have to offer and the skills and tools you may have when working towards your future.

The summaries are below:

Dreams of the Goal

The title of this theme came from the notion that you should be able to clearly visualize (from beginning to end) your destination. This theme has chapters that focus on what a big picture looks like and how to go about identifying how a singular purpose or role fits into a larger one.

Chapter One: Roles of Leadership

The purpose of this chapter is to identify what is important with regards to leadership, the motivations required to have maximum success, and to demonstrate what plays a part in determining your leadership activities.

Chapter Two: Moments of Leadership

This chapter demonstrates that leadership is the sum of a series of moments that require leadership. The description of leadership follows directly from the previous chapter. The chapter goes on to explore how your overall leadership abilities are affected by those moments, and the manner in which they should be perceived.

there may be ways to create checkpoints and recognize when goals have been accomplished. This chapter explores what a plan looks like and some of the qualities that it should have.

Chapter Ten: Responsibility

Responsibility is comprised of two words which are response and ability. This simply implies that you must be able to adapt, flow, and respond in order to approach success. This chapter explores what influences your ability to respond and to adapt.

Part Three, "The Transition Stage", discusses the process of communicating your strengths and ideas to others. Communication is perhaps the most important aspect to accomplishing anything. Imagine finding a book which possesses the answers to all things in the world: cures to our incurable diseases and the future. Imagine, however, that you could not read it. In that light, the book renders itself to be absolutely useless, and so are its ideas. This also true for people who are misunderstood or not understood at all. They render themselves absolutely useless, and their ideas will never be utilized by any effort offered on their part.

The summaries are below:

Transition Stage

This theme is meant to describe the process of communicating your thoughts to another person, and to gauge how another person is interpreting your communication.

Chapter Eleven: Internal to External

The purpose of this chapter is to identify what stimulates your own thoughts about communication. It is also meant to help you synthesize full concepts, and then deliver those thoughts to someone else. This is particularly important for networking. Realize that when you speak, you are revealing more than the words you say.

Chapter Twelve: Voice

In this chapter the goal is to understand what control must be exercised with your voice. Imagine three situations: a silent man, a talkative man, and a man who evaluates his surroundings and targets his words. All three will cause you to arrive at a different opinion of the aforementioned man. How you use your voice will help you direct the opinion that is formed about you.

Chapter Thirteen: Energy

"Energy" is all about how information can flow from one entity to another. In this case, energy describes how your communication is packaged. Your feelings regarding a certain subject are conveyed in a message's physical delivery. It also discusses how connected everyone is to everything that exists and that all things at some point may be, at the least, perceived.

Chapter Fourteen: Communication

Communication is an art that is ultimately going to determine the results of how someone else responds to what you may be saying. This segment describes how to communicate and what you should communicate.

Chapter Fifteen: Effect

The effect is the end result of all the communication from one to another that occurs. The "Effect" chapter deals with achieving the most from your communication.

Part Four, "And the Puzzle- Emergent Properties", explores channeling the special effects of working with or within a group. It is important to channel the energy of the group into a direction that is organized, manageable, and effective.

The summaries are below:

And the Puzzle- Emergent Properties

Emergent properties are hard to predict by analyzing the small parts of a larger functioning thing. An emergent property is a property which a collection or complex system has, but which the individual members do not have. An example is the relationship between a living entity and carbon atoms. A failure to realize that a property is emergent, will lead to the fallacy of division- that the individual parts must possess the capability of the sum of the parts. Emergent properties are, however, evident and obligatory. It is important to be able to gauge and target these emergent properties especially when it comes to group dynamics.

Chapter Sixteen: The Whole Piece of the Puzzle

Identifying how you can work with others is very important to overall success since each person is equipped with his/her own special talents and abilities. By working together and properly managing emergent properties, a product has the potential to be greater, more comprehensive, and unpredictably more beneficial. Emergent properties should be encouraged by you when working in a group, and this segment discusses how to accomplish that.

Chapter Seventeen: Necessary to Serve

The mindset you should have when establishing and executing a task is that the task is ultimately meant to serve some greater purpose. Every individual should employ this mindset in their team. Having the mindset of "serving" allows for certain creative elements to flourish and of course, for the identification of a specific role priming an optimal environment for emergent properties.

Chapter Eighteen: Dalton's Theory

There is no empty space. This literally means no person is meant to singularly occupy space. Every person has a specific contribution to make and it should be valued when this contribution is discovered. This segment is an analogy prescribed by the scientific theory attributed to Dalton.

Chapter Nineteen: Aggregate Resources

This chapter is based on the Theory of Abundance. It is a mindset that the world is infinite and that much of it is a matter of trade. The possessions of an individual continue beyond his or her familiar environment but incorporate the entire world as the market. It is a difficult concept to grasp and put to practice, but many successful people simply believed it and so their limitations were much fewer than those who did not.

Chapter Twenty: The Whole Picture Part 2

This chapter focuses on your reflection of everything discussed in previous chapters and prepares you for the next theme. Try to get a good look at how you are working within all of your groups and how those groups play their roles in society.

Part Five, "Community Activism", examines the process of accomplishing goals. Much consideration should be applied to what you intend to actually accomplish. This theme explores what it means to be active in your community. Community in this sense is all-inclusive (from your personal life to the world).

The summaries are below:

Community Activism

Community activism in this sense is broad. It simply means being active in the community. It may be for business, school, charity, or any other activity deemed as an interest.

Chapter Twenty-One: Differentiation, Purpose, and Talents

As mentioned before, each person in a group has a specific role and group work is involved in discovering those roles. This segment contends that there must be a separation of roles in order to prevent confusion and promote responsibility. Use your designated project as the context for this chapter.

Chapter Twenty-Two: Cogito Ergo Sum

"I think, therefore I am," is part of an old axiom. The adage continues to be that we are because you are and you are because we are. This chapter discusses the significance of an individual being an active thinker. When someone is able to think, by default, they become important. They can be influenced or influence others, and that concept is fundamental to the functionality of any group or individual activity.

Chapter Twenty-Three: I and Me

This chapter references a previous mention that an individual is a divided entity. There exists the component that creates with the mind and feels, and the component that creates within a substantial world, with substantial meaning. It is the full circle of creating something composed of matter.

Chapter Twenty-Four: What

The compelling statement here is "What are you going to do?" You are nearing the end of the entire curriculum and it is now important to consider what you are going to accomplish. You can put all of the things you have discovered and created into practice. Determining the "what" is easier than you may believe.

Chapter Twenty-Five: Methodology

Now that you have determined what you want to do, come up with a plan for execution. Remember the qualities of "The Plan" and "Concentrate your Forces" in order to really get started.

The book was compiled in a manner that would allow you to really be aware that both leadership and personal development take time and involve a process of evolution. There are stages, but the stages may involve different things for different people. I have confidence that this book will meet you halfway, regardless of how you may look at life. Remember that it takes time and focus to reach your goals, and that advice can be fitting for whatever you may be pursuing.

As for the completion of this book, acknowledgement should be extended to the many staff members at the Georgia Institute of Technology who assisted in the development and editing of this book. Mr. Len Contardo of the Alumni Association and Dr. Wesley Wynens of the LEAD office are two major proponents for the successful distribution of this book. Acknowledgment should also be given to the co-founders of GTStartUp, Parul Kapur, Sean McGee, Jeremy Feaster, Manimala Karusala, Elizabeth Blumer, Parker Vascik, Jasmine Lawrence, and Timothy Lin. They have all contributed meaningful additions to the curriculum associated with this book. Further acknowledgment is extended to the Sosumaritans of Society of Step who allowed for the initial teaching of this curriculum. It was through them that I developed my confidence in its content and felt the need to share it with the world. The book's structure was inspired by Pastor Bryan E. Crute of Destiny Metropolitan Worship Church. My initial journey to create the original curriculum began with the seeds of wisdom planted by Vanguard Leadership Group. Editing credits are extended to my mother, Valerie Richardson and to my friend, Gregory Philips. My father, Willie Richardson is recognized for his time and resources in positioning this book for a successful journey. I am grateful for the continued contribution of encouragement and support from my brothers Rico and Galen, and my grandparents, Nancy and Willie C. Richardson, and Doris and Leonard Schexnayder.

I would like to thank my family, friends, and community, in both my New Orleans area and Atlanta area bases, for their love and continued support.

LP25: Influence

Part One Introduction

Dreams of the Goal

Figuratively, a dream represents some of your greatest desires for success. This theme is about dreaming of your goals. You should be able to clearly visualize, from beginning to end, where you want to go. This theme has segments that focus on how a big picture can be crafted and how to go about identifying how a singular purpose or role fits into a larger one.

Lifting your eyes to the horizon will always benefit you because you will be able to anticipate impending circumstances and properly prepare for them. They may help you, hinder you, or do nothing at all; but you will know how to gauge them, direct them, and properly respond to them if you keep looking forward. What does this mean in a practical sense? It means having awareness about your surroundings and an understanding of other people. Perhaps you would like to become an engineer, a doctor, an entrepreneur, or work in one among many other important jobs that will supply a steady foundation for you and a sense of job security. When you are considering a potential career track, it is imperative to keep in mind the prospective qualities of the job as there are many careers that had once existed just to vanish thirty years later. Also, take note as to whether or not you are willing to make the sacrifices needed to succeed in that particular career. If you are not, chances are, it is not something you actually want to pursue. Part One focuses on helping you identify and define what it means to have a career and what sacrifices are necessary. Truth is that you most likely do not realize that you already have all of the answers, but now, it is time to be honest and diligent about your present and your future. When you dream of your goals, you partake in the process of making them a reality because you will have made the dream as realistic as possible.

There are many inspirational quotes you can gather from different sources. Wealthy and wise leaders of humankind's past have all offered many. Pick one that describes who you are, and make it your motto. Keep that motto in mind as you read the next five chapters. It will keep your spirits high and you will begin to place context to each of the following pointers.

Chapter One

Roles of Leadership

The purpose of this chapter is to identify what is important with regards to leadership, the motivations required to have maximum success, and to demonstrate what plays a part in determining your leadership activities.

Roles of Leadership

Note: "What is a leader? I see it as the biggest multitasker on the team. The leader has to do a number of things efficiently and effectively." (Young Leader)

Yes, being skilled in multi-tasking is an important quality to embrace. As you go through life, many affairs are going to require your attention. Your friends and family, schooling, extra-curricular activities, career, community service, and of course yourself will all have a share of being on your list of preoccupations. Within each of these categories, there are different considerations. At any job, you may be required to answer phones, schedule meetings, maintain great working relationships, complete your tasks and or goals, find ways to improve your work performance, and tend to your health so that you can be physically prepared for your job. Anyone who says that multi-tasking is unnecessary is a part of another world. Especially as we move into a more connected and technologically savvy society, multitasking is a skill that you might as well accept as a necessary part of life. The caveat with multitasking is not being able to understand the tricks to doing it well, and what should and should not be multitasked.

As a leader, which we will define, it is also important that you understand there will be many influences and facets to your success.

The operational definitions for this chapter are below:

Leadership is deemed as the position or function of a leader. A leader has the ability to lead. Leadership is an act or instance of leading, guidance, and providing direction.

Effectiveness has several important meanings including an actual operation or force; the effort adequate to accomplish a purpose or producing the intended or expected result; it also means to produce a deep or vivid impression; it means to be prepared and available for service.

Efficiency is a notion that can only be discussed when considering the amount of effort invested. It is the ratio that exists between the energy developed versus the energy invested. In the definition of leadership, note that leadership is identified as the position or function of a leader.

'Leading' for the purposes of this chapter, means guiding or moving in a particular direction. So putting the two together, when you are in the function of guiding, then you are, in effect, leading. When you offer advice as a friend, a consultant, or head of an organization, you are leading. You are using tools of communication and products of your own thoughts to try to convince yourself or another person of a belief. When a group of people are seated in one room, each one assumes a specific position, usually self-determined. The interactions that follow are the manifestations of these self-determined roles, and a good leader understands how these interactions are related to what each person thinks and believes.

The second proposed definition is that of effectiveness. Create a mindset that if your leadership is to portray effectiveness, then it must be operational. It must actually produce an intentional effect. Intentional effectiveness is rooted in the idea that there is a certain amount of premeditation to your actions. If you are not intentional in your actions, then you will find yourself encountering a series of seemingly unpredictable circumstances. While it may be a fun way to experience your life, it is not a good method to use if you are trying to be effective. It is actually quite ineffective, and you will lose the confidence of others if you are leading a team. The definition also describes effective as producing a deep or vivid image. This should be your way of measuring your effectiveness. Are you able to communicate and deliver an idea with a lasting impression? The views that leave an impression on us are usually provocative in nature and appeal to the basic human sense of love, hope, or fear.

Finally, the definition introduces the idea of servant leadership. As a leader, you are subject to your decisions. Your decision to participate or disengage, or to move east or west will ultimately paint the picture of your leadership. To what degree do you acknowledge the things to which you are a servant to? Being subject to your decisions means that you understand who and what your decisions affect and that you consider those factors in the decision-making process. Asking questions such as, "Who am I helping?" may begin to open the door to your understanding of your servant leadership.

The final operational definition is efficiency. When determining efficient leadership, take note that initial energy must be offered, otherwise, efficiency cannot be determined. This means you should be ready to work as a leader. You should be willing the think, decide, and execute. Efficiency in engineering terms is the ratio of energy developed to the energy invested or total energy available. Out of what is accessible, what has been produced? Efficiency requires thinking outside of the box. Perhaps developing a new method to accomplish a similar task may accomplish efficiency. Use society's search for a new energy source as an example. Fossil fuels, nuclear, and coal, all produce different efficiencies and their effectiveness considers the consequences for each method's efficiency.

As a leader in the technological age, you should consider a few things...

I. **You are always expected to be a leader.**

Under all circumstances, expect that you will have to be accountable for your actions and the ensuing consequences. Recognize that in all situations, you have made many decisions and consequently have participated in the act of leading. Instead of using the pervasive notion of leading others, use the idea that making decisions is leading. You are leading yourself. When you decide to speak out, it is because you decide that what you have to say is merited. The *choice* to sit back is a choice made by you. An effective leader considers the possible consequences that can occur from a decision and considers what is influencing the decision. An efficient leader then thinks, decides, and acts on what he or she deems is the best route. You must begin at step one, however, and realize that all you do and where you are, is the sum of the many decisions you have made in your life. Taking accountability in that facet will open the door for you to begin identifying the direct causes and effects of those decisions. This is where there is potential for growth and where you can decide to pursue the goals that you dream.

So in all troubles, begin by asking, "What part of it was my fault, and what could I have prevented?" At the end of the day, each person is responsible for his or her own actions. This is not because there is no such thing as being a brother's keeper, rather it has more to do with the idea that most people are concerned with their own well-being, and if they have any energy remaining, they will be concerned for the welfare of others. Relying on the availability of others is not an efficient choice. So now that you are always expected to be a leader, what does that mean in the context of how you think, decide, and execute?

Composure: *"Law 35 -Master the Art of Timing -Never seem to be in a hurry – hurrying betrays a lack of control over yourself, and over time. Always seem patient, as if you know that everything will come to you eventually. Become a detective of the right moment; sniff out the spirit of the times, the trends that will carry you to power. Learn to stand back when the time is not yet ripe, and to strike fiercely when it has reached fruition." (48 laws of Power)*

    A.   <u>Understand your surroundings.</u>

The 48 Laws of Power by Robert Greene is to the point. Composure is an important aspect to your leadership. When you are leading a group or yourself, maintaining a clear and focused mind is going to help you navigate through unfamiliar territory. It is important to not be so distracted by unfamiliarity that you miss what is occurring around you. If you become extraordinarily entangled in the mechanics of your job performance or your academics, you will miss the other opportunities that may enhance your experiences and potentially bolster your career or academic status. If you are in a class and are solely focused on the material that you are learning, without gaining clarity of what is expected, you will place unnecessary and unexpected limitations on your performance. Clarity on placed expectations is just as significant as the knowledge you bring to every test. Not understanding the rules of the classroom is like trying to play chess with Monopoly's rules.

Perhaps you are studying management. By taking advantage of an internship or a mentor in the field, you will gain perspective on what you do in the classroom and vice versa. Perhaps in an office setting, you neglect to meet with your boss and ask him for clarity on some of the expectations. Perhaps you have discounted the value in befriending your co-workers and your boss. Keep in mind that people recommend, hire, and promote those they trust. Knowing the vision of the company you work for will add layers of satisfaction to your job routine. You should reflect on your dreams of the goal. Take the time to consider and understand the job market, people, influences, and opportunities. You will gain a definite advantage in working towards your effective and efficient leadership. Each day the world changes in how it processes information, handles intelligence, and engages in business. You must adapt to multi-tasking at this level. Note, however, that the basic wants and needs of people do not really change. Most people seek to firstly have security for themselves and their families and then secondly to satisfy the ego. You can use this to your advantage and it will help when trying to understand more complex systems. Similarly, the struggle between security and ego may also be a distraction in your personal life, and cause you to lose your composure. When observing your surroundings, keep these things in mind.

Pride and Ignorance: *"A proud spirit, therefore, is deadly to leaders. It will kill their effectiveness ... for it breeds two dreadful diseases of the soul. The first is ignorance. Pride makes a person self-sufficient and unteachable. It blinds them to their own needs. It causes them to ignore the good advice and counsel of others." (Be the Leader You Were Meant to Be)*

    B.   <u>Identify your leadership weakness (es).</u>

This process is the most laborious of them all. How do you go about identifying your weaknesses? Everyone is great at offering the advice, but actually trying to find the weaknesses is another concept all in itself. The quote sets up a great context. Pride and ignorance are two very distracting elements. In life, you will encounter awful circumstances, and you must be willing to learn from each one. You will also have to learn from the experiences that offer you great joy. Train yourself to think about what you are experiencing while you are in the midst of emotional moments. Use your pride to predict the responses of your own ego and the ego of others.

Reflect on the list of what you are prideful about. When others tell you "You are such a great ---- or such a handsome man or woman", do you feel a sense of encouragement? If so, it qualifies as an asset you are prideful about. Make a list of these qualifiers. This is the first half of your list of weaknesses. Keep in mind that at some point, all weaknesses will be used against you. The example above indicates that your vanity is reliant upon another person's subjectivity. There is no shame with it, but by knowing that someone can gain your trust by offering a compliment will help you better sort through another person's motivations in offering a compliment. These vulnerabilities will be used against you. Understanding what you are prideful about opens a window to what others are prideful about, because people function based on similar social cues.

Ignorance is the manifestation of using your own ideals as a comprehensive standard. It is our main way of offering judgment to others. While your convictions may be true and unwavering, they may not be true to someone else, rendering you ignorant to who they are. It allows them to use your own idealistic standards against you. If ignorance is the blind acceptance of your idealistic standards to the exclusion of others, then the words used to describe these standards can be noted as "judgment words". When you use adjectives, they are the judgments you are delivering. Even if they are readily accepted as applicable, they are still judgments, i.e. 'The sky is blue'. Use judgment words to identify your ignorance. You can gain insight into your perspective of the world, as language reflects thoughts. To better understand what this means, you can refer to what takes place in a courtroom. Lawyers spend their time trying to convince a jury of the *innocence* of a client and the *faulty* claims of the other party. They appeal to the jury's sense of justice and mercy. The lawyer uses many judgment words that have been accepted as true. When defending the client, they use judgment words that compel the jury to believe or trust the client. 'Fairness', 'righteousness', and 'justice' are commonly used. Rarely is the list of facts void of any adjectives or words with strong connotations. Lawyers lead the conversation with vividly described images. Perhaps the defendant was *wrongly* hurt, or the *innocent* child should be cleared of all possible punishments. Lawyers appeal to another's ideals; otherwise, they are sure to lose the sentiments of the jury. As for the judge, a good lawyer is also aware of his surroundings and works the system to find the most sympathetic court and the most "fair" judge. Be aware of the judgments you make in your mind and use this as a way to gauge how you think. You can better understand others by identifying their judgments. Identify your judgment words and add them to your list of weaknesses.

Attention: *"Everything is judged by its appearance; what is unseen counts for nothing. Never let yourself get lost in the crowd, then, or buried in oblivion. Stand out. Be conspicuous, at all costs. Make yourself a magnet of attention by appearing larger, more colorful, more mysterious, than the bland and timid masses." (48 Laws of Power)*

    C.   <u>Opportunities are everywhere.</u>

Pay attention to your surroundings. When you are focused, the right opportunities become prominent. When you seize these available opportunities, you draw attention to yourself. While this may present a fear, others will begin to place their trust in you and expect you to live up to certain standards. Keep in mind; however, that this is the way to push progress. Imagine if a person decides they want to help others. If he is never actually affecting others, how can he accomplish what he set out to accomplish? When you are pursuing your goals with fervor and focus, people will recognize it and actually work to make it happen. Many scientists have contributed to our current technological age, but only a few are actually noted for their discoveries, and even fewer have discovered something of use. The others fall into an unacknowledged oblivion. Perhaps you are only in your field for the sake of advancing science or for helping people? Well, to answer your thoughts: to get to the point of helping people, others have to feel that you can actually help them. You can demonstrate this when you have their attention. What would happen to a presidential candidate who received no media attention but wanted to advocate and help design laws that would save the country? How could the candidate accomplish what he or she set out to do if that candidate never took advantage of the systems in place to allow for a successful campaign? Not only does the candidate lose, but he also loses the opportunity to affect the country.

This does not mean that you must sacrifice your own standards or morals to impact the world. In effect, it is a way by which you can take your standards and escalate them to the point where they actually matter. Imagine you are in a crowd of people shouting at one person, and you begin to shout alongside them. Each person is shouting something different. Will the person you are trying to shout to actually be able to discern what you are shouting? On the other hand, you could hold a poster or sign with your words, or find a way to be the only person doing the shouting. Maybe, you can wear a ridiculous outfit that causes the crowd and the listener to spot you. All of these options will yield a different result than simply shouting alongside the crowd. In practice, perhaps your method of standing out in the conventional way is not actually allowing you to function as an individual who brings value to a situation. Rethink the opportunities you have taken advantage of and perhaps how they have brought about the correct attention for you to continue towards success. When applying for law school your application needs to stand out. In a job interview, the employer has to feel he or she trusts you and in order to do that, you have to stand out. Beware that, when it comes to drawing attention to yourself, you must be strategic and careful. The 48 Laws of Power also discusses the importance of guarding your reputation.

Make it your goal to stay ahead of a curve by doing two things: counting your blessings and also paying close attention to trends. As we move into a smaller, more accessible and complex world, the way business is done and ideas get transferred is changing every day. So, maintain a clear mind in recognizing trends in jobs, services, and products. In business school, this kind of forecast is known as the product life cycle. Getting a job selling VCRs may not be lucrative today, but being on the cutting edge of robotics or computer modeling systems may yield substantial monetary gains within the near future. All jobs, services, and products have life cycles. It is your responsibility to understand the cycles and factor them into identifying potential opportunities.

For finding the right opportunities, realize that situations may not be as they seem. How you interpret a situation will guide you to a certain conclusion. When interpreting situations, you can only use the background knowledge you have. The brain functions by developing what are known as schemas. These are patterns or groups that the brain uses so that it can determine how to appropriately respond. How you were raised, your religious or non-religious background, the people you have encountered, the information you have acquired, and what you have been told about your position in society, each affect the schemas you develop. Take the time to identify your schemas in moments of danger, failure, accomplishment, and love. After identifying your schemas, realize that the motivation to pursue and identify opportunities stems from them. There are a few fundamental concepts that should form the foundation of your journey. These are known as standards. They will allow you to determine whether or not you are changing too much. You will have the opportunity to create your own in addition to those introduced in this chapter, and embody them as principles in later chapters.

Standards: *Allow each day to present me with a learning experience.*
Remain receptive to all points of view because truth is embedded in everything.
Continuously mold myself into becoming my best.
Carry myself with dignity.
Accept the consequences of my actions.
Resume responsibility for my character.
Love my fellow man/woman.
Distract my attention from gossip and stereotypes.
Believe in the greatest ability of myself and others.
Become a role model for my community.

D. <u>Expect yourself to live up to the Standards of Leadership.</u>

The Standards of Leadership listed are meant to provide a starting ground for your standards that you will create. These are open and vague enough to begin.

Allowing each day to present a new learning experience is vital to your growth. You encounter new information and perspectives every day. Do not take these for granted. Remember that you are encountering this experience for a reason. There exists an opportunity to grow, you just have to be focused enough to recognize it.

Remain receptive to all points of view because truth is embedded in everything. This principle is a bit tricky. It does not mean that everything should be recognized as true. It implies that everything is true for someone. In any given statement, even within a lie, there is truth in discovering the intention of the lie. The fact that a person lies indicates that other unapparent thoughts occurring compel the person to decide to lie. Therefore, that individual had to accept certain beliefs as true for them to arrive at lying to be the most viable and acceptable option. In essence, it means that people only do things once they have justified it for themselves. Understanding that and how it affects judgments will create room for freedom in your ability to predict and engage others- especially when it comes to their needs.

Continuously molding yourself into becoming your best means that you should have no moment of true boredom. If you constantly evaluate and reflect upon your weaknesses and the new experiences life creates for you, you will see yourself evolve. By using this as a standard, you will find that each day will bring about a different and more refined "you". So, in your studies, try to identify the habit you could enhance or avoid. If there is something you wish you did more of, just do it. Of course, it takes more than just verbally deciding to change. You have to focus on your motivations and determine why you do or do not do something. By starting at this point, you can then change your habits.

Carry yourself with dignity. This is imperative. You should be poised in your decisions and should live with little to no regret. Hindsight is 20/20, but in the moment, you made the best decision you could have possibly made. You should definitely reflect on preventing poor decisions and acknowledge when you have wronged someone, but be sure to maintain your sense of dignity with your admission.

Accept the consequences of your actions. This really goes without saying. Once you grasp the idea that you are expected to be a leader, the next step is to recognize how your decisions result in multiple outcomes. You should fully accept the consequences. You should be aware of your shortcomings, faults, and ignorance, as you will ultimately be indebted to them. If you do not have the tenacity to be responsible, even if it is secretly, you will never learn from others. You will find yourself repeating the same errors many times over.

Resume responsibility for your character. The implication using the word "resume" is that taking responsibility for an error is a process. Even within the circumstance of a mistake, you must continue to take responsibility for your character. As for your character, you must know what makes you quick to anger, extremely happy, or insatiably jealous. Then, you must take full responsibility for your shortcomings. Errors are not just in an action, but are also in your personality. It behooves you to become familiar with these flaws and embrace them and understand where they come from so that you can begin your refinement process.

Love your fellow man/woman. Under all circumstances, you should respect other people. Every individual is comprised of desirable and undesirable qualities. Taking the moment to understand another individual will do more wonders than any form of coercion. Understanding someone does not indicate that you agree with their stance. It simply means that you are able to determine the judgments and rationalizations that a person used to arrive at their state. Respect is a very high form of love, and you will gain access to your dreams by offering it to others.

Distract your attention from gossip and stereotypes. Participating in these activities will always end up with someone getting hurt. Most likely, that someone will be you. Gossip and stereotypes, in this list, are classified as false statements or fallible conclusions that are used to identify or categorize others. By using false statements or fallible conclusions, you will be led to a false sense of confidence and any invested work will prove to be ineffective. Do not confuse causation with correlation when it comes to classifying others.

Believe in the greatest ability of yourself and others. Hope for the best, but prepare for the worst. You should not rely on others to actually perform to impress you, but rather to satisfy their own egos. When someone does not perform up to their potential, believe that the person has the capability to perform but has not been properly incentivized or placed in the appropriate situation. With this mindset, you can see where your shortcomings are and also how to garner the most out of your leadership.

Finally, become a role model for your community. When others encounter you, an archetype should come to their minds. How you are perceived, how you look, and your brand, should deliver the same message. For whichever activities you are engaged in, aim to become the model for that activity. This is how it should be done. Keep in mind that while others may not be inclined to help you, they are still watching you, and gathering information about what to do. So, to add the altruistic flair to this entire curriculum, make sure you are setting a standard that is good for the world, and not bad for the world. It will be the last impression you give when you go to the grave. Your mark will leave an empty mold for someone else to occupy.

These standards are suggested mainly because the tools and tricks that are discussed in this book can be used to really benefit the world, but may also cause undue harm. The tools of leadership are neutral, but the intentions behind your actions will ultimately influence the outcomes. Follow the standards of leadership.

II.   **If you are a leader, then you have followers.**

This may be the oft most forgotten part of leadership. There are people following you. If you are leading yourself, then you are also following your own decisions. That is what it means to follow your own path, or make your own life. You define how you will live by your decisions. Taking the time to really understand your followers and your ability to follow will help in matters of rebellion, development, and achievement. There are some very important characteristics to being a follower and being a leader with followers.

Hierarchy: *"This principle embodies the truth that there is always a correspondence between the laws and phenomena of the various planes of Being and Life. The old Hermetic axiom ran in these words: 'As above, so below; as below, so above'."* (Kybalion)

A.   Followers will mimic their leaders.

The Kybalion can be quite esoteric in its explanations of worldly things, but the basic premise is that the parts of the whole, to some extent, exemplify the whole. If an organization is viewed as a moving body, much can be learned about the leaders by speaking with the followers. Much can be learned about the followers when a discussion is prompted with the leaders. When there is a disconnection between the leaders and the followers, it further provides insight into the kind of leadership the person at the top possesses. We also deem the organization 'disorganized' because of the dissonance. As for the quote, it plays on the idea that in the same way dysfunction and success occurs on lower levels, it also occurs at higher levels. Smaller organizations combat the same issues that larger organizations do. The difference is in the scale and the complexity. The unforeseen elements to this kind of evaluation are emergent properties. These are properties that are specifically properties of the entire structure, but are not displayed by the individual elements of the structure. Much will be said about this Correspondence Principle in later chapters. With regards to this chapter, it is important to keep in mind that when accomplishing something well, hierarchy becomes a pivotal aspect to strategic implementation. Each person has a role and while roles should be of equal importance, they do not share the same burdens of responsibility nor do they consist of similar method or volume of work.

Imagine a child learning to walk, which words to say, or facial expressions to make. The child takes cues from the parents. Did that person smile and make me feel good? I should do it again. Did that action give me a response I liked? I should do it again! It really is as simple as that interaction. We read social cues to determine whether or not something is acceptable. This is important because in part it allows others to feel comfortable around you. We are comfortable with things we can expect or predict. Change presents potential unknown variables and may result in our dissatisfaction. When dealing with people on small and large levels, this is true. The scale is different, and so some customs may be altered, but for the most part, we mimic those to whom we must answer.

Imitation is the highest form of flattery. Every person longs to feel some form of acceptance and belonging because humans are social creatures. If a person shows no want for acceptance, then there are perhaps other considerations that need to be made. Having the leader, parent, or boss acknowledge their work is very much craved by most people. In this light, when followers "mimic" their leaders, it is usually for attention or acknowledgment. This is true on any level of the hierarchy. Even the CEO of a company must answer to his shareholders. When the JP Morgan CEO and Chairman could not account for a large amount of lost money, not only did shareholders want answers, but the public wanted some sense of accountability to be forced into the banking industry. When you shame your boss(es), you put yourself at risk for losing their respect and loyalty. Rebellion is imminent, as it will be fueled both by the need to satisfy the ego and by the need to be secure.

Loyalty: *"Work on the Hearts and Minds of Others -Coercion creates a reaction that will eventually work against you. You must seduce others into wanting to move in your direction. A person you have seduced becomes your loyal pawn. And the way to seduce others is to operate on their individual psychologies and weaknesses. Soften up the resistant by working on their emotions, playing on what they hold dear and what they fear. Ignore the hearts and minds of others and they will grow to hate you."* (48 Laws of Power)

    B.   <u>Understand your followers.</u>

In order to properly work on the hearts and minds of others, you must take the time to understand others. When you cannot understand the rationalizations of another person, it is the same as being ignorant to them. You have heard the idea of "walking a mile in another man's shoes". This encompasses what it means to understand your followers. What are their weaknesses? What are their desires? What are their fears? By answering these questions you will gain insight into the motivations of those around you as well as yourself. In marketing, if you appeal to basic needs or convince someone that a specific item or service is important to them, then that person becomes loyal. If you do not take the time to understand others, you will find that your efforts to accomplish anything will yield a fruitless garden. Animosity will overcome your followers and they will rebel against whatever you have to offer. This is true even of ideas that are to the benefit of your followers. Your leadership will come to ruin if you betray the trust of those who follow you. Remember, at a minimum, you are always leading yourself. Remember that ideas that are true are always true. So understanding followers does not just apply when you are leading a group of people. It also applies to when you are leading yourself. If you go against your individual psychology, you will find execution very difficult. Thus, it is just as important to take time to understand yourself as a follower.

When you communicate to others, be sure to include one or both of the two main concerns in the context: ego or security. Money is something that appeals to both needs. "Ego" deals with a person's sense of belonging or desire. "Security" encompasses physical and emotional security. When these needs are satisfied, you gain the loyalty of others. When communicating to other's needs of security and ego, you have to give a little of yourself so that the person you are speaking to feels more comfortable about what you are offering. If you want to find out someone's motivations, reveal a little about your own, and their doors will be wide open for further discussion. How you reveal your motivations is an art in itself. If your motivation is to cause harm or discomfort, you will not meet the security needs of your audience. When you draw someone outside of their comfort zone, they then have to trust you to lead them, or rather guide them. Their security and ego depends on your good decisions. You can imagine this kind of interaction in this way:

You convince a person that they must be blindfolded while you guide them through a forest. You explain that you are guiding them towards a pot filled with money. You tell them that the blindfold is needed in order to make sure that they stay protected and not be distracted from your guidance by the musings of the forest. If you do this correctly, any person will willingly be blindfolded and be guided by you through the forest at your advice. People will do this because they feel they will retrieve what they feel they deserve. They have been influenced and their needs understood.

Control: *This curriculum stresses internal (discourse with oneself) and external unity (discourse with others). In order to accomplish this type of harmony, the curriculum focuses on the four dimensions of our lives: physical, spiritual, social, and mental. Being a member simply means that you will live in harmony with the principles of StartUp: focus, power in expression, strength, individuality, and creativity. (StartUp)*

    C.   <u>Be an effective and efficient leader and follower.</u>

It is important that you are able to describe your leadership. Effective and efficient are meant to reflect the aforementioned definitions. While the quote may be metaphorical in nature, it simply means that obtaining self-control requires being able to predict your actions. What are your vulnerabilities and what are your strengths? Under which circumstances will you thrive, and in which activities should you participate? The act of following and leading requires the avoidance of pride and ignorance becoming weaknesses. You must master your emotions, and understand how to use them to elicit desired effects. Of course, this kind of introspection will occur after you envision yourself as always in the act of leading. Note that all of your decisions will stimulate multiple effects.

As for the "dimension" reference, it is a suggestion for how you can view the world. These dimensions will be further explained, but they refer to four tiers: social, physical, mental, and the spiritual. The spiritual in this sense deals with motivations and experiences. It is where one gains their reasons for persistence. These tiers go all the way to the social which includes how the rest of society interacts with the object or person under observation. As an apple tree bears apples that other entities consume, so does a person have creations with which other entities will interact. When you perceive something, you are observing, making assumptions, analyzing, and drawing conclusions on it. You repeat this process for events recognized as being similar and modify your conclusions. Then, you arrive at your world perception and identify ways in which your world may be improved based upon how you see it. The idea here is to recognize your world view so that you are able to see the world as broadly as possible and comprehend as many lenses as possible. Then, you will have the ability to be effective and efficient because not only are you considering other possibilities, but you are also implementing solutions. This is an important characteristic of leadership. It is the main difference between self-authorized leadership and title-authorized leadership. Both offer authority, but self-authorized leadership includes the idea of participating in some position of influence, while maintaining appropriateness and leading with accordance to a vision. It requires imperatives designed by you.

The other important take-away from the above paragraph is the idea of focus. Focus is different from narrow-mindedness. Focus means that you are concentrated on some fixed point. This does not mean you will not have to multi-task. To maintain proper control over your circumstances, there must be some amount of focus on your end-goal. When you focus on your end-goal, you consider the other factors that may influence the end-goal. Do your current activities bring you closer to your focus? Think of a diagram concerning lenses and optics. The focus is a point of convergence. It is where everything is able to culminate to one point. Depending on whom you are and your lenses, the focus point will be different.

III. Your Leadership must have a purpose.

Thus, you should clearly define or identify with your end goals. Hopefully, you are not leading just to lead. It is not called leading at that point. You are just occupying space and engaging in title-authorized leadership. If there is no rhyme or reason to your decision-making, then you are leading without a purpose. If this is the case, beware that you will be replaced very soon. There must be some marginally added value to your presence as a leader. Perhaps it is to discover new territory or to improve the internal organization of a larger system. Perhaps it is to bring great credit to your boss. What will your leadership bring to the table? If you do not determine your leadership's purpose, there is the off-chance that you may haphazardly bring value. There is no efficiency in that route, however. In the process of haphazardly producing results, you will miss valuable opportunities because of your lack of control and misunderstanding of others around you.

Ambition: "*I want to put a dent in the universe.*"
(Steve Jobs)

A. A purpose is a final destination.

There is much talk about purposes, and it always seems like something that is a goal beyond reach or hard to determine. Do not get too caught up in trying to find the perfect word or phrase to describe your purpose. Think of it as a final destination. When you see yourself as an older individual, what are some of the things you would hope to have accomplished? These are the final destinations. Envision yourself there. When you can clearly feel, visualize, and hear everything that is involved with your final destination, it is as if you mentally highlight the path that may get you there. When making decisions, you should imagine your final destination. You should also imagine the different opportunities and challenges that you will encounter and see if you are ready for the kind of sacrifices that will most likely have to be made.

If you do not imagine your leadership with a purpose, it is as reckless as going on a road trip with a map in which you cannot read the streets nor have a final destination in mind. Sure, the ride may be thrilling, but you will pass by all of the turns that might take you to a place you would really want to visit. Those streets are the opportunities and the final destination is your purpose. As a matter of fact, you will encounter more challenges and many of them will be unnecessary. If you make a turn that is too far in the wrong direction, it may prematurely end your road trip for you and whomever else is in your company.

In the quote, Steve Jobs makes a proclamation of putting a dent in the universe. While this goal may be a bit vague-sounding or too metaphorical in nature, it still gets the point across. It becomes a standard. Are my activities going to lead me to cause some kind of change? Am I falling in line with the natural flow of the world? For Steve Jobs, these questions would have produced great reflections on whether or not 'a dent is being made in the universe.' What do you want to do? What is your final destination, and what are you doing to get there? Are your activities bold enough?

Objective: My concern is to ensure the growth and development of each person who reads this book. The focus is to help you determine your purpose and make sure that you have the resources necessary to fulfill your purpose. (J.M. Richardson)

This is the objective or the final destination of this book. It may happen that you complete the rest of the chapters and find that you have not been affected at all. That is a choice. You must make a decision to be affected, and dedicate the appropriate time to personal and professional development.

There are no quizzes for this chapter.

Chapter Two

Moments of Leadership

This chapter demonstrates that leadership is the sum of a series of moments that require leadership. The description of leadership follows directly from the previous chapter. The chapter goes on to explore how your overall leadership abilities are affected by those moments, and the manner in which they should be perceived.

Moments of Leadership

Note: "The race will free itself from exploiters just as soon as it decides to do so. No one else can accomplish this task for the race. It must plan and do for itself." (Mis-education of the Negro)

The story of man exploiting man is an old one. It is wise to assume that history will repeat itself as it already has so many times. The idea of this chapter is that you must understand that in every moment, you can learn something about your inhibitions and your liberties. Experiences and beliefs truly shape how well you survive. Cultures and groups with a strong identity rooted in historical importance or tradition will find itself lasting from one generation to the next. A group's ability to self-determine its identity affects the individual moving parts of that group's expectations, experiences, and beliefs. Many studies have been used to show the effect that experiences can have on behavior. Something to keep in mind is that the world is becoming a more mixed one. With such mixing, there will be a period of cultural clashing that will eventually evolve into immersion. Language, mannerisms, and expectations currently vary by wide margins, but expect this to change as time unfolds. The world will be a more accessible entity, and almost nothing will occur in a vacuum. Pay attention to the context in which you are defining yourself.

Imagine the opening quote with "the race" being replaced with the words "you", and replacing "It" to "you". Much can be gathered from this statement. Assume that the only person in this world that cares about you is yourself. Others are consumed by their needs and wants. Therefore, if something is going to happen for you, or if you are going to lead something, then the keyword here is "you". If you make an error, you will have to assume responsibility and do your best to avoid issues. Now, it is not true that your good works will occur solely as a result of your effort. Cause and effect relationships affect more than general events, but are directly involved in influencing your success.

There are always many levels of participants in a successful venture. This statement simply urges you not to rely on another individual and apply pressure when you have the ability to leverage a specific outcome. When engaging in applying pressure, remember your standards. If you are doing unjust harm to an individual to appease your ego or security needs, chances are you will face proportionally excessive consequences for your crimes. (The reason behind the excessiveness will be due to the fact that rebellion is fueled by irrational emotions.) As you are making your way on your journey, remind yourself that your circumstances are of your doing. This is not for you to preach to another, but it should be the platform on which you begin to reflect on those moments of leadership that have ultimately led you to your current status.

The other important aspect to this quote is the idea of decision making. With discrimination or slavery there are some very significant psychological tools at play. For either to properly work, the individual discriminated against must be convinced that discrimination is appropriate and necessary. If the individual does not subscribe to it, then he or she will rebel against it. It works the same way in your life.

In order for you to operate under a certain mindset, it is simply because you have accepted it to be true. What are some of the paradigms with which you live? If you are not content with your current circumstances, you must accept that it was a series of your choices that contributed to them. You are accepting your situation.

The operational definition for this chapter is below:

A <u>moment</u> can be defined in many ways, but the most captivating is thus: a definite period of time.

People make judgments based upon what they see. So, your leadership is represented by the moments in which you were required to demonstrate your leadership. These moments can either be presented to you or created by you, but you must take advantage of them and use them to help you strive toward your purpose.

Things to consider if you are a leader...

I. **I will be required to testify to my beliefs.**

There are many schemas that we create to describe ourselves. We see ourselves in a light that is usually unblemished and steady. We would like to believe that we are great or perfect, and so when it comes to our decisions, we practice a certain amount of self-righteousness. There is a confidence that exists in the core of who we are as individuals and, thus we feel empowered to actually make a decision in the first place. As a result, it is hard to admit to wrongdoing or an improper choice. This stubbornness may be effective for friends and family, but you will be forced to handle the repercussions of such obstinacy. By not recognizing your potential to commit a crime or act pretentiously, you will fail to control yourself when the opportunity occurs. If everyone could live and function the way they imagined themselves to, then the world would truly be a better place. Acknowledging that you could hurt and help is the first step to self-control. If you continue to be naïve about your nature, there will be a day when your weaknesses will be challenged. If you believe you are capable of owning or managing a business, or mingling with a large crowd of individuals, be sure to understand why you believe that, and whether or not you actually believe your proclaimed belief.

Reflection: *"Each day look into your conscience and amend your faults; if you fail in this duty you will be untrue to the Knowledge and Reason that are within you."(A Spiritual Treasury)*

A.   I will have to lead myself.

One of the moments to developing your leadership, is the one you spend contemplating on yourself. What makes you happy, or sad? What do you fear and what do you love? What are your insecurities and where did they come from? Answering these questions will help you understand what drives your decisions, and will help you prepare for situations that may affect you in otherwise, unforeseen ways. In all situations, the responsibility of a decision rests upon you, and you will eventually receive and deal with the consequences of the emotions that occupy your mind. If you are too fearful of potential repercussions, then you will find yourself debating the best case scenario that causes the least amount of resistance.

So if fear drives you more than love, you may lose out on the things you claim to want because the fear of the prospective consequences clearly outweighs the love of success. You can avoid many errors and cornered defeats by fully understanding yourself. The truth is that, other people will take the time to understand you, even if you do not. So, while you are pretending to possess few weaknesses, all of your friends and enemies are becoming aware of your quips and quirks, and will be able to influence you in ways that will result in your feeling of powerlessness. You will be tested by others, and at those moments, your true beliefs will be revealed.

It is absolutely imperative that you understand that you are always expected to be a leader and that there will be moments when your leadership will be tested and defined based upon the results. Imagine the circumstance of a CEO searching for seed funds who finds himself sharing one untruth. In order to maintain his appearance of credibility, out of fear of rejection, he must continue to be dishonest. Each of these moments, define his tenure. The lies will erode the confidence others may have once had in him, and he will eventually become exactly what he was afraid of becoming. He would be rejected by the community. Had he understood what was motivating him, he could have prevented those consequences.

Growth: *"Have you ever visited a pottery factory? When the pottery is placed in the kiln, its colors are dull and muted. After it has been in the fire- when it comes out of the oven-its colors are vivid."* (Be the Leader you were Meant to Be)

B. I will face very difficult times.

Along with moments of testifying to your beliefs, there will be moments that are filled with heat and pressure. These moments, however, are opportunities for success. You should gladly welcome them as challenges to prove to yourself who you are. These pressurized moments should push you to your breaking point, and if you prepare wisely, you will prevail and be better for it. You will be more useful, polished, and valuable, as is a crystal. The other element to this is time. It takes time to reach a final form. You should always be malleable, but convicted. Conviction is by principle and malleability is by understanding. Conviction and stubbornness differ by the width of understanding. You can erase your stubbornness by understanding the perceptions of others. As aforementioned, possessing the ability to understand others and yourself will allow you to grow. Pride can be an unwanted result to having convictions. The best safeguard here is to keep an open mind that others also have their convictions, and that your standards are not the world's standards. Practice by trying to "justify" another's beliefs. This exercise will yield you greater insight into your own convictions.

II. I must seek my opportunities for leadership.

The image of someone wanting to prove their strength comes to mind. He goes from one place to another, initiating fights with others in order to show others that they should fear him, and revere him for his strength. As primal as it sounds, it is exactly what we do. Our resumes are a list of fights that we have participated in, and hopefully won. We go from one opportunity to another seeking to prove ourselves to ourselves and to others. Be cautious of the fights that you pick. They should reflect exactly what you want to be known for. This does not mean to defer a job because it is not what you see yourself doing, but it means that if you take that job, shape the job so that it matches who you are. Create an opportunity within the opportunity. This is the process for seeking opportunities.

While you are actively making decisions that will position you for opportunities, realize that serendipity does play a vital role in the presentation of an opportunity. Something to keep in mind, however, is that moments of serendipity occur many times over time and expose you to an abundance of opportunities at any given time. It is upon you to identify and leverage that opportunity.

Perspective: *"Said one oyster to a neighboring oyster, 'I have a very great pain within me. It is heavy and round and I am in distress'. And the other oyster replied with haughty complacence, 'Praise be to the heavens and to the sea, I have no pain within me. I am well and whole both within and without.' At that moment a crab was passing by and heard the two oysters, and he said, 'Yes you are well and whole; but the pain that your neighbor bears is a pearl of exceeding beauty.' (A Spiritual Treasury)*

> A.   Obstacles are opportunities for success.

Recognizing potential opportunities is crucial to potentiating and leveraging them. According to the story, the oyster with the pain could only recognize the pain, and not the beauty of what that pain could produce. You must train yourself so that you can see every obstacle as an opportunity. If you find yourself doubting your capabilities to overcome a difficult problem, take the time to step back and evaluate what may come from triumphing over the presented obstacle. As a matter of fact, having an end goal in mind will allow you to prepare yourself for opportunities disguising themselves as obstacles.

The result of learning through an obstacle is that you have a story, and can then proceed to more difficult and complex problems. In a nutshell, you become more useful as an individual, and as a leader. Use an obstacle as an opportunity to find mentors. In the story, if the crab had not told him the reason for the pain and the outcome of its endurance, the oyster would have been left to complain and miss its value.

LP25: Influence

Think about the events that have occurred in your life. Understand that each situation is a consequence of other situations, and that each has shaped how you look at life, and how you handle new circumstances. Imagine if you had never encountered those experiences. What would you value then? What might you be doing differently? What habits might you have developed? After that exercise, you will gain some perspective on how your life pieces together, and you will be able to comprehend how obstacles are opportunities for success.

Sequence: "*Every Cause has its Effect, and every Effect has its Cause; everything happens according to Law; Chance is but a name for Law not recognized; there are many planes of causation, but nothing escapes the Law.*" *(Kybalion)*

B.   <u>Any decision you make has a cascade effect over time.</u>

Order and chaos are simply degrees apart. System order describes the degree to which each of the elements connects or relates to one another. If you want to run for office in the United States of America, a particularly *ordered* route may be:

1. Be born into a wealthy family with a background in public office
2. Go to a school where you can maintain a network of family friends who also have a background in public office
3. Intern for someone in public office
4. Attend a prestigious college and affiliate yourself with a political party
5. Obtain a law degree and maintain relationships with others who are involved in public policy or public office
6. Develop a unique record of success in your profession
7. Create professional relationships
8. Run for local office in your area

This example demonstrates intentional order. As you read this list, however, you may have had thoughts like, "How can I control which family I am born into?", "How can you just go to a prestigious school?", "Would not I need money to do some of these things?", or "How would I just work for someone in public office?" You are so right! These are uncontrollable factors. Instead of such an ordered list, you are subject to chance and opportunity. In that light, life is actually chaotic. So then things must be unconnected or unrelated. However, this section is about the importance of sequence in life. It means that if A happens, then B must happen. Because B happened, C will happen. If you read this book, then the book is read. These connections are infinitesimally small, but they add up yielding a multitude of orders. By itself, an order is predictable and guaranteed. When these orders interact with one another, the result is chaos.

Chaos could be described as the result of everyone's "order" working and colliding with one another. These unpredictable factors for some are simply the injection of the order by others. This is important to take note of because as you make decisions, like the leader that you are, you will be subject to what seems to be chaos. The trick is to understand the orders that are interacting with one another and perhaps you will be able to make predictions that could impress Nostradamus. So, you can stack your deck by becoming an expert in systems – or interacting orders. These systems could be concrete: business cycles, engineering processes, or policy tracks. They could also be more intangible: human emotions, human behavior, or human actions. Understand how these systems interact with one another and how each system is connected.

Because you have an aptitude and desire for an end goal (a final destination), this sort of high level thinking will help you keep perspective, which in turn will help you find opportunities in situations that will challenge you as obstacles, and which in turn will yield your success.

Idealism: *"It can be argued that the quickest way an infant learns to speak, move, and even think, is by imitation. They look to their parents, siblings, or anyone else around them as examples." (Young Leader)*

LP25: Influence

C. <u>I am always learning how to become more successful.</u>

When you find these opportunities, it is imperative that you know nothing is truly new. In this book, there is nothing that has not been written or taught elsewhere. So, before you embark along a decision's cause and effect stream, reach out to those who have had similar experiences. This does not mean you should limit yourself to their advice. It means to build upon what they may have to offer. If you are creating a new product or want to embark on a new research project, identify someone who embarked on the same initiative. There are others who have created entirely new areas of study. Read their books, watch their shows, and then decide to do even better than they did. It is not from a competitive standpoint, but rather as a validating testament to their lives. Their stories were put to good use. You will be able to prepare yourself for even bigger opportunities because you have safeguarded yourself from some of their obstacles. It is like being ahead of your peers in a class because instead of learning addition when they are learning it, you already know what it means to multiply. Addition may have been taught to you at an age in which you were the most open to learning it. Therefore, you feel no inhibitions when the teacher introduces it.

The other important concept to utilize from this is the idea of idealism. Idealism is not a bad word. Many successful people functioned through persistent idealism. This does not mean to not be aware of the situation in which you are present, but to use it to your advantage. There is a story of a woman who really wanted a position at a large company. She did not know how to make her resume stand out, so she sent a shoebox to the person responsible for new hires. The shoebox had one shoe in it with a note. The note read, "Well, since I already have one foot in the door..." She was hired soon after. This technique is not for everyone, but you should be idealistic in how you approach circumstances. If you have a book and you want to get it published, well then get it published! Show up to an editor and let them know, "I know you are in this business because you enjoy the value that books can bring. Read my book, and I promise you will be encouraged by the value that it brings."

You will at least get him or her to read the book, but the rest of that interaction is the "systems" part of this scenario. As mentioned before, it is important to understand systems. In contrast to your idealism, these systems represent the realism. Your realism should complement your idealism; it should not obstruct it. If your realism overshadows your idealism, you become cynical. People just do not like cynical people, because they serve as a reminder for all of the negative consequences of the human emotion of fear. However, because people possess fear as an emotion, too much idealism will make you incredible (without credibility).

Striking a balance between the two will help you when striving toward your goals. You can gauge your balance by how you respond to questions. If someone asks you for advice on a new idea, what is your focus? Are you excited about the possibilities for the idea? Are you listening carefully to determine all of the shortcomings? Do you feel worried or insulted? Do you see plans or resources? See below for the traits:

Realism	Idealism
Feeling insulted or nervous	Excitement
Shortcomings/ Obstacles	Possibilities/creative ways to make it work
Plans	Resources
Systems	Identify method to attract attention

You should possess a mixture of the above characteristics.

III.   I must reflect on my leadership.

Specular reflection, in engineering terms, is a phenomenon exhibited by light in which the angle the wave is incident on the surface, equals the angle at which it is reflected. The other interesting quality of reflection is that the images are chiral- you cannot superimpose the images on top of each other. How does this translate into leadership development? Well, it means reflections are always going to be a bit skewed, but are great when identifying objects behind you. They also indicate when you should change yourself, specifically your appearance, in some way. I am sure

LP25: Influence

before you leave in the morning for class or work that you look into your mirror. You probably make sure your clothes match, and your hair is brushed. If you do not do this every day, hopefully you at least check a mirror before you go on a date or to an interview. After looking in the mirror a few times, you get used to the reversed directions. This is how your reflection on your leadership could work. It will probably be a bit skewed to reality, but you can use it to manage your flaws and prevent something coming from behind and surprising you.

Reflection: *"Who is not a companion to his spirit is an enemy to people. And he, who sees not in his self a friend, dies despairing. For life springs from within a man and comes not from without him." (A Spiritual Treasury)*

  A. <u>Meditate on my character.</u>

Be deliberate about your reflection. It should not be the consequence of interference, but it should be self-instructed and consistent. Meditation involves studying with an objective in mind. It implies focus and concentration. You want to consistently study your character. Your character is the compilation of everything that makes up who you are. What are your values? How do you make decisions? What matters the most to you? What motivates you? What is the purpose you dream of and why? If your name were the title of a book, what would your current chapter be and what would the content be in the book? Would others be able to read it? If you take the time to truly understand those aspects of your life, your mirror will become cleaner, and you will be able to navigate yourself. If you know the saying, "you are your worst enemy", part of the meaning and lesson is that you should understand yourself and then be able to predict and manage yourself accordingly.

The consequences of not spending time and figuring out your flaws are the same as going into an interview without checking the mirror. You will be embarrassed, you will appear in a way you never thought you would, and you most likely will not get the job.

In the previous section, it was discussed that there exists a true sequence in the world. You must internalize that your situations are really an expression of how you view your worth. Just like any good investment, it takes time and work to grow. It must be fed new resources and evaluated for progress. If you are performing these tasks, then you will reap the benefits, referencing the quote: *"for life springs from within a man and comes not from without."*

There are many deeds to be done in this world, and you are capable of accomplishing the greatest of them, but you are also capable of bringing terror upon others. If you do not understand your breaking points, or your motivations, it will only mean harm for those whom you love, and people you have never even met.

Pride and Ignorance: *"But not to acknowledge a mistake, not to correct it and learn from it, is a mistake of a different order. It usually puts a person on a self-deceiving, self-justifying path, often involving rationalization (rational lies) to self and to others."* (7 Habits of Highly Effective People)

B. <u>Acknowledge my mistakes.</u>

Have some caution with your actions. You do not have to display your mistakes, but you must acknowledge that things may turn for the worse in any given situation because our world is filled with interacting sequences. Self-righteousness can be easily spotted. If you find yourself saying, "I would never do that" or "how could I ever think that way", you are exhibiting the traits of a self-righteous person. It is great that you have a high regard of yourself; however the danger is that it is falsely derived. As mentioned before, you are completely capable of an array of deeds. It may take a lot for you to "think that way, or do that thing", but there is a point in which you will. Being self-righteous about it will bear no fruit for you. As a matter of fact, it will lead you down a pathway that will cause you to lie so that you can reinforce your ego. Practice admitting, at least to yourself, that you were wrong with small things and then work your way up once you are more comfortable. If you have an impulse to pass judgment on another's actions, stop yourself, and wonder why he/she may have committed that action, and determine under which circumstances could you see yourself doing the same. Having this ability is a step into learning how to reflect on your leadership and meditate on your character. It will open up a great opportunity to learn from new and familiar situations, and from people who are young and old. It will offer yet another moment of leadership.

Chapter Three

Dimensions of Life

This chapter attempts to find a holistic way to describe the world. It involves analysis (separating information to understand the pieces), and synthesis, (applying the pieces to develop a method by which you can organize and manage your surroundings). With regards to leadership, it is important to be able to interpret your surroundings in order to make better decisions. Our thoughts may only go as far as we can understand.

Dimensions of Life

Note: "Independent thinking alone is not suited to interdependent reality. Independent people who do not have the maturity to think and act interdependently may be good individual producers, but they won't be good leaders or team players. They're not coming from the paradigm of interdependence necessary to succeed in marriage, family, or organizational reality."(7 Habits of Highly Effective People)

When considering how to view your world, it is a fallacy to adopt a system of dependency. When you enter into a situation, you carry with you an order. The sequence of events in your life and the decisions you have made are brought onto every project in which you engage. In this light, you are an independently functioning person. You have thoughts, feelings, skills, inclinations, and relationships that come along with you. When you are hired by a new company, those are the things you bring with you. It is also a fallacy, however, to only consider your independence. As mentioned before when discussing chaos, your order must interact with the order of others. This is the interdependent system that is being referenced. It is not just reality. It must be your mindset. Even something as simple as attending a class, involves decisions made at the national level of the government. Decisions made there affect what resources are available to your school or college. This affects the leadership of your school and influences their decisions. These decisions may result in fires or new hires in the school faculty. Added pressure will affect the performance of your teachers, and will ultimately influence what you learn in the classroom. An interdependent mentality however does not end the story there. As an interdependent person, you have the ability to influence the system and not just be influenced by it. You can go to any of the decision points in the system and either change what is available or create new options for what is available. This is what an efficient leader does. The point demonstrated here is the interaction of these orders. In order to optimize your efficiency, you primarily view the world in one of a few lenses. This chapter is about those particular lenses that you can use as evaluative measures for what you want to accomplish, what you think you are accomplishing, and what you are actually accomplishing.

The operational definition for this chapter is below:

Interdependence is mutual dependence or in the state of depending on each other.

A mentality of dependency limits your ability to influence a situation. It means no one relies on your success, thus you must rely on their good will to care about you. If you make another interested in your success, however, you have created a small interdependent unit. The other individual now has motivation to see you succeed because that success is in their best interest. This is why the "joining a team" mentality works. Simply put, if everyone has a vested interest in the positive outcome of a project, they will be more willing to work and put in resources to make sure that it is successful. The workplace environment is evident of such a paradigm. Workers who feel invested in their jobs or projects, yield better results than those who are functioning off of the mechanics of scientific management.

Things to consider about interdependence...

I. **Think in four dimensions of life.**

The best way to comprehend the point in this chapter is to think of the dimensions as parameters. Parameters are characteristics that are unique and independent, but can be mathematically positioned in a way to demonstrate relationships or create models. The results of the model are affected by prescribed parameters. For a square, the model of its area considers the parameter of the length of a side. For the volume of a tire, however, multiple radii and cross-sectional area are taken into consideration. The important concept is that models are meant to describe an entity and parameters are used to manipulate models. So, this chapter is meant to model life. The parameters are what this book is deeming as the four dimensions. It is important to consider all of the parameters and to that end they are analyzed independently of each other. However, if life presents a change, then each of the parameters are also changing. The parameters are, by nature, interdependent.

Another important idea to consider is the utility and purpose of creating and applying models. Models allow for the opportunity to evaluate and estimate results. This is important because with models, you can make better decisions. The closer a model is to the actual reality, the less un-factored uncertainty is present. This concept of uncertainty and parameter choice also goes into the complexity of the model that is being created. There are some parameters that are perhaps impossible to obtain: Heisenberg's Uncertainty Principle discusses just one aspect in the mechanics of subatomic particles. So, the more high-level the parameters become, the more useful they are, but the trade-off is that they are harder to configure. If there were to be a disavowal of the proposed dimensions of life, it would be due to the complexity involved in each of the parameters.

Accessibility: "*As an interdependent person, I have the opportunity to share myself deeply, meaningfully, with others, and I have access to the vast resources and potential of other human beings.*"(*A Spiritual Treasury*)

LP25: Influence

A. <u>The Social Dimension allows for collective groups to operate for the greater good. It is the outside perception.</u>

Normally, there are three dimensions that are presented in philosophical books. One that is however, discounted is the dimension that involves shared interactions. It is everything that is a part of the cause and effect interplay of systems. A fruit is known to be good based upon how it interacts with a person. Eating a fruit is however, the product of many processes that must occur. A fruit is the bearing of a plant, and the plant is said to provide a fruit as its benefit to the world. When discovering your Social parameters, your fruits are the products of many internal processes with which others do not engage. It is in the Social Dimension of your life that others are able to gain meaning from you. If you only want to share weak fruit, then it is your decision to do so. That will be all that is shared. If you choose to share or produce plenty of fruit, then the world will eat of it. Their judgments will be based on their experience with your fruit: its taste and its nutritional value.

Purpose and value are expressed in the Social Dimension. Imagine a book that cannot be read by anyone. What value might it possess if there is no hope that it may ever be read? Life can be evaluated based upon the value that a certain action or object provides. When you evaluate yourself in this light, you can see the benefit and harm that you bring to others, and can adjust accordingly. Groups are able to make functional decisions from doing a "Social Dimension" evaluation. It works by using the sum of the parts and their interactions with other entities. In business, transactions occur amongst multiple parties. Strategy, organization, marketing, financing, and management decisions all can be made by looking at the interactions between the company and its customers.

For an individual, this translates into determining your perceived value. How do others feel around you? What do you give others? What do you do for others? What do people do for you? Why do people treat you the way they do? The last question is very important to consider. Any time you interact with someone, they can only make judgments from what you share about yourself. Your words and actions may be very revealing and allow others to make even more significant discoveries about yourself. Others then relate what you present to their own experiences and then create expectations. So, if you are being treated a certain way, try to understand what you are conveying. It is here that perceptions are created. When considering your communication, perceptions are just as valid as truths. They come from two places: predominant perceptions and convicted perceptions. Predominant perceptions are the easiest to alter. They are derived primarily as a result of fads or phases. They are adopted to "fit-in". Convicted perceptions are, however, tied into the ego of the individual who possesses them. The ego can be offended or exalted. You should be aware of the ramifications for what you say and what you do in the Social Dimension.

Calculation: *"Lead them into the moment-an intensified present in which morality and, judgment, and concern for the future all melt away and the body succumbs to pleasure." (Art of Seduction)*

B. <u>The Physical Dimension describes your sensory perceptions. It is what you do.</u>

The Physical Dimension is all about existence. That a thing exists and can be described is a part of the Physical Dimension. It is the object or person with which you interact. It is void of the interactions that may exist between the thing and another. All perceptions can be altered, at least temporarily, by changing the Physical Dimension. Evaluation in this dimension does not rely on the interaction of the object but singularly on its existence. A plant that bears fruit is simply a plant that bears fruit. Favoring, eating, and digesting the fruit would fit into the Social Dimension. The fruit you bear may not benefit anyone. Thus, its value is rendered useless. Still, it does not mean that you have not offered fruit. In business, the Physical Dimension consists of office space, office items, properly filed paperwork, and a product. Decisions regarding personal preferences and structure can be made based on evaluations in the Physical Dimension. What are the available items?

Your talents would be described in the Physical Dimension. You sing, dance, write, create, speak, swim, workout, walk, run, and the list can go on. The Social Dimension determines the perceived value. The Physical Dimension determines what is being valued. These talents can be noticed by simply paying attention to your most common conversations. If the relationship between the Social and the Physical are that the Social dictates value and the Physical presents the entity to be valued, then when you are interacting, the things you present are a part of the Physical.

Just as others have the ability to pass judgments, you are also able to do so. You can use this to your advantage by taking your Physical Dimension attributes and passing judgments on them. Try to imagine yourself from the outside, and dictate your value to yourself. What do you commend yourself on, and what do you denigrate? The Physical evaluation can give you a window into your own perceptions and prepare you to not only calculate an appropriate reaction or initiation, but to also prepare for the reactions and initiations of others.

Depth: *"The Seed. The soil is carefully prepared. The seeds are planted months in advance. Once they are in the ground, no one knows what hand threw them there. Disguise your manipulations by planting seeds that take root on their own. (Art of Seduction)*

    C.   <u>The Mental Dimension is a very powerful dimension which to be on one accord. It describes your intelligence and "how" you do.</u>

The Mental Dimension is more conceptual in nature. It involves the uncontrolled inner-workings of a particular entity. It is the design of the product. To continue the analogy of the fruit bearing plant, the Mental Dimension would be the kind of seed that was initially planted. A sunflower seed may never become a rose. Therefore, it should not attempt to be a rose, but to be a sunflower that bears the physical attributes of a sunflower. The Mental Dimension can be crafted by your genetic material or by behavioral instructions exercised by your guardians. When evaluating in this dimensions, it is important to realize what influences you. Perhaps it is your region of birth, sex, or age. The Mental Dimension is the sum of all of those influences. It is here where you can grasp that you are capable of devising strategic plans to either cause harm or benefit. You can determine what motivates you and what limits you. The Mental Dimension evaluation is very complex. It involves understanding your thoughts and desires. For you, at what point do consequences offer less risk than a potential reward?

Some products of philosophy also include the Emotional Dimension, yielding a 5-tier method by which you may analyze the world. This book however, has consolidated the Emotional Dimension to exist within the Mental Dimension as they are inextricably tied to one another. Your ability to reason and be intelligent is directly influenced by your desires. It can be analyzed using the same methods of the Mental Dimension, but emotions themselves are objects influenced by the four dimensions outlined in this chapter. As mentioned in the beginning of this chapter, there are many ways to view the world, and the proposition of four dimensions is simply one of them.

By understanding and evaluating this parameter of life, you can predict the involvement and motivations of others. Thus, when one mentions the idea of planting a seed, they mean that they are influencing another's views of their design or motivations for their decisions. While perceptions may be influenced in the Physical Dimension quite easily, altering the Mental Dimension can be devastating for an individual. Diversions in this dimension are much harder to craft and involve a deep understanding of how emotional systems operate. The things you fear, love, and hope for are all blueprinted into this dimension. When communicating in this realm, you are maneuvering in the Mental Dimension. How you view yourself here affects how you display yourself (Physical Dimension), and how others interact with you (Social Dimension). If you are willing to take the time to comprehend this parameter, you can begin a process of behavioral reprogramming.

In business, the vision and mission statements are a part of the Mental Dimension. The vision and mission statements often vividly express what the company believes it is qualitatively worth and capable of achieving. Every operating decision you make should be to accomplish the vision/ mission. These statements are the fundamental beliefs of the promise that the business holds. Clearly, if the Mental Dimension is so fundamental to the many decisions businesses make, so is the dimension also pivotal to the decisions you make about yourself.

When referencing "how" you do, the statement is offering a method for identifying the mechanism that is the Mental Dimension. To begin identifying what the Mental Dimension consists of, think of how you interact and the influences that drive those interactions. Is it that you may be afraid of loneliness? Perhaps you are afraid of rejection. Beginning with your fears, hopes, and loves will assist in discovering your Mental Dimension and begin to evaluate it so that you may make better decisions. Once you identify your motivations, you have the option to change them. *How* you believe something can be changed by understanding *why* you believe something.

Intelligence is referencing how your experiences play into your understanding. Knowledge obtained through other people, books, or experiences all can be incorporated into intelligence. Your ability to recognize patterns and make predictions based off of those patterns is crucial to your survival. The Mental Dimension is not concerned with why you must survive, but it does believe that it must, and is left to determine how.

Motivation: *"Faith is a knowledge within the heart, beyond the reach of proof." (A Spiritual Treasury)*

> D. <u>The Spiritual Dimension has the greatest importance and influence. It describes your intellect. It explains "why".</u>

Keep asking yourself why. What is the deeper meaning? What makes people care? Think of the entire universe. Picture each of the planets and the stars and asteroids that surround them. Imagine how dark it is. Picture the sun. Picture the Earth, which is like a marble to a baseball. Imagine yourself on the surface of the Earth in your little room with a ceiling reading this extremely small book.

Think of the vast oceans and never ending sky with seven billion people carrying on conversations, eating, sleeping, dying, laughing, and playing. Imagine the many people that have come and gone on this planet and the lives they led. Replay the wars, the pandemics, the meteorological catastrophes and the world wide aid missions. Imagine the changes in technology: transportation, communication, and health. The world is vast.

Every system is arbitrary. They are explained and proven by metrics. "One" has a meaning because it has been dictated. In learning mathematics, you can progress from addition to multiplication, and then to exponents. The building blocks for each step are based in a successful adoption of assumptions as you progress higher. If any of the assumptions were to change, the entire system would be compromised. In engineering, axioms, postulates, and laws can be used and not broken. We accept that magnetism, electricity, and gravity, are all in existence and an engineer has the ability to manipulate them. They do not have to be fully understood, to accomplish something with them. However, the greater the understanding, the more manipulation is afforded. In every aspect of our lives we display a phenomenon known as faith. Whether it is in a higher being or in our own perceptions, we want to believe that there is truth in something. As mentioned in the standards of leadership, a leader understands that there is truth in everything.

Our biggest truth is in the concept of existence. As a child, you may have questioned, what if I am the only one that is alive and all other entities are products of my imagination. You quickly learn that it cannot be the case unless our minds are able to create, configure, and separate new entities. If you could create your world, you would be able to predict it. Nevertheless, there is a link between you and other entities. This link affords you some predictability. Evolutionarily speaking, you have the ability to speak ask questions so that you may understand and predict others. You play mind games to realize the motivations of others and look for windows to comprehend their options when given false decisions. You rely on a system when you participate in these mind games. The system is the most basic assumption that you can make in your setting and

LP25: Influence

allows you to configure survival and need obtainment. Your reliance on the system is faith. Albeit a god, God, or consequence of science, you faithfully rely on the system to work each and every time.

When you walk, eat, sleep, work, and play, you rely on the system. In general, we are attracted to religion because it offers us a deeper understanding beyond the Mental Dimension. It is the Spiritual Dimension. In this dimension, your primal beliefs lie and determine everything about who you are and what you do subconsciously and unconsciously. The system had to come from somewhere. In the fruit metaphor, the Spiritual Dimension is the planting of the seed. There was intention in the planting and in the design. The seed cannot change. Had it never been planted, there would be no sunflowers.

In business, there is confidence that the business system exists and that the core assumption is true: if you provide for a need, people will take it. How it actually happens is up to the design, the product, and how the business interacts. However, the assumption that people will take what they need or that people must survive are just that, assumptions. Such an assumption may or may not always be the case. As for the world we live in, it is. It tends to work out that when people are compelled to buy, they buy. When they are left with a choice to live or die, they usually choose to live.

Intellect implies a sense of intuition in addition to your intelligence. Intuition is much more mysterious. It can be explained as an intelligent response that is the result of understanding the flow and position of the operating systems. In which systems do you possess faith? What assumptions have you made about them and their existence? *"Why do people want to survive"* is a basic question. Its corresponding question is, *"What is my purpose?"* This is the hardest dimension to alter. However, when this realm is understood and changed, it has the greatest impact. If you find yourself in repeat situations that you do not want, you should refer to your Spiritual Dimension. There is perhaps something you believe about yourself that you do not want to believe. The surfacing perception however, will be the one that is controlling your subconscious and your unconsciousness in addition to your consciousness.

Something as simple as shyness or obesity usually takes residence in the Spiritual realm. Your shyness may come from your belief that you have nothing important to say. It is important to be honest because this realm only recognizes honesty. It can distinguish when you are providing falsities. Determine what you actually believe because you will receive exactly what you want.

II.   **These dimensions are interdependent. They are interlaced and stacked and each has its cause and its effect.**

These dimensions are considered focuses. You can focus on evaluating yourself in any of the four. The latter requires the most effort, but the former offers the greatest tangible risks/ rewards for a short amount of time. Your focuses will determine how people treat you, how you treat others, and how well you are able to predict yourself and others. Unknowing masters at these evaluations became some of the world's greats. They played the world like a chess game. They all fall to some inevitability or vice, however, and it would be wise to understand the perceptions: what, how, and why. Perhaps your fall may be prevented or accounted for.

Keep in mind that the Spiritual influences the Mental which in turn influences the Physical. The Physical then influences the Social, and from that, you may construct the world we live in. Our focuses and orders meld together to create our systems. These systems, in turn, may be influenced by our focuses and orders. If you can control multiple orders, you then have the ability to create your own system.

Function: *"You will kindly remember, however, that the Three Great Planes are not actual divisions of the Universe, but merely arbitrary terms used by the Hermeticists in order to aid in the thought and study of the various degrees and forms of universal activity and life" (Kybalion)*

LP25: Influence

A. <u>They describe your leadership.</u>

The quote references three dimensions: the Spiritual, the Mental and the Physical. Recall that there are many ways to evaluate life both qualitatively and quantitatively. The proposition of these four dimensions is simply an arbitrary method of doing so. Using the four dimensions to construct conclusions about yourself and your surroundings is complete and highly relatable. Every complex problem and simple object can be analyzed and reconfigured to some degree by the application of the prescribed parameters. By using them to describe your leadership, you can better define the kind of leader you want to be and be better able to discern and engage in opportunities. Each dimension acts a filter for both experiences and communication.

Your leadership in the Social Dimension is what you will be known for, since it is the social facet that interacts with others. When you think of great leaders, you dwell on the effects of their accomplishments. These accomplishments are the manifestations of the subconscious and the unconscious aspects of those leaders.

In the Physical Dimension, you think of what they did, void of value or reason or rhyme. You think of their organization and calculated moves. Conquering lands, changing legislation, building a school, filing a paper, designing an airplane, cleaning a room, raising a child, and even buying an item are all considered actions or completed tasks. These things are attributed values once moved into the Social Dimension.

In the Mental Dimension, you think of their influencing motivations and their underlying character. How did they achieve their accomplishments? Was it with sternness? Did they do it with luck or confidence? Were they conceited? Did they feel entitled to their accomplishments? These emotional states of existence become actions and reactions when moved into the Physical Dimension.

Finally, in the Spiritual Dimension, you wonder, what was the reason for them being put into the system? What craftiness went into the design? Was there a goodness or evilness to their deeds?

What makes them different from another? These fundamental beliefs, morals, values, become emotional expectations in the Mental Dimension.

Thus, you should reflect on yourself in the same capacity. Run evaluations on yourself in all of the dimensions to create a full picture of who you are, and what it means to think of yourself as a leader. As a reminder, you are always a leader because you are always making decisions and are accountable for those decisions. A decision to do nothing or keep quiet is still a decision. Be aware of your leadership.

There are no quizzes for this chapter.

Chapter Four

Win-Win Mentality

The purpose of this chapter is to determine what a good decision looks like with regards to short and long term ramifications. The win-win mentality option pursues no compromise and is an indirect pathway to becoming a leader of respect and admiration. You can be a leader who changes position at the publics' interest or personal whim; but to be the greatest leader, it takes something of a different essence.

Win-Win Mentality

Note: "The Principle of Win/Win is fundamental to success in all our interactions, and embraces five interdependent dimensions of life. It begins with character, and moves toward relationships, but of which flow agreements. It is nurtured in an environment where structure and systems are based on win/win mentality. And it involves process; we cannot achieve win/win end with win/lose or lose/win means." (7 Habits of Highly Effective People)

When presented an opportunity to plan, there is a certain mentality you possess while participating in the activity. Much of what has been discussed has been in regards to understanding your surroundings by reflecting on your perceptions. Taking a step further, win-win mentality is about understanding your options. At any given time in a relationship or situation, you are presented with a multitude of options: false options, unpleasant options, and desirable options. All of the options are analyzed based on the benefit/harm analysis that they provide to you. However, you have the ability to create options that provide even more desirable results than the ones that are usually presented. This chapter focuses on training your mind to be in the habit of deriving its own options that are desirable, according to your standards.

What are the benefits of the win-win mentality? Firstly, you will establish an environment of trust and loyalty. Others will perceive that you are highly concerned with their well-being in addition to your own. So, even when you are not able to deliver satisfactory results, they will suppose it was the best option possible. In leadership, or decision making, loyalty and trust are extremely important. Many revolutionary changes can occur over long periods of time, but the benefits of the specific plan or goal you may be trying to implement may be compromised by the impediments that arise within the short term. Most people can agree on a vision, but it takes a lot of work to get people to agree on the details. So, building trust and loyalty can afford you time and acceptance so that your revolutionary changes are possible.

The other benefit to practicing a win-win mentality is maneuverability. When a win-win mentality is employed, the playing field for strategy becomes more ordered. By anticipating moves (the reactions and actions of others), you can prepare for multiple outcomes and heighten your ability to maneuver around obstacles. You practice this when you have mentors who give you advice. They receive benefits of validation from the relationship they have with you. You receive their resources. When they provide and you consider the caveats of certain activities, you are practicing a planning mentality. You can plan your preparation and anticipate your weaknesses and how they may be used to hurt or help you. Win-win helps because it requires you to plan. This chapter argues that approaching problems with the motivation of seeking a win-win solution will return the most benefit for all parties involved.

The operational definition for this chapter is below:

"Mentality" is a word to describe someone's outlook on life, or more importantly, their intellectual capabilities or endowment.

Things to consider about your mentality...

I.   **Practice the Win-Win Mentality.**

In order to practice something, you must understand what it is. As aforementioned, a mentality is an outlook. It is a manner of thinking, and can be traced to the mental dimension of the previous chapter. Mentality describes a manner of information processing. While information may vary in size, content, or meaning, the manner in which we process the information has a significant effect on our lives and our decision making capabilities. Your mentality should be something that you develop and constantly evaluate in order to check your perspective and adjust your perceptions. Win-win implies success or victory. The win-win combination signifies that firstly, a relationship exists and secondly that both people in the relationship are gaining a triumphant success or victory.

There are other forms of mentalities you may possess. Most people function in lose/win, win/lose mentalities. This kind of mentality has been ingrained in our brains, perhaps by evolutionary design. Zero-sum game theory plays to validate these thinkers. In a nutshell, it means that if someone wins, then there must be a loser. In competition, business or in athletics, if someone wins a game or a customer, then a competitor loses the game or the customer. This is the simplest of all mentalities you may possess. It is a performance-heavy mentality. The options to win or to lose are present and one or the other will happen regardless of what you do or how you prepare. In a basketball game, the players on both teams have put in a tireless number of hours to improving their skills and studying the plays and skills of their opponent. However, there is no consistent way to predict who will win the game and who will lose the game. There are multi-million dollar industries that thrive on this type of uncertainty. As a matter of fact, no effort is really put into the planning stage. Performance is planned, but the systems coordinating the game are not objects of the plan. While planning may increase your odds of winning, planning is not requisite to participate in the game.

Lose/lose mentality is for those who feel sorrow and want to spread their sorrow. "If I do not win, then no one will win." These mentalities are dangerous and self-destructive. Competition can at least be friendly. In lose/lose, you will not only lose your opportunities, but you will lose your relationships and any credibility you may have had will be written off as a lie. Lose/lose players are always victims and search for more victims to add to their inventory. Avoid having this mentality and those who possess it. If a person uses this mentality to process information, they will find happiness fleeting, and you can do nothing to help them as they find complacency in the consistency of constantly being a victim. This complacency is a byproduct of our need to make things predictable. Note that predictability is important for survival and allows us to make decisions. If nothing exhibited causality or predictability, we would find ourselves in a state of constant fear and paranoia.

Win-win is planning-heavy. It requires that you have identified options, players, and key factors. You then have to stage your subsequent actions and decisions so that you can gain an outcome that benefits all participants. This mentality cannot be employed without planning ahead and understanding what other factors are involved. If the planning is not completed, then the mentality falls back into the win/lose, lose/win because there will be someone's need that is not being met.

Finally, what is practice? Practicing involves consistent and deliberate engagement of some tool or activity. Practicing a mentality can qualify as both.

Consideration: *"Instead of looking for the best alternative for the long term, people who are defensive lose the ability to get past their own involvement." (Young Leader)*

    A. <u>It makes us more creative.</u>

Win-win mentality is a planning-heavy mentality. It requires that several orders are explored (an order is a series of cause and effect relationships). The emotional orders of the individuals, the orders of the systems at play, and the order of their changes over time should be the variables at the top of the list. There will always be unconsidered factors, but the more you can safeguard against uncontrollable factors, the better the result will be. When a difficult problem has many degrees of freedom, it is upon the solver or the mathematician to creatively devise assumptions. In a transport system, those assumptions may be with regards to shape, area, flux, time, or some other parameter. The goal of these assumptions is to do two things: decrease the number of unknowns, and synthesize equations to mathematically model the process. The same happens with a win-win mentality's approach to problem solving.

Considering the factors does not mean to simply acknowledge their existence, but to be able to parameterize it enough so that the unknown factors will not apply or are best approximated. This kind of problem solving involves a high amount of creativity. How well do you develop options and models that were not originally given in the presented problem? This approach involves thinking outside of the box, or rather:

Think

Perhaps it takes a change in perspective. When looking at problems, there are a few ways to achieve viewing through another lens without having to reevaluate your belief system. However, many times our beliefs are the inherent philosophical incongruences that cause us to not interpret a problem in a more robust manner. Speaking to others will help to provide insight from other angles. Asking questions that require open-ended answers will help in discovering factors that may not have even been considered. These factors can then be incorporated into the win-win plan. Not being able to imagine beyond your own involvement in a ploy, plan, or project, will limit your ability to make appropriate risk-taking decisions with the available resources.

Reflection on long-term cause and effect relationships is also imperative for practicing win-win mentality. You must develop a sixth sense for changing tides. You should reflect on the mentality of those around you. Otherwise, they will create obstructions that you will not see coming. Perhaps they are intimidated by you or are unconvinced of your ability to persevere. Either way, by ignoring their mentalities and how they will come into play as you gain accolades will bring about your own ruin. Over time, people, places, and circumstances change. Sometimes, they change abruptly. In your creativity, do not simply solve your problem, but try to frame it in the context of an even larger problem. There, your solution will have a greater impact. In economic policy, for instance, it may be great to increase subsidies on a commodity, but over the long-term, it may cause more havoc.

Results: *"A relationship where bank accounts are high and both parties are deeply committed to Win/Win is the ideal springboard for tremendous energy. That relationship neither makes the issues any less real or important, nor eliminates the differences in perspective. But it does eliminate the negative energy..."* (7 Habits of Highly Effective People)

    B.   <u>We obtain the most positive results.</u>

Win-win is planning heavy and results focused. Who benefits? How many people benefit? How many people are harmed and how can you prevent their harm? The kind of options you create should be positive. If there are loose ends, keep trying to tie them up. When you can no longer find a losing party, you have reached your maximum creativity. The options created are then evaluated for their overall benefit. While it is impossible to always make everyone happy, this mentality will allow you to reach the most positive results. One of the fastest ways to derail a win-win is to have a win-lose mentality on the team. The win-lose mentality requires much less work or if it requires equivalent work, is meant for the demise of another party. Either way neither provides good business or personal karma, and efforts should be taken as a leader to mitigate the influence of that individual's win-lose mentality.

The created options should be positive.

As an individual: Be sure to balance your idealism and realism as aforementioned, and begin to move forward with a plan. You should constantly reflect on it and develop it as it should be flexible. Your options should benefit you on multiple levels and those that may be affected by your decision.

LP25: Influence

In a group: Once you cannot creatively configure new and usable parameters, introduce your idea or plan to the group. Anticipate your group's reactions to your idea. You should be flexible in your presentation so that each individual may perceive a certain amount of buy-in, as explained by the "join the team" strategy of presenting ideas. Keep in mind that you are aiming for the best possible option, and the participation of the rest of your team will be necessary to create it.

Reputation: *"Seeking to understand requires consideration; seeking to be understood takes courage. Win/Win Mentality requires a high degree of both." (7 Habits of Highly Effective People)*

C. <u>We will always approach circumstances in this way.</u>

When a person engages in an activity on a consistent basis, it begins to develop that person's reputation. Your reputation is directly tied to your actions and expectations. It is indirectly influenced and altered by others. The reason to always approach circumstances in this manner is to accomplish a few objectives.

1)   Practice

By practicing this mentality with small endeavors or decisions, it will become a habit. Never appear to be indecisive, however, as it will encourage fear in anyone who chooses to follow you, including yourself. The time it takes to consider options and devise new ones should be perceived as the application of diligence and intelligence and not uncertainty. Imagine a man who quickly and wittingly is able to create a solution to a problem that many others have attempted to solve. He will be regarded highly for his astuteness and gain loyalty. The practice will allow you to develop that mentality and apply it more effectively and efficiently so that it may be put to good use. You will be able to anticipate the perceptions and actions of others due to your new multilateral way of seeing a problem. Think: a pyramid appears to be a triangle when viewed from one angle.

2)   Results

Creative and positive results are desirable results. Creative means original and in business where originality becomes a competitive advantage, creativity can be good. "Positive results" are results that are beneficial. In finance, business, policy, entertainment, information management, accounting, engineering, research, and every other professional category, positive results are a necessity.

3)   Reputation

In the Social Dimension, a reputation can be liquid. It can be used to hurt others, help yourself, or harm yourself, in the case of blackmail, and to help others, as does an endorsement. Your reputation can help chart your route to your dream. Reputation, as aforementioned, is directly influenced by your actions and your expectations. Win-win mentality will build your reputation as someone who is trustworthy, progressive, and diligent. Refer to the table below to see which adjectives may become associated to your leadership as a result of your mentality.

Win-Win	Win-Lose	Lose-Win	Lose-Lose
Diligent	Stern	Pessimistic	Vindicated
Loyal	Intelligent	Useless	Rationalizing
Intelligent	Loyal	Sacrificial	Useless
Trusting Followers	Competitive	Competitive	Risky
Progressive	Callous	Pawn-like	Dangerous

For the win-lose relationship, this type of individual is mostly concerned with the best outcome for himself. At the pinnacle of practicing win-lose mentality, you will become great at what you do and accumulate much success throughout your life. Since you have become obedient to your trade and made decisions accordingly, you will appear with a certain amount of sternness and intelligence. Others will commend your ability to serve yourself in an outstanding manner.

At the same time however, others, will assume you do not have their best interest at heart and will deny them an opportunity if there is the perception that it will threaten your success. In this way, the followers of a win-lose personality will go to great lengths to prove that they can be trusted by such a leader. They are, however, functioning out of fear that they may be forced to become a competitor. So, they usually live dual lives of outwardly supporting you and secretly trying to identify a way to move you out of power and enforce their own practice of win-lose. They will spurn you once you lose power as they always secretly believed you were self-serving and callous.

A lose-win relationship is a relationship in which the individual is self-sacrificing for the benefit of others. While this may seem a noble approach, understand that the individual who is self-sacrificing also has individuals who rely on their success. Others who watch a person functioning with this mentality will be forced to play on the individual's weaknesses. This kind of mentality is usually justified with a sense of self-righteousness and rooted in an interpretation of philosophical or religious piety. These deep-seeded beliefs can easily be used against a person because it allows for a certain amount of predictability. When someone is predictable, they can be forced to take options. A win-lose mentality will use another's lose-win mentality to achieve its objectives. It is only useful to be on the competitor's side of a person practicing the lose-win mentality. Playing on this person's team in which your individual needs are not met, will yield a fruitless relationship. You cannot truly grow. This case does not apply to individuals who work to make their bosses look good. These individuals are actually gaining a lot through the relationship, and it qualifies as a win-win relationship, if done correctly.

Another caveat of the lose-win relationship is one in which the individual becomes so consumed by his own self-righteousness and lack of success, that he or she begins to become a pessimist- that nothing beneficial for me should come out of my deeds. Deliberate self-sacrifice will scare others and will make you an obvious pawn.

Finally, the lose-lose mentality is the mentality of "If I cannot have it, then no one can". This leadership type is purely one of a movement. It can be extremely powerful, but dangerous. Working towards the demise of others in lieu of your failure is extremely motivating, but will lead to the most extreme set of adjectives of all adjectives in the Social Dimension. This type makes excuses and rationalizes everything without accommodating the investments of others (many times the investments are considered, but in the context of destroying them). Many individuals will see these types as useless as they provide no beneficial value in the Social Dimension and are extremely risky. They are much harder to predict since as a collective, people usually do not reflect on the opinions and methods of "evil-doers". We focus on the mentalities of those who do well and do good deeds. Understanding the ability to do "evil" will allow a win-win mentality to master a lose-lose mentality.

Every situation is truly unique and may provide temptations to revert to another mentality. The lesson of this chapter is to express the opinion that the win-win mentality will provide the greatest benefit and will assist you in doing the most with your skill set and personality.

II.   **It requires a relationship.**

Properly practicing a win-win mentality requires a few ingredients. What is a relationship? A relationship is an agreement between two or more parties to participate in some accordance with each other. The agreement may be implied or explicit. Relationships go awry when one party does not realize they are in a relationship nor understand the terms of the relationship. Relationships are important to reflect on: they consist of individuals with different interests, experiences, expectations, and orders. When two people are trying to establish a relationship, both parties begin with familiar territory. Conversations usually border along a brief description of a day and perhaps the weather. Someone then decides to take a leap of faith on a similar interest based on the detail of the brief description of the day. Over time, each person begins to identify with and anticipate the other person. This is where win-win mentality begins.

Discussion: "Win/Win Mentality is not a belief in the Third Alternative. It's not your way or my way; it it's a better way, a higher way." *(7 Habits of Highly Effective People)*

A. <u>All parties must be understood.</u>

In the case of beginning a relationship, each person's interests have to be determined. For a win-win game to be played, the objectives should be explicit. Otherwise, there will be parties who will not have their expectations met. This kind of accord is developed through open discussion. All concerns can be voiced and explored. The goal should be for everyone to voice their "vision". The details can be configured and pieced together. For discussion, there should be a main objective to achieve. There are some cautions with discussion:

1) Problem-solving can become ineffective or inefficient if an effective time keeper and note taker are not in place.
2) Emotions will run high if there is a disagreement in approaching a problem, so maintaining focus on a meeting objective is necessary.
3) There will be a mixture of games being played (win-win, win-lose, lose-win, lose-lose) during a discussion, so maintaining a t-chart on benefits and pitfalls will help to keep the group thinking more creatively.
4) Everyone will not explicitly state their interests or objectives, so encourage the group to provide their opinion on specific ideas by asking compare and contrast questions for presented ideas.
5) Strong personalities and power holders will influence the explicitness of the opinions of weaker personalities and subordinates. So, approaching the strong personality first to win them over should work in your favor. The other line of approach includes approaching the other members first, but you will risk ostracizing the strong personality and further create a dichotomy in a group. The approach can be intentional or inadvertent. Either way, you should be prepared for the recoil.

In discussion, however, everyone is simultaneously going into an agreement, and setting objectives so that a plan of action may ensue. In win-win mentality, the solution is not a compromise solution. The solution is very methodical and anticipatory. Much of the planning will be done individually, but the objectives should be clear in the context of the discussion. Everyone should be able to propose options and then the final decision should be a combination of many reflections and considerations so that the desired results may be obtained.

Comprehension: *"...Seek first to understand, then to be understood. This principle is a key to effective interpersonal communication" (7 Habits of Highly Effective people)*

    B. <u>Understand "why" a party wants something and not just "what" they want.</u>

There are two important components of comprehension: passive sensing and active sensing.

Close your eyes and try to be silent. You will begin to hear many sounds in your surroundings. You may hear others having conversations, perhaps a television or video game, the humming of the refrigerator, or even of the electricity going through the wires in a light bulb. You may hear your heart beating. With your eyes closed, you will start to feel things over your skin and imagining things that may be going on around you. You will try to reconstruct your environment because your brain wants to perceive your surroundings. It is said that dreaming is simply the brain's way of seeing when there are no physical constraints on its interpretations. Your brain does this without you consciously compelling it to do so.

When you are hearing a conversation, the same thing occurs. What you are receiving goes through a series of filters, all of your dimensions, and searches for what it wants to hear and then pings an understanding to them through categorizing the information. Your brain stores the information in schemas and then is able to recall information based upon the connectivity of those schemas to

LP25: Influence

other schemas. This is important for understanding because it is in those connections, that you are able to devise empathy. You can begin to understand the "point of view" that others may have. There are many scientific studies on this. Your brain begins to imagine you as the person and tries to imagine the options from that person's point of view. At that point, you can then understand someone else's ideology. In win-win, you should be hearing all of the time. Your brain will take over and do the rest.

In active sensing, you are applying an intention to your action. Hearing is passive, but when objectives are attached to it, it is then active. Hearing, speaking, feeling, seeing, and tasting, with a mission in mind is how you can participate in discussions. This becomes really important when dealing with multiple parties. There will be plenty said, but there is also much said in silence. Use silence strategically. When you have an idea for what you are looking for in the group's verbal and non-verbal dialogue, it will become obvious to identify who in the group is uncomfortable and who is satisfied. Body language and unconscious reactions to words will all demonstrate the true progress towards a goal that is occurring by a group. There is also a sixth sense that you can develop after properly empathizing with another individual. You will be able to capture the vibes of how others are feeling about a particular topic. While you are actively participating, it is important to identify not only what another person is commenting on or demonstrating; you should also be aware of why that person may feel a certain way. This may be accomplished by prying deeper into how a person arrived at their created option, and what they feel could be gained or lost from choosing it.

By reading these vibes, you can do two things: one is a win-win approach on your individual basis, and the other is a win-win for the group. By mentioning that you understand their concerns, but you would like to let someone else offer their commentary on a particular topic, you will free the room to let the weaker personalities engage in discussion. The second thing is to identify whether or not the options the group is offering accomplishes a win-win option. If not, then you can appropriately adjust the talking track so that everyone is focused on the same objective. Finally, when considering a win-win option and handling the discussion in a win-win manner, it is not necessary to actually give it the name "win-win". You should find some unique way to phrase how you feel about the solution and use that. (Branding, when done incorrectly, can be very dangerous and destructive to your reputation.) Discussion is not accomplished without actually understanding the other parties.

You can complete the chart to begin the process of understanding the other parties involved.

Party	Desired Outcome	Resource Required	Reason for Desire

III. <u>Shortcuts do not exist with a Win/Win mentality.</u>

There are no shortcuts to excellence. A shortcut is a perceivably shorter route to a destination than a more common one. Reasons people may take a common road over a shortcut include lack of knowledge, aversion to change, or risk involved in uncertainty. Metaphorically, it is an option that requires less time, effort, or resources than other options when accomplishing an objective. With win-win mentality, understand there are no shortcuts. You will have to put effort into understanding others and develop the skill in shaping a win-win option. The result, however, will be one that not only promotes your agenda and well-being, but also creates inspired and loyal followers who will blindly trust your reasoning and methods.

Resources: "The third character essential to Win/Win is the Abundance Mentality, the paradigm that there is plenty out there for everybody." *(7 habits of Highly Effective People)*

A. <u>Compromising is not an option.</u>

There is always more to consider with a mentality of abundance. With a win-lose or lose-win mentality, the concern is that resources are finite or limited. The full spectrum of Abundance Mentality will come later, but understand that when creating a win-win option, it is not simply a plan of compromise. It is a plan that considers as many facets as possible, and attempts to achieve an objective while meeting the expectations of all parties. A compromise, on the other hand, qualifies as a shortcut. A compromise is a consequence of a win-lose mentality. "If I give some, then you can give some on your demands. We will sacrifice together for the greater good of the plan." Whereas a win-win says, "This plan benefits everyone, and for those who will be indirectly affected by it, it has created a way to still utilize their skills." Some may argue that the heightened use of technology has replaced jobs in our current economy and is partially to blame for the economic downturn. The win-win solution involves the efficient training of the displaced workers to further use and grow their skills in other more engaging ways.

A compromise includes a severance package or unemployment benefits. The previously displaced workers would be out of luck in having a new job but could be paid for their previously completed work. The company would be able to lower their overhead costs by installing computers and laying-off the workers. Here, both parties are temporarily content, but the workers are left pondering their utility and begin developing insecurities about their hiring value. Over time, these disgruntled workers may return to the company and protest the use of computers replacing jobs and stifling the economy. This becomes bad PR and bad PR can return low profit margins.

A non-compromised option can always be configured. Perhaps, the situation is that others have an interest in taking you out of power. A Win-lose option is to convince the others that they are wrong and that you are an asset to the group. A Lose-lose option is to destroy the entire team. A Lose-win option would be to acknowledge their request and step aside. A Win-win option involves a technique known as reconstructing the narrative. Reconstructing the narrative means to change the topic of discussion.

Usually, when all parties are represented within one group, each person focuses on their objectives or interests. As an effective leader, whether self-authorized or title-authorized, you must reconstruct the narrative. Identify a larger, more basic issue that is a common thread of agreement for all parties. Ask questions that help each person return to their vision/ interest building state and then begin to conjointly develop a new vision and a single objective. If this process, evident of a win-win, is not utilized, expect the discussion to devolve into either a stalemate or a compromise. Neither will get you what you desire. You can use questions such as:

    a.   How did we get to this point?
    b.   If we were to focus on one remedy, which department should that focus be channeled to and why?
    c.   What are some external consequences to our actions leading up to this meeting?
    d.   From where is our imbalance stemming?
    e.   Are there any other groups that are experiencing a similar problem?

Note: Make sure that everyone has the opportunity to answer. Be sure to present the image that everyone in the group is interdependent of each other. Everyone brings equal power to the discussion.

A resolution to the stated scenario may begin by questioning why your absence is imperative, and identifying a way in which you actually can be an asset. Perhaps, letting you out of your current position, and occupying a different, more suitable position for your skill set will accomplish everyone's goals. Creating such an outlet allows the rest of the group to consider your talents elsewhere. Craft a vision around your option, and you will be sure to buy yourself some time and perhaps be happier.

Refinement: *"Maturity is the balance between courage and consideration." (7 habits of Highly Effective People)*

    B. It requires <u>maturity.</u>

Practice makes perfect. The practice of this mentality will refine you. You will know when to listen and when to speak. You will learn how to anticipate and identify the motivations of others. The application of this mentality, no matter how complex the circumstance is, requires maturity. Maturity is a psychological term that is used when describing one's ability to respond appropriately, or in a socially acceptable manner, in particular circumstances. One of the keys to maturity is control. Another is calculation. Another is empathy.

Control in reference to maturity is the ability to not act on an impulse and decide when and how to respond. Emotional control is perhaps the most difficult as emotions are innately present and fueled by our impulse to survive. If you feel threatened, rapid changes occur in your body to protect yourself. If you are in an environment that provides an imbalance of fear, love, or hope, you will be less able to adapt when the environment changes. Consistency breeds predictability which breeds comfort. Practice control by imagining yourself in very different environments: encouraging, degrading, and unfulfilled promising. You will develop a stronger sense of yourself and your spectrum.

Calculation is more external. It requires measured decision making. Risk and reward-weighted decisions are involved in calculation. It is also prophetic in nature. Clearly, many of the parameters used for calculation can change in any given circumstance. This is especially true across diverse cultures. Some mannerisms are socially acceptable in the United States, but are extremely taboo in the Middle East. Calculation requires time to learn about others and their expectations or norms.

Empathy is the intellectual identification with or vicarious experiencing of the feelings, thoughts, or attitudes of another. According to an etymology dictionary, "em-" means "in" and pathos means "feeling". Empathy is dependent on your ability to sense another's mindset and imagine the application of their circumstances to your life. Empathy goes beyond simply envisioning the literature, but to interpolate your own feelings associated with the presented circumstance. It means to relive the decisions and emotions the other individual made and felt. The result is not to excuse the other individual's behavior, but to empathize with it.

With these three facets (control, calculation, and empathy) in mind, you can develop your maturity and effectively apply the win-win mentality to any situation.

Chapter Five

The Future

It is imperative that you have a goal for every action. Envisioning a future is a great source of motivation and will provide the appropriate reasons for cautiousness. This, in turn, will help with navigating around obstacles and opportunities. This chapter also proposes the tools and friends needed to escort in your desired future.

The Future

Note: "Substance means: that which underlies all outward manifestations; the essence; the essential reality; the thing in itself, etc. Substantial means: actually existing; being the essential element; being real, etc. Reality means: the state of being real; true, enduring; valid; fixed' permanent; actual, etc..." (Kybalion)

A substantial reality is a reality with considerable value or meaning, and when considering your future, it is the imperative way of imagining it. Something of substance indicates that it has meaning in realness. It is vivid or important. In law and in science, substantial evidence is persuasive, tangible, and maneuverable. Reality is existence. The substances that exist are the manifestations of ideas or the combination of elements to make an entity capable of interaction. To reference the dimensions, the Social Dimension is the manifestation of the Spiritual Dimension. The Substantial Reality is the Social Dimension that should be envisioned when reflecting on the Spiritual Dimension.

There are many uncertainties when considering the future, and we are always planning our lives based with it in mind, albeit the immediate, or the extended. One of the reasons procrastination exists is because we value the existence of a future. We envision ourselves engaged in a task or in our dreams in the context of the future. Perhaps we dream of wealth, fame, or family. When we go about planning for what has yet to come to pass, we usually take tangible steps in order to have the envisioned substantial reality manifest. The same is true for every aspect of our lives. In planning for the future, however, there are a few ideas that should be taken into account.

The operational definitions for this chapter are below:

Vision is the act or power of sensing with the eyes or with sight and the act or power of anticipating that which will or may come to be.

A supervisor is one that directs or oversees a person, group, department, organization, or operation.

Super is a prefix occurring originally in loanwords from Latin, with the basic meaning "above, beyond." Words formed with super- have the following general senses: "to place or be placed above or over" (superimpose; supersede), "a thing placed over or added to another".

As banal as it sounds, you should supervise your life. Super means "above or beyond", and vision is the act of seeing. So, the idea behind supervising your life is seeing beyond the current state of affairs into the future. A supervisor looks over an entity of discussion. Imagine a map in which there is an outlined destination. From the top, you can see where the pathways are. You can compare the routes by length and time. You can see if there are obstacles in the routes, and plan to navigate the best possible route. Once the pathway has been understood, you can then travel the route and arrive at your designated destination. Now, imagine the route from one dimension, a front end view. All you will be able to see are multiple paths and it will be nearly impossible to anticipate obstacles or compare possible routes.

As we navigate through life, we tend to focus on front-end views. What is going on right here and right now in my current situation? I am given a choice of going left or going right. I can jump over the fallen tree or I can crawl under it. When we take an aerial view, however, the entire pathway becomes clearer and easier to maneuver. So, when being a supervisor, keep in mind that you are not simply looking at a situation, but you are looking beyond or above it. Using this approach in planning for the future will be positive for your leadership, both as a leader to yourself, and as a leader for others. Create a vision complete with a starting point and a destination. Then, follow it.

Things to consider about a vision....

I. **<u>You must have a goal.</u>**

As in the case with the map, having a destination is vital to your success. Designating a final destination allows you to evaluate your current position. Find a blank sheet of paper and draw two blocks: A and B. Make B your destination. Make A your initial point. Your B should be an end goal. Label your Point B with qualities. What does the B look like? Now, label your point A with its attributes. Your Point A answers, "What do you look like now?" There is most likely a difference between the two, but this is one way to demonstrate that you can begin to plan how you can happen upon your final destination, literally, and figuratively. The end goal is the driving factor in the map and there are some special features to your point B.

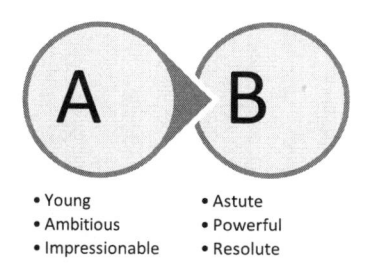

A	B
• Young	• Astute
• Ambitious	• Powerful
• Impressionable	• Resolute

This difference is translated into a path to get from Point A to Point B. The plan/map has many facets to its development which will be later discussed in the book.

Completion: *"Do not go past the mark you aimed for; in victory, Learn when to stop. The moment of victory is often the moment of greatest peril.*

In the heat of victory, arrogance and overconfidence can push you past the goal you had aimed for, and by going too far, you make more enemies than you defeat. Do not allow success to go to your head. There is no substitute for strategy and careful planning. Set a goal, and when you reach it, stop." (48 Laws of Power)

A. <u>I have a purpose.</u>

Your Point B is your purpose. The reason behind beginning the journey is to arrive at point B. It should be crafted with a permanent image in your mind. Having a point B in mind is extremely important as it will indicate where your planning stopped (plans are described in depth in Part Two). Going beyond the Point B leaves much room for uncontrollable factors to play a part in your failure, as no precaution was taken. It is the same as landing a plane and then walking. Depending on where the plane landed, without additional information, your ability to survive and succeed is drastically compromised. When crafting your Point B, you should use archetypes. If someone says, "Mother," an image comes to mind. This image is what can be known as an archetype. It is a universally acceptable and understood symbol and is usually associated with a standard. Some archetypical words include:

Angel	Chief Executive Officer
God	Brother
Politician	Mother
Doctor	Father
Police Officer	

While some of the associated standards are not realistic, envisioning your end goal as an archetype will do much for establishing a vivid impression, or vision, of your Point B. The more completely the Point B is described, the more realistic options you will have when it is time to configure the path.

Another consideration regarding your Point B is the interaction that it will have in the world. What is the worth of a mosquito if it is not considered within its larger context which is the world? Beyond simply creating an archetype, determine the value and worth by understanding the interactions that you will encounter at your final destination. If you envision yourself as a chief executive officer of a large engineering firm, what kind of CEO are you? Are you actively involved in the product development, do you handle negotiations around the world, and where do your contracts come from? Are you patient, impatient, liked or feared? What does your large firm produce or manufacture? What conversations might you have on a daily basis? What would you be expected to understand or know? What is your expertise? Is your company providing a large benefit to others and what is their annual profit margin? What would you do with the profits? Would they be retained earnings or help fund charities? How do you make decisions? Build the image of your final destination so well that it almost seems tangible. Do this so that it may begin to manifest into a substantial reality.

Finally, your Point B should be a culmination of all of your four dimensions. If your spiritual, mental, physical, or social parameters contradict each other, you will be destined to failure. This is understood in the notion of individuality. You were created in a specific and unique way. What you offer is different from others because many factors are involved in determining your current status. How, where, and when you were raised are all important in determining your purpose.

So, if you find yourself jealous of another, then take a moment to reflect on your own possessions. It is not that they are more valuable than you. The truth is that you provide a value in a different form. Although food is important, man cannot live on bread alone. He must have many other things that provide value for his life to be fulfilled. He needs water and love. If love were jealous of water and water jealous of love (the thought is humorous), then what world would we be in? As a side note, jealousy will prevent your individual growth and create discord in your life. Quickly identify your jealousies and begin to explore your own individuality so that you may more completely envision your purpose.

Ethic: *"'How did you learn to read?' the girl asked at one point. "Like everybody learns,' he said, 'In school.' 'Well, if you know how to read why* *are you just a shepherd?'" (The Alchemist)*

B.   I have roles to fulfill.

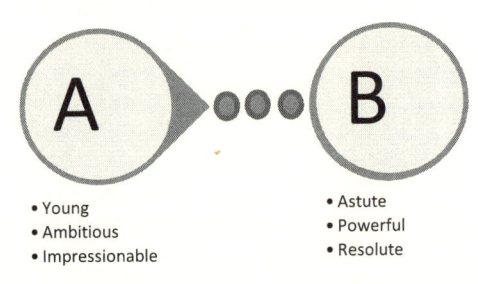

- A
  - Young
  - Ambitious
  - Impressionable
- B
  - Astute
  - Powerful
  - Resolute

Recognize that the process between points A and B involves occupying many roles. Roles are temporary positions that you fill within the context of achieving your purpose. There is a reason to every role that you engage. This particular quote references an incident in The Alchemist in which a seemingly poor shepherd boy is reading. The girl interrogates him due to the cognitive dissonance of seeing a shepherd boy reading as reading was a skill associated with wealth or a higher status. The lesson to understand in this part of the book is the importance of occupying a role and the humility associated with the occupancy of that role. Perhaps you intend to be the world's most important leader. You are, however, currently a janitor. This does not mean that you are traveling the wrong path, or that the current job is beneath you. You should view it as a stage, however. It is a level in which you must obtain necessary attributes and relationships in order for you to arrive at your destination. Regarding the travel metaphor to a final destination, each role is as a gas stop is to arriving at the final destination. You must fuel yourself, and you cannot be partially fueled. Along the way, you will have to stop and ask for directions, fuel your car, and learn your environment so that you can navigate yourself along the streets. The aerial view will allow you to navigate yourself correctly, but you still must actually drive the route you plan.

So, in the case of the reading shepherd, the books he read and the skill to read became pivotal for his eventual arrival at his "personal legend". He ended the story with a family and wealth, but he learned much on his journey through filling the roles of a shepherd, a tribal constituent, a merchant's assistant, and many others. Each role then proceeded to assist with the next. The same is true for your life. There are roles you play, such as: child, parent, student, worker, manager, etc. You should be willing to embrace your current role and maximize the opportunities within that role by learning the craft that is being taught. If you are teaching someone, learn how to teach to the best of your ability. Envision yourself excelling in every role you partake in. You should understand the terms of your role. What is expected of you, what do you have the capability of doing, and what are you willing to do? You should take the time to develop your work ethic and ability to build relationships. You should be an asset to whomever you enter into a relationship so as to develop their dependency on you and to gain the most out of that particular relationship.

The other element to this quote is condescending encouragement. The girl ends by saying, "Well then why are you just a shepherd?" While her question could be interpreted to mean: you could do so much more since you can read, the tone of the phrase means: you are wasting your time reading if all you are going to be is a shepherd. The latter is usually construed as discouragement, especially if we have no control over whether we are a shepherd or not. Retrain yourself, however, to understand the value that is inherent within every role. The boy understood his value by replying with the importance of learning how to care for things that were dependent upon his guidance. Sheep cannot tell the difference between safe grounds to feed and those with danger. A shepherd, however, works long days and ensures the safety of his sheep by staying aware of the surroundings and protecting them from potential predators. His reward is based on the health and survival of his flock. Do not take your life experiences for granted as they will be needed on recall for the rest of your life. If you had a poor childhood, realize that you experienced it for a reason. The qualities you can develop during such a phase will be important for your success in the future.

II. <u>You must see the journey.</u>

When planning your future, it is imperative that you not only envision your Point A and your Point B, but envision the journey in between. Imagine the types of obstacles you will encounter, and what you will have to learn along the way. Envision what pathways will lead you to your Point B from your Point A. As Alice in Wonderland was wandering through her forest, she encountered all sorts of puzzles, traps, and interesting characters. Your life will not be too different. If you plan to attain massive amounts of wealth, the journey will be filled with multitudes of road blocks and traps. Financial gimmicks and dream gurus will try to test your patience and sense of hope or faith that will lead you down a path of misery. Individuals who specialize in mind games will play them on you: stalling techniques, tools of propaganda and persuasion, and too-good-to-be true deals claiming to be free of charge. People will present shortcuts that are actually filters in disguise. They filter out individuals who:

1) Do not know their worth
2) Have no intent on developing a true ethic
3) Are not sure of what they want, need, or love
4) Are seeking shortcuts because of the fear associated with failing

You should not blame the crafty individuals you meet. They are actually blessings in disguise reminding you of where you could or should be. They are doing what they do best. Blame yourself for falling prey to one of the four aforementioned types. Fix it, and move on.

Approach: *"Plan all the way to the end: The ending is everything. Plan all the way to it, taking into account all the possible consequences, obstacles, and twists of fortune that might reverse your hard work and give glory to others. By planning to the end you will not be overwhelmed by circumstances and you will know when to stop. Gently guide fortune and help determine the future by thinking far ahead." (48 Laws of Power)*

    A.   <u>I must understand the playing field.</u>

In order to safeguard yourself from those four individual types, you must understand the rules of the game which you are playing a hand. Imagine your friends want to play Monopoly. When you all

LP25: Influence

sit down, you try to apply the rules of Chess. The result is inefficiency. I doubt the game could even be started, and perhaps an evening of teasing and arguing would follow such idiocy. This idea is also captured in the quote: "If you only have a hammer, everything looks like a nail." Seems simple enough, but when we return to our lives, we sometimes forget that just because we may recognize that a game is being played, all scenarios do not play the same game. The rules change, and it would work to your advantage to be flexible and privy to the rules that govern the games. If you know what a politician is doing (you learn this from the use of empathy from the previous chapter), then you can interpret "between the line" speeches.

Playing fields are systems in their entirety: the involved parties, processes, and expected reaction-action orders. It would be a fallacy to assume that all systems operate under the same ethics. So, when viewing the pathway's from Point A to Point B, you can understand each pathway's intricacy by observing its associated rules. In Alice in Wonderland, this is also evident- although ironic.

Clearly, however, there are some basic assumptions that can be made for all playing fields. Almost all of our systems are directly related to the three main emotions of humans: love, hope, and fear. They are all related to a need for survival. From there, the conclusions to the assumptions begin to change. There are some who think of self-preservation. Others have divided themselves in a way to think of the survival of larger groups of people. When a person feels threatened, there are a range of reactions that they can follow. Know who you are dealing with so that you can best anticipate their moves. If they have been trained, be cautious. In business, there is a difference between meeting someone who is seasoned, and a freshman. On average, it would be much easier to play mind-games on one of them. Much of the planning process will come from applying the chapters Win-Win Mentality (Chapter 4) and The Plan (Chapter 9).

When this quote references "all the way to the end", it is referencing your Point B. Envisioning how a pursuit may twist and turn is very important, and recognizing the interacting orders is vital to your success. *"Gently guiding fortune"* is a technique. You should never be too outlandish in your pursuits. It will breed insecurities in bystanders. Just as you get jealous, others do too. When you excel, you remind others of their inadequacies. Gently guiding involves a careful and calculated method of achieving goals. There should be a rhyme and reason to your success that others can easily grasp and partake in. Beyond just following paths, you have the ability to change them. You can add and take away where necessary, but it must be a calculated action. Organic happenings are subject to Darwin's survival of the fittest. You are giving "chance", which is unrecognized order, power to influence a situation. A win-win mentality will allow you the maximum protection from the interference of "chance" because of its planning-heavy techniques.

Certainty: *"Enter action with boldness: If you are unsure of a course of action do not attempt it. Your doubts and hesitations will infect your execution. Timidity is dangerous: Better to enter with boldness. Any mistakes you commit through audacity are easily corrected with more audacity. Everyone admires the bold; no one honors the timid."* (48 Laws of Power)

   B.   <u>I will be making life-changing decisions.</u>

As a leader, you will be making many decisions. Every decision has a cause and an effect associated with it. This causal relationship will influence entities that you may not even be aware of. When justifying your path and making changes to it, realize that these changes have effects associated with them. Most of them will strongly impact your life. They may work to increase your options, or to limit your opportunities, but you should keep a mental ledger that accounts for your decisions.

When making decisions, you should be cautious, but when communicating your decisions, you should be bold. If you indicate any doubt in your communication, your followers will begin to doubt you. Your confidence will strengthen those who listen, and even if you are wrong in your statement, another strong statement will mitigate the effects of a bad decision. In order to accomplish such boldness, you should spend time reflecting on your decision before you communicate it. You should convince yourself that the option you are deciding to follow is the option you agree with 100%. When it is time for you to deliver your decision, everyone will have open ears because it will be obvious that you are committed to your decision, and for many, that is a prerequisite for its success. The reason this is subliminally true, is because boldness is tied into the ego. In order to save face, the audience perceives that you will try to do everything in your power to prove that your decision was the correct decision. If someone asks you, "Do you want to do this job?", and you have decided you would like to, your answer is, "I would be happy to do this job, because I know the value that I will bring to you and your project." Be bold.

The way to beat a lie detector is to really believe your lies. Such control requires much reflection because with words, you may get away with lying. Your body, however, will betray you. Your heart rate increases, your brain starts using its creative side, and you become sweaty. You voice quivers, your eyes rummage, and your veins thicken because of the increased pressure. Your words begin to stumble on top of each other, because you begin speaking too quickly. You realize it and so you try to slow your speech down, making your listener feel uncomfortable and question your intentions. Your listener identifies what is occurring and walks away remarking how they feel uncomfortable around you and thus, they do not trust you. Decision communication is an art. If you do not believe in your decision enough, your body will communicate it as though it were a lie. Others will believe it to be so, too. It should be said with enough concreteness and conciseness that there is no room to pull it apart before being considered. It should also be said encouragingly and objectively enough so as not to offend the listener. The balance is confidence, and not arrogance or reticence. Arrogance and reticence are consequences of an insecure individual who evaluates their worth in accordance with the worth of others. Confidence however, is conveyed without words.

III.   You must have friends.

Of course when thinking about your future, there are several things you will need. One of which is friends. They are reliable to a certain point, and will be essential on your pursuits. There are two kinds of friends that you should have on your journey. Any others are not necessarily friends, but acquaintances. The more friends you have, the more complex your planning will become. Strategic usage of your friends will allow you to manage an extremely successful journey. Once an individual becomes a friend, there is nothing which prevents them from converting back to being an acquaintance. At that point, their actions will solely consider their interests, and not those of the relationship. You should not blame a friend for tending to their personal desires, but you should be aware of a particular friend's predisposition or susceptibility to reverting outside of the friend relationship.

The friendship should work to the benefit of both who decide to enlist in the agreement, as mentioned with the win-win mentality. Interests and objectives should be clear and susceptibilities can usually be configured from these initial interactions. Constantly evaluate your friends for their allegiance, and reaffirm their comfort with your allegiances. There will be circumstances in which you will be on the lookout for your own interest, and not the interests of your friends. Know that point and know your friend's points.

To create a friend, communicate an image of the relationship. Speak in vague words that align with hopes, fears, and loves. This will open the door to them to also share their hopes, fears, and loves with you. Never tell all of the details. Details will usually betray the symbiotic relationship as conflicts will emerge, and you will ruin any prior progress made. As a friend demonstrates their allegiance, slowly share some details so as to encourage them to be even better friends, but always leave out some information. In this manner, you will always keep a repertoire of friends, but will protect yourself from acquaintances. It is not good for a leader to be alone. A lone leader goes unchecked and usually functions under clouded judgment because he is constantly trying to understand why he is alone. It is distracting. When you meet a lone leader, befriend him by speaking in terms of fear and hope.

Apprenticeship: *"Quite obvious to you at this point a mentor is someone who guides or trains a pupil at some skill or craft." (Young Leader)*

A. <u>I have a mentor.</u>

One kind of friend you must have is a mentor. The only way you may have a map to use in aerial view is because of the mentors with whom you surround yourself. The concept is the same with charting topography. It requires another item or person to view and map the ground. A satellite may run a signal and use the change in speed of the return signal to map out what is in the nearby area. Books are the metaphorical equivalence of satellites as they are entities that can give you an abundance of information about a particular subject. Keep in mind that books are written by people. Authors have lives and opinions, and many times these experiences can bleed through the text. Knowing the author and their background is just as important as knowing the content of the book. It can help you with discriminating between advice worth using and advice worth reading. Some opinions may not apply, but there is deeper insight you can gain by knowing that the opinion exists. Some books provide greater insight into the meaning that other books are trying to convey. Missing out on a good book will limit your fluidity in traversing your pathway.

Many times, in the metaphor of the satellite, people are sent to ensure that the satellite is gathering accurate information. They verify the accuracy by walking the actual land mass and mapping steep or gradient inclines and discriminating between water and land areas. They then either confirm the findings, or establish new information for the map. Before a golf course is able to be used, engineers approach the green and use lasers to properly classify each hole by par and ensure that the actual green matches the expected green. The point here is that maps are only made after being reviewed first. A mentor is someone who has traversed some part of your figurative map and can provide you with details on its figurative layout and features. Mentors are the first type of friend when travelling on your journey to your future. A complete version of a map is only possible after consulting many different topographers. This is also true of your life journey. A clear vision of it is only possible once you have been given the consultation from mentors.

The map is made after walking it a few times. Use your mentors to make the task more efficient. When learning from others, there are a few particulars to keep in mind. Firstly, the information being given may have inherent faults. Perhaps a company's topographer was only able to walk four feet into a new territory before he was quickly captured by natives in the area. Since he was taken hostage, the company sent another topographer. He traveled another route to avoid the natives, but ran out of things to eat and so the company had to rescue him. Then, a third topographer entered the territory through another clearing. All three will have similar information to give you about the territory and there will also be differences. The one taken as a hostage will probably tell you to never enter the territory. The second will probably say you must bring a lot of food with you so as not to starve. The third will give you the topography surrounding only one pathway and tell you that it is probably the best path since he made it through without any problems. While all pieces of information may be true, they also are equally likely to be only true in certain instances. It is up to you to be able to practice discernment with the advice of mentors. They are speaking to you in terms of their lives and experiences, which may only be similar to yours. A true map of the territory would come from listening to the similarities in their stories. In scientific testing, when using multiple data points, Analyses of Variance (ANOVAs) are performed to cross-analyze results. An ANOVA will determine whether or not a specific result occurred enough to be viewed as a cause and not a random match. An example is demonstrated below:

Experiment One
A coin is flipped once, and a thunderstorm occurs.
The conclusion is that whenever a coin is flipped, a thunderstorm occurs.

Experiment Two
A coin is flipped 10,000 times, and each time, a thunderstorm occurred, yielding 10,000 thunderstorms in the same place.

For the first Experiment, the ANOVA would show that there is a high chance that the two occurrences only happened by chance, and not necessarily a result of a direct cause-effect relationship. For the second experiment, however, the ANOVA would indicate a very small variance between the results and show that there is a high chance that the first occurrence is the direct cause of the other. When cross-analyzing the wisdom of others, it is important to do mental ANOVAs. What are the chances of detail "A" being accurate and under which circumstances does that direct relationship occur? If you do not sort out the incongruences of your mentors, and blindly apply all of their advice regardless of validity, then you will have to accept the consequences of those imprudent actions. You cannot blame others for your failings in discernment. Tread carefully, as it is your life and you only live this life once. Regardless, mentors are an invaluable asset when taking your journey. There are no bad mentors, only an array of mentors. You can learn something from anyone. Sorting through the advice they give may be difficult, but you must be willing to spend time analyzing the risks involved in your decisions. Then, be bold with your decisions.

If you do not take the time to sort through the information that a mentor may give you, then you will eventually make decisions you do not whole heartedly believe in. Once this happens, you will hold grudges against your mentors for "forcing" you to make certain decisions. It is best to determine who you are and what you want before immediately taking the advice of a mentor. If you do happen to make a decision that concludes poorly, then you must accept ultimate responsibility for it. As long as you blame another person for your actions, you will never grow or learn, and will reaffirm yourself that you have limitations within your ability to make decisions. You will erode your confidence in future circumstances.

Practice: *"Empowerment can best be explained as the distribution of power onto others in a way that allows them to create an even stronger power base for themselves." (Young Leader)*

    B. <u>I have a mentee.</u>

As you learn something new, it is important to practice it. "Practice makes perfect". The adage is prevalent because it is true. In order to practice the new information you gain from mentors, you can do two things: meditate and find a friend to mentor.

When meditating, you are searching through your life and identifying where you can make personal improvements and position your strengths and passions. You should be reflecting on your circumstances and try to apply new wisdom to old situations. Empathize with your past so that you can become aware of your own judgments and justifications. It is here where you can learn to anticipate yourself and control your tendencies.

With mentoring, you can express your newly devised wisdom to another, and discover its manifestation into a substantial reality. If your advice works, then your mentees should thrive. They should benefit from your wisdom. If they falter, however, then chances are you should review your current mindset and aptitude to apply wisdom.

Feedback received from your mentee can take one of two forms: positive or negative. In mentorship, you should share your ideologies. Your mentees will mainly learn from your habits and the things you do not say, however. It is akin to creating a mirror. You can gain greater understanding of yourself and correct your mentee by correcting yourself. You can also commend yourself by commending your mentee. With mentees, be sure to practice patience and empathy. These friends are the most loyal because they are dependent upon your wisdom. They assume you have their best interest in mind and you should do your utmost not to abuse it. Mentees are very valuable and can become your future bodyguards when you are successful.

A caveat with the mentee relationship is that you can spurn them and create enemies. This technique can be used both to your advantage and your disadvantage, but either option is definitely a possibility. If a mentee feels betrayed, they will hold the grudge against you and work against you. Be sure to disseminate open ended and multilateral advice so as not to have a mentee feel pressured to accept it. If you become too engrossed in their affairs and convince them to accept advice which then turns awry, the first person they will blame is you, their mentor, for "making them do it".

IV. **You must have tools.**

Beyond books, there are many other tools that you can use when preparing for your future and venturing on your journey. Recall, this entire theme is regarding how to view the world. It explores which kinds of logic and emotions should be applied to circumstances, your approach, and what the future actually represents. The future is the manifestation of your four dimensions and is your substantial reality. The more vividly you imagine your future to be, the more of a substantial reality it can potentially become. Your future will become your way of life as you will develop a second nature muscle in identifying trends and opportunities that will keep your present full of adventure and new learning experiences. You have already established a few mental tools within this chapter, and a tool that can be consulted as a mentor. As a refresher, the mental tools are:

1) An aerial view of your journey

This skill is difficult and requires the active use of information provided by mentors. Practicing involves thinking in long terms. If you are making a decision, ask, "How does it affect you one year from now?" What are some potential hazards and risks involved by deciding one way or another? Who will benefit and who will be harmed? Does this decision get me closer to my end-game, my Point B, my purpose?

2) The ability to judge yourself from the outside (to step outside of your body since you have the dual nature).

With children, this concept is known as Theory of Mind. Most people do not develop it until the age of four, but it is having the ability to understand that other viewpoints exist. The same reason a child believes that his mother is the only mother that exists is because he assumes his life and standards are the only ones that exist.

An experiment was performed with a group of students in

determining their ability to logically approach a problem or question from the viewpoint of another. A teddy bear was seated next to the first child. A box of crayons was displayed for the child. The box was opened, revealing crayons. When the box was closed, the child was asked, what was in the box. The child remarked, "Crayons." The child was then asked, what does the teddy think is in the box?" The child remarked, "Crayons." The teddy was then removed from the area. Next, the crayons in the box were replaced with a new item. The child was asked what was inside of the box. The child responded with the name of the new item. Then, the teddy was brought back into the room. The child was asked what the teddy would think was inside of the box. The child responded again with the name of the new item. The results of the experiment overwhelmingly went this way until the researchers tested children over the age of four. These children overwhelmingly responded that the teddy would think the crayons were in the box and not the new item because the teddy did not "see" when the items were exchanged.

Our ability to think like another, or experience as another does, is a developed skill, and can continue to be developed.

While these tools are great for establishing a journey, there are still some tools to use on your journey that must be discussed.

Forces: *"Conserve our forces and energies by keeping them concentrated at their strongest point. You gain more by finding a rich mine and mining it deeper, than by flitting from one shallow mine to another- intensity defeats extensity every time. When looking for sources of power to elevate you, find the one key patron, the fat cow who will give you milk for a long time to come."* (48 Laws of Power)

    A.   <u>I know my resources.</u>

Many people use a lack of resources as an excuse for not accomplishing their goals. These resources could include relationships, money, objects, people of desire, land, basic necessities, education, social status, appearance, genetic makeup, intimate elements, mediums of communication, loyal followers, or a support infrastructure (network). Resources are influenced by forces, which are motivations in the four dimensions. How well we allocate resources is a testament to how we view the value of our resources and our possession of them. By focusing the forces to a single point of interest, you can create a goal that is aligned on all levels, and increase the chances of succeeding in that goal. When you focus on something, your mind is obsessively concerned about it. As with a man who has a hammer, all things look like nails, opportunities will be easy to spot because you are focused on a goal with a method in mind. Your win-win mentality and four dimensional perspective should not be compromised by your focus, but they should rather guide your focus. As a lens guides the light to the inner-workings of your eyes, so will your forces guide your focus, so that it may be seen more clearly.

Resources should be strategically positioned. You must keep in mind that others who need resources will seek to have yours. The goal is not to be stingy with your possessions, but to be critical about who receives them. Understand what they will do with your resources, and be careful when completely absolving yourself of the sovereignty of your belongings. While you may have used your resources wisely, the receiver may have no intention to do the same. The other element to this section is in the search for resources. If possible, it is better to find one source that provides much than many sources that provide little. The exception to this is when you are seeking the vested interest of many. In this scenario, you want all participants to have some risk involved with a transaction so that the total risk is distributed. Any deal without risk to a buyer is likely to be abused. Finding one source, a true patron, can be very useful. Patrons usually give you more than one resource. They can provide monetary gain, status, and a network. In exchange, you must perform services at the whim of the patron. If you have two or more patrons, interests become more complicated. This is not to say that you should not have multiple streams of income, but stay focused on your end goal, and utilize your resources so that you may accomplish it.

Resources can be used in multiple ways:

End-Goal Obtainment

Resources can be directly used to buy a house, or stage an event, or win an election. Most people think of money this way, "When I get rich or wealthy, I am going to…" While the notion is filled with hope and keeps the short and long term goals conscious, it is not the complete vision of resource utilization. This is the most prevalent mechanism by which we view resources, and it causes us to either excuse ourselves from actually accomplishing our goal through steps that could be taken today. It also provides us comfort in knowing the civic and personal good we may one day do with a lot of money. At the end of the day, however, what is done with a little is what a person does with a lot. If you can be a great steward of a mediocre salary, then you have a greater chance of being a great steward of a large salary. Set resource goals and apply your resources to accomplishing small things if you only have a small amount. If you have a large amount, do the same. Never catch yourself disseminating resources you do not yet have. It is a sure way for others to take advantage of you. If you are in debt, it means your value has been negatively valued. That is enough of a weakness for another individual to offer you a deal you cannot refuse, and then you must owe them. There are many discussions involving good debt and bad debt, but in general, having outstanding resource promises, holds you subject to someone or some entity. Even your citizenship does not come freely. So, as you are handling your resources, identify what resources can be applied to short-term goals, and then accomplish those short term goals. Practicing this with just a little will leave the door open for having more at a later time. Not to mention, in the process, you are actually accomplishing goals.

System Influence

Resources are also used to influence a system. Salaries are paid to incentivize workers to do a specific job. Bribes are used for either protection or a guaranteed contract. Resources are used to do this because the global nature of resources is that they are always in demand. Someone else wants your land and sees a specific value in it. Therefore, you may be the happy medium for them to accomplish their end goal. The transaction of resources represents the transactions of interest. Much can be learned about an individual once they have been asked what they are looking to exchange. Imagine hostage situations. The first question in negotiation is, "What are your demands?" These demands are then analyzed to understand motives and willingness to carry out a threat. Resources can be used to influence a system, and this is what is known as leverage or power. When you have something to offer that is in demand and of limited accessibility, you have leverage, and the effective power to have your interests met. This is one of the reasons why you should understand your unique talents and offerings so that you may find yourself more influential. "Power" can be understood to mean having insight into a system. If you can understand a system, you can directly influence the system. Your actions with leveraging will have a ripple effect that you should not only be aware of, but deliberately use.

Resource Pool Growth

The final usage of resources includes growing a smaller set of resources to a larger amount. This transaction is usually known as investing. In investing, resources of a certain value are strategically applied in order to attract more resources or increase in value. Investment styles are very personal and, at a minimum, require some analysis of risk, and additionally the use of intuition. Numbers, if tortured enough, can be made to say anything. So having an intuitive sense for how a system is working would be much to your benefit. True intentions can be hidden behind a great display of puppetry. To understand your resource pool or its ability to grow, seek out mentors and convince them to help you as a mentee, by soon becoming a prodigy of theirs.

Gifts: "*So here are a few things that can be considered traits of creativity: 1. Ability to relate a vision. 2. Talent in some unique way. 3. Recognition that there's art in just about everything. 4. Desire to be fantastic.*" *(Young Leader)*

B.   **I know my creations.**

The final tools you have on your journey are your own creations. These are the entities or circumstances that you manufacture with your resources. You should know what you are capable of creating, and use those skills in your job. Note that any learned skill can in some way, shape, or form be applied to any job. What qualifies as a creation? Manufactured works that require creativity are included in the definition of a creation. The quote proposes a few guidelines for determining creativity. The first is the ability to relate a vision. Realize that everything you envision is created in your mind. You understand it well because you thought of it. However, when communicating the vision to another person, you are required to understand how the person would be able to understand it too. Imagine if you and another individual spoke two different languages. You could not simply explain your thoughts to the other person using your language. You must be creative in relating your vision. Perhaps a translator is needed or you can use pictures. Maybe, you learn their language and the language's nuances to clearly describe your vision. Whatever the transaction requires, in translating a vision from yourself to another, you must be creative.

Another way to look at creativity is through a particular talent. A talent is some act that you perform that is either superlative to or different from others. Talents can be used for bad or for good, but they are a part of your creativity. The most common forms of talent that are associated with creativity are those within the arts: writing, drawing, painting, singing, speaking, etc. You can also have a talent in advising people in their affairs as a good consultant or counselor. Talents are diverse and span a vast array in kinds. How you use them, is where creativity is important. Attaching value to a talent requires creativity. Painting is only important because we ascribe to the value that has been presented in it. If a talent is no longer creating wealth, it is imperative to be creative and reconstruct the values associated with the talent. At one point, we had a need for draftsmen. Then, once computer programs were created to do the same job in at least half the time with twice the quality, the value associated with the profession of being a draftsman was severely diminished. The idea is not to give up and curse the system for

LP25: Influence

devaluing your talent, but to get creative with your talent and make it invaluable. That is creativity.

Art exists in everything. There is ebb and a flow to all systems, man-made and nature-made. Understanding the ebbs and flows will offer you much opportunity to be creative. The ebb and flow are present in the design and the building blocks of all systems. If you are looking at the human race's emotional system, an individual's ebb and flow is a building block of the larger system. You can run a campaign utilizing the human mob mentality by understanding how an individual can feel pressured into thinking a certain way. Using your knowledge of systems is creativity.

Finally, a desire to be fantastic is pivotal. If you have the desire to be fantastic, that means you are constantly seeking opportunities to turn your resources into creations on your journey, and to do it efficiently and intently. Being in this mindset is a definite trait of a creative person. Fantastic people are always trying to expand their horizons and heighten their ceilings through the creative allocation and focusing of resources.

Creativity and resource management are essential for your journey. Maintain a clear perspective of your journey by taking an aerial view and seeking mentors to help define the pathways of the journey. Do not be afraid to be bold with your decisions, especially if you have spent sufficient time imagining your Point B and envisioning what you want. Your future depends on the decisions you make today and the mindset you carry with you along the way.

There are no quizzes in this chapter.

Part Two Introduction

How Do I Play a Role?

You should be able to clearly define your role within a broad picture. This theme goes deeper into the generalities of everything in the world working together, and discusses your particular application of forces and focuses from an internal point of view.

Understanding your forces and focuses includes knowing your strengths, passions, and resources. It also means knowing what your motivations are. The dimension you are extremely dependent upon, will determine the results of your most prone actions. You can only create a plan and learn how to communicate with others once you have sufficiently analyzed your own assets and liabilities. This theme is meant to cause you to deeply reflect on what motivates you so that you can be prepared for the third theme: The Transition Stage. You must have internal accord before you may have external accord.

At the end of this theme, you are expected to have identified exactly what your purpose is and begun exploring how it applies and exists within, with, or above the current systems of the world. This theme focuses on learning within context. You have been given the tools to gain perspective on life, but now you must gain perspective on your life. Imagine yourself as a puzzle piece. You are cut in a specific way and are designed to represent a certain part of a larger image. No matter how large or small a piece is, each puzzle piece has a specific location in the completed puzzle. Each piece has a unique purpose. If one piece is mis-matched the remaining puzzle pieces are affected. The surrounding pieces will be affected and the image will be distorted. By determining your proper position, you help to complete the larger puzzle.

Many roles make up a purpose, and it is important to create an archetype by which you willingly and excitingly align yourself. As you read the next five chapters, be sure to refer to your designated Point B so that you can begin sketching a journey. By doing this, you can remain focused on the end-goal instead being mentally mired by your weaknesses and regrets. This chapter is meant to give you the freedom to contemplate your past decisions, both actively and passively made.

Chapter Six

Who Am I?

The purpose of "who I am" is to understand your rationales behind actions and decisions. This chapter is intended to strengthen your notion of what it means to pursue your passions and to identify your specific limitations.

Who Am I?

Note: "Do not accept the roles that society foists on you…Be the master of your own image rather than letting others define it for you." (48 Laws of Power)

Whatever predicament you find yourself in, realize that it is of your own doing. Your decisions, understanding of systems, and control over yourself have permitted your current circumstances to operate and consume your life. If you yield your power over yourself to others, they will surely take advantage of the disorder in your life and corner you into an opportunity or role that you cannot resist. If you are desperate for money or love, then society will use such desperation against you. However, if all that you desire is proposed on your terms, truly on your terms, then you will lose your powerlessness. When in negotiations, offer your highest desire. If you are going to work at a fast food restaurant, let them know what you are aspiring to be or do, and what value you can bring to them through those achievements. If you allow another regimen or schedule to be imposed upon your daily routines, those regimens will become you and you will temporarily lose the ability to determine your own image.

If you feel as though you are sacrificing who you are or what is good for you because of another's rules or rhetoric, then you should consider why. Is it that the other's rules are truly working for your benefit, or are those rules derived from the ruler's own fears and insecurities? If the ruler is instead working for your benefit, you should consider why you may want to rebel and try to understand whether or not the proclaimed benefit is good for you. The ruler may be correct in this instance. If the ruler, on the other hand, is acting out of fear, then create your own terms and foster your own growth and individuality by cornering the ruler into a box using fears and insecurities. Present false options which allow you to work to your benefit and the ruler's (with a win-win mentality). He will become loyal to you. Never let another individual have absolute control over your journey. Once they assume that type of power over you, they will consistently use you as a pawn to accomplish their own objectives. Many of which may adversely affect you. All of which will destroy your sense of identity.

Most people are afraid of power until they realize what it means to not have any. Imagine a life in which all of your decisions were inextricably connected and directed by another entity or individual. Your freedoms are reduced to breathing, eating, and procreating. You have no right to justice, and you possess no right to harness the potential of others to complete a project. People claim they would rebel in such an environment of slavery; however, we dependably and willingly release our freedoms to other individuals so that they can anticipate our actions and remove our sense of responsibility. The result is a loss of identity. Preserve your identity by establishing your own standards, rules, beneficial desires, actions, and mutual relationships.

The operational definition for this chapter is below:

<u>Identity</u> is described as the condition of being oneself or itself, and not another.

The act of not being another requires much effort. An apple is different from an orange, and cannot be an orange. An apple must be an apple just as an orange must be an orange. In the same way, you cannot be another. When you try to be a duplicate of another, you will consistently fail. Role models are not meant to be defining, but rather guiding. When two people communicate, each is attempting to share an identity. They communicate their expectations and justify those expectations with stories. Your identity rests upon your ability to carefully be yourself. If you are too much of yourself at one time, then you can demean the reputation of your identity, as others also want the opportunity to share their identity.

Identity preservation, as aforementioned, includes establishing your own standards, rules, beneficial desires, actions, and mutual relationships. What are your current descriptions of each? After reading what each term means, try to configure your own. You can use the Standards of Leadership presented in Chapter One to begin.

> *Standards are a list of morals to which you will hold yourself responsible.*
>
> *Rules are mechanisms by which you can achieve your standards when forced to make decisions.*
>
> *Rulers set rules over entities and individuals.*
>
> *Beneficial desires are desires that will benefit you within all of the four dimensions: Social, Physical, Mental, and Spiritual.*
>
> *Actions are practices you engage in or make a habit of in order to disobey or obey your designated and agreed upon rules.*
>
> *Mutual relationships are relationships that afford all parties some desirable benefit as a consequence of the relationship.*

Things to consider about identity....

I. <u>My limitations will discourage me from becoming myself.</u>

Perceived limitations are the bane of your identity. Once you accept a limitation as true, you are liable to compromise or alter your identity. Limitations come in many forms and will influence you one way or another like a mouse in a maze. Every time the mouse runs into a wall, the position of that wall becomes a learned obstacle in the mouse's mind and eventually the mouse arrives at the predetermined location. Every time the mouse runs the maze, it is reminded of the predetermined route. Much of life is traversed in this manner. When we hit a wall, we turn and look for another route noting where each obstacle is placed. These obstacles become learned behaviors and responses. Eventually, the only track we choose is the one in which the person studying us wanted us to follow the entire time. These limitations in life however, are not made of walls. They are made up of thoughts and beliefs, which can be paraded through and manipulated. Limitations can be derived from any of the dimensions and require different methods of management depending on its source. Recall the discussion on rebelling against a ruler. The case is not to always rebel. In some cases the limitations will benefit you. It would be wise to become familiar with the sources of limitations so that you may distinguish between those that will benefit you and those that will cause undo harm to your identity.

Here is an exercise: In order to truly apply the content in this book, you must follow these guidelines. Read the entire book, and then meditate every day on each sentence. You must fly at least twice around the equator of the Earth. Visit each country and learn the languages of all of the countries. Teach the content in the book to a group of four year olds, and allow them to practice the content by following you. Then, you must read the book one more time, and you will be the most successful person in the world. Throughout the above story, you may have actually imagined yourself doing each thing. You probably even imagined the faces of the four year olds as you were teaching them.

Mainly, however, your mind most likely preoccupied itself with thoughts such as these:

1. Well, that is ridiculous! How is that even possible?
2. This book is not even that novel!
3. This must be a joke, and an unimaginative one at that.

The exercise is self-talk. Most of the talking we do is in our minds. It is made up dialogue and never makes it to the rest of the world. So, much of what influences us comes from within and invariably lies within our own sense of self and what we feel we are capable of doing. Your morals and ethics rely on your ability to self-talk, and to self-talk in a self-promoting way. According to how well you perceive yourself in alignment with your positive self-talk translates into how you see your worth. There is a factor x, which consists of the percentage of positive self-talk you actually believe. This is your total worth. So, how do we derive our positive self-talk? We derive it by taking all of the possibilities and subtracting the limitations (P-L).

W (worth)/ X (factor X) = PT (positive talk) = P (all possibilities) −L (limitations)

(This equation should be used for metaphorical purposes only. It is not meant to yield true numbers.)

Worth: *"The thought of inferiority of the Negro is drilled into him in almost every class he enters and in almost every book he studies.....As another has well said, to handicap a student by teaching him that his black face is a curse and that his struggle to change his condition is hopeless is the worst sort of lynching. It kills one's aspirations and dooms him to vagabondage and crime." (Mis-education of the Negro)*

A. <u>Limitations come in the form of prejudices.</u>

As mentioned, limitations can come in many forms. One of which is the form of a prejudice. With the civil rights movement, many mental set-backs for the race came from the propagated idea that as an African American, you were inherently inferior and incapable of accomplishing certain achievements. Such a prejudice was reinforced by texts, social surroundings, and rules. Jim Crow laws helped to sustain the ideology that a mixed culture would be prime fodder for crime due to the inherent differences between the different races in the United States. This ideology extended to other cultures beyond the "Black-White" divide. The infiltration of prejudices can be counteracted by the defendant's own cultural beliefs. Most individuals gain their cultural insight and strength from family or history. Without family or history, individuals can be broken down to believe anything, especially, if there are existing texts and environmental factors to support the new belief (history includes all forms of culture). In this way, some cultures have been able to escape persecution and recast themselves as sustainable and influential entities. In the grand flow of history, all is bound to repeat itself. Cultures exist to support an individual's pursuits, and the individual furthers the culture through actions and decisions.

In this relationship with one's culture, it is easy to see how an individual can limit himself or herself based upon the beliefs purported by the culture. Limitations are created by prejudices. So, at the end of the day, how you view yourself is in part influenced by individuals you have never met. Some settle here and say, "Just because I am _____, I cannot have _____, because _____doesn't like _____." Such an explanation may be absolutely true. It is not sufficient, however. As mentioned, prejudices may be counterattacked by firstly noting that a prejudice is a suggestion, and then secondly, creating a new paradigm by which you can whole-heartedly believe in. It is easy to simply say something is wrong, but to believe it requires a whole new effort. You have to evaluate your actions using the spiritual dimension and change your ideas at the most primal level. Chapter Ten is focused on such mental reprogramming. Once you have reprogrammed yourself to give more positive self-talk, the "limitations" part of the "worth" algorithm must be decreased to compensate for it.

Progress: *"You can die from someone else's misery- emotional states are as infectious as disease. You may feel you are helping the drowning man, but you are only precipitating your own disaster. The unfortunate sometimes draw misfortune on themselves; they will also draw it on you. Associate with the happy and fortunate instead." (48 laws of Power)*

 B.   <u>Limitations come in the form of other people.</u>

This applies to even your best friends. Do not invest your time in those who dwell on their shortcomings. This does not mean that you should offend them, but you should not dedicate your time and energy to those who cannot see past their own faults. Their hindrances will slowly become yours as does a contagious disease.

They dwell in their small worth because their positive talk is so miniscule. They focus on their limitations, and will serve to induce you to believe that their limitations are yours too. Having a circle of naysayers, ill-advisors, or sick doctors, will leave you patiently waiting for a ruler to condemn you to failure.

Misery-stricken individuals serve as great reminders of how your mindset can influence your circumstances. Because, as humans we must be correct in our self-perception, we become what we believe. If you believe you are an unlucky soul, you will become and continue to be an unlucky soul because you are trying to justify your own belief. You will find yourself seeking opportunities to be unlucky so that you may claim yourself to be victim to a system of persecution. You should realize, however, that at the root of these systems are people with insecurities and they can therefore be influenced. Nevertheless, if you surround yourself with powerless people, they will begin to raise you to believe you too are powerless. They will limit you and curse anything you do that shows otherwise.

They may tell you that you are not smart, wealthy, bronzed, clever, gendered, or refined enough to accomplish a task. Even discussing a "Point B" may be foreign to these individuals, because they are so focused in the ploys of their "Point A." These unhappy people are different from the realists. A realist not only identifies an obstacle but plans a method to circumvent the obstacle. An idealist plans a method to use the obstacle as a stepping stone to greater heights. An unhappy person cries about the obstacle and uses the obstacle as a method to attract an audience who will cry with him.

Their focus on the obstacle harms your ability to develop perspective and properly judge a situation. Things may not go as planned, but unhappy people only plan on failure. Consistent focus on failure by others around you will eventually force you to plan your failure. Surround yourself with people who have a conscious sense of worth and a minimal number of limitations.

Encouragement: *"....I am going to feel worse than I did before you arrived. Because I know the things that I should be able to accomplish." (The Alchemist)*

    C.   <u>Limitations come in the form of me.</u>

The final source of limitations is self-provoked. Many times, your comprehension of a life lesson can be the difference between success and failure. When you walk in front of the mirror, you begin to scan your reflection for troubled areas. You attempt to perfect yourself, and that means you must also see flaws. Some of these flaws are not able to be fixed, and those are the ones you are the most insecure about.

The quote references a part of The Alchemist in which the young boy happened upon a merchant. In the book, he suggested that the merchant rearrange his store's display so as to attract more customers. The merchant, in response, became frustrated because he had already considered rearranging the store, but never did. There are many things you tell yourself throughout the course of the day that will help you become better. Yet, you allow yourself to procrastinate or convince yourself to do otherwise. This is where you limit your progress. Many times, you subconsciously tell yourself you would not be able to handle success or would not know what to do with it. This is why it is important to fully envision your "Point B" and then encourage yourself to its attainment.

These limitations can also be present as past grudges with which you may still be grappling. As they linger, you constantly reflect on what could have been done differently to prevent whatever may have caused such grief. While contemplation may offer you some consolation on the issues, it is only temporary, and the next few moments will be filled with anger and resentment. If you hold on to such an exercise with your emotions, they will only serve to tire you. It is best that you accept the decisions made as the best ones possible for both yourself and the person you are holding a grudge against, and move on. If you do not, you will not have enough strength to tackle the issues you face today and will further spiral out of your self-discipline. You cannot linger on your emotional scars. Let them be a part of your new identity and use those scars as a way to be more aware of similarly posed impending crises. If you find it difficult to "let go", reach out to the individual with whom you hold your grudge, and clear the waters face to face. If it is an issue you can fix, then fix it. The point is that you should use your strength wisely. Strength is only part-way infinite. It seems infinite because the source is hard to describe, but you will run out. As all of your energy has been invested into holding grudges, you will have little to spare for determining your purpose and eliminating your limitations.

You can be your own worst enemy. Imagine where you would be if you took your own advice. Every time you persuade yourself to do otherwise, or convince yourself that you are not worth anything, you are limiting yourself. When you have an idea or feel a sudden motivation to do something worthwhile, you should encourage yourself to follow through. When you are watching television, and suddenly you get the thought, "I should go to the gym." Get up, get dressed, and go to the gym. Do not waste time trying to convince yourself not to move. Compel yourself to act. It takes practice, but if you imagine yourself completing or doing the task, then you will have an easier time actually initiating it. When you are done, you will feel even more encouraged the next time around.

II.   **Purpose is vital to understanding who I am.**

Purpose is your final destination. It is your Point B. Once you determine your Point B, you can begin to really see who you currently are. Instead of comparing yourself to other people, compare yourself to your standards. Identify your weaknesses and strengths in that manner, and your development will go very far. Who you are revolves around your purpose, and once you determine your purpose, it will be much easier to see your shortcomings and fortes. What you truly believe your purpose to be, will affect your thoughts, actions, and dispositions. In consequence, these same thoughts, actions, and dispositions will be a reflection of what you believe your purpose is. They have a mutual relationship. The purpose does come first, however. Use this segment to determine your purpose and from there begin to program your thoughts, actions, and disposition.

Utility: *"Today I understand something I didn't see before: every blessing ignored becomes a curse." (The Alchemist)*

    A. <u>My situations are determined by my analysis of what my purpose is.</u>

There are two ways to analyze this quote. Both are valid. The first interpretation is that what you do not treat as a blessing will fester because of misuse. Therefore, blessings will be used against you, or used to limit you. Some blessings are obvious to use as blessings, whereas, others are written off as curses. Your perception of your blessings is directly influenced by your upbringing and your surroundings. What are things you take pride in? This list is also a list of what you place a lot of value on. What frustrates you? These are your curses. Re-examine your curses and retool them to be your strengths or your blessings. Insert at least three of each here:

Blessings	Curses
1)	
2)	
3)	

For each one, list how they could be used to your advantage. To which areas of your life could the blessing and curse be applied?

Blessings	Curses
1)	
2)	
3)	

The other interpretation is that the unused blessings will become regrets, and the regret will haunt you for your entire lifetime. So, if you have an opportunity that you really want to take advantage of, and decide not to out of fear of failure, you will regret it. As you age, you will constantly refer to that decision as though it is the basis for your lack of success even at old age. These are the "if only's". Create an opportunity and make the most out of it. You will likely succeed or at least learn from the experience and open other, more appealing and desirable opportunities.

As for the lesson in this segment, how you view your end goal directly influences your current situations. The Point B is not just the exercise of having a Point B, but it also means believing in your Point B. You must envision it, live in it, and know that one day you will meet it. The dream will become a substantial reality. How you live your life will provide a testament for what you truly believe about yourself. Perhaps you dream of home ownership. If you really believed it, then you would not engage in activities that take you further away from that dream. When you contradict what you say, you make it even harder to pursue the things you claim you will have. All opportunities will seem to be hiding from you, and the reality is that you are just not looking for them. Utilize your blessings and curses by positioning them. Being conscious of what they are, will help you prevent your downfall.

Imagine that you are on a list of individuals being considered for a team by a team captain. The team could be an athletic team, academic team, or some talent group. As a member of the list, you begin to analyze yourself. You think of why the captain may or may not pick you to be a part of the team. You then imagine what it would be like if your name were called and the expectations associated with being picked. Your heart rate increases, and you mentally prepare yourself to be a confident pick. Then, you realize the captain only has room for one more pick, and your name is not called. Suddenly, you transition into thinking purely about why you should have been picked over the others. This process is a short version of what you should go through when thinking about your purpose and your goals. Imagine you are being called to be your "Point B". Why should you be your Point B and why should you not be picked? Why would someone be picked over you? The reasons you should not be picked are your weaknesses and the reasons you should be picked are your strengths. The differences between strengths and weaknesses are opportunities.

Point B to Point A:

Difference 1)
Difference 2)
Difference 3)

Turn your weaknesses into opportunities by re-evaluating them as potential blessings.

Discipline: *"A life of obedience by leaders is the greatest motivation to the people who follow them. They see their lives and are challenged to greater heights of commitment and obedience." (How to Win Friends and Influence People)*

    B.   <u>Other people see my purpose when I am headed in the right direction.</u>

Discipline is incredibly important when determining your purpose. Meditation and focus require that you are able to discipline yourself enough to know how to perceive yourself from the outside. Reprogramming requires the same amount of discipline, as your habits and beliefs have had many years to establish a home in all of your four dimensions. The special thing about internal discipline is that the outside world will remark on it when you are displaying it correctly. Imagine a beautiful woman whose smile is slight and reassuring. She uses her words carefully and every sentence has an abundance of meaning, certainty, and conciseness. Her gaze is enough to communicate fear, love, or hope, and her posture is welcoming, but stern. Imagine a dashing young man who displays no anxiety and who asks the correct questions at the correct time. He is slow to commit to an emotional reaction, but when he does, they are poignant and useful. When seeking to influence another, such results are an imperative. A disciplined person looks, acts, and thinks a certain way. The more internally disciplined you become, the easier you will be able to envision your purpose. Other people will always be around to reassure you by commenting on how even-tempered and charismatic you are. Not only will they comment on your discipline, but you will gain disciples, or followers. The challenge to obtain balance is too great to resist. They will aspire to model your mindset because of the promise that is carried along with discipline. A man who masters himself cannot be mastered by another.

Talent without discipline is easy to be jealous of and hard to reproduce. What do you think when you see someone else rewarded for hard or smart work? Do you ever wonder how they did it, or where their inspiration came from? Do you think about the persistency they must have committed to in order to succeed? A true musician must practice their craft tirelessly until they feel it sounds perfect to them. The musician learns the craft of music. Learning the craft includes learning the instruments, the language, the theory, the history, and the current state of the industry. The craft is supplementary to the artist's own confidence in his music. Once the artist feels as though he has sufficiently disciplined his fingers, breathing, and voice, he ventures into the world to share his discipline in his talent. Those that were great spent many hours perfecting their craft. Identifying your talent and purpose is half of the battle. The other half is discipline.

One thing to keep in mind about discipline is balance. You must maintain a balance with yourself. You should neither go too high, nor too low. You neither commit, nor become recluse. You are neither too trusting nor too suspicious. You do not immerse yourself to the point of no return, and you do not run away from issues so that they might disappear. You are instead the epitome of balance: your center of mass is in perfect alignment with your actions, thoughts, and disposition.

What is/are your talent(s)?

Fill in here:

Freedom: *"The trouble is that they do not think for themselves." (Mis-Education of the Negro)*

    C.   <u>When I do not think for myself, the others will think for me.</u>

True freedom is frightening. You must take responsibility for your decisions and acknowledge the consequences that will follow them. Freedom, however, is freedom. It is considered the intangible gift for which men and women have lost their lives. People have even fought for the freedom of their children knowing they, themselves, would perish. What is it about freedom that is so appealing? While it may be terrifying, it ensures that you will have choices. Many of us willingly forfeit our freedoms, and then complain. We do not take the time to mentally free ourselves and wonder why there are people who dictate our worth. As aforesaid, a man who masters himself cannot be mastered by another. It is true that what is on the inside counts and what is on the outside matters. This is because what is on the inside can really determine much of what is on the outside. Take a look at your surroundings sometime. Think of how each object in your room has influenced who you are today, and the influence it continues to have. We attach meanings to objects, and claim that these objects have sentimental value. We do the same with occurrences. These are known as superstitions. We let other entities and actions facilitate the formation of our actions and beliefs.

For most of us, if someone wanted to make us mad, he or she would just have to be annoying. If the person wanted to make us happy, he or she would just have to say, "You look nice today." We are severely limited by our desire for comfort. While there is absolutely nothing wrong with being happy because someone says that you look nice, you should understand that every transaction has some motive behind it. They are all involved, to some degree, in manipulating another's mind. In verbal communication, you have one person influencing the emotional state of another person without even touching them. The person receiving the emotional stimulation undergoes multiple biological changes in the brain and in the physical body. These changes, in turn, are released as a form of communication that can be read by others. Recall that all emotions can be derived from fear, love, hope, or some combination thereof. Not only can your emotions be altered, but your options and consequently, your decisions may be altered. Use your responses carefully. If you are willing to hand over your freedom, other people will gladly take up the gambit and play with you as you concede.

Chapter Seven

Concentrate My Forces

When pursuing a particular passion, it is necessary to utilize your resources appropriately. It is not good to expend them on frivolous causes and this chapter is meant to discuss the balance that should exist between your priorities and your resources.

Concentrate My Forces

Note: "Iron sharpeth iron." (Bible, Proverbs)

In a previous chapter, it was explained that your forces should be focused. Fleeting from one shallow mine to the other is comparatively fruitless to finding a deep one that will allow you to mine for life. This is true. Your resources should come from one main source, and the source should be in the likeness of the resources. In the quote "iron sharpeth iron", it is of great necessity that a focus be refined by entities that are of the same nature to that focus. If another material is used to try to sharpen iron, it will either break the iron or be broken by it. Iron can only be sharpened by iron, and so when you are developing your purpose, you must surround yourself with like-minded individuals who can sharpen you and make sure that you stay on track with your designated purpose. The quote does not imply that iron is never in the company of other metals, but it does imply that it can only be sharpened by something in its likeness. This chapter explores how forces and focuses interact with one another. A force is something that provides or channels resources. A focus is the method by which those resources are administered. The focuses are comprised of the four dimensions. You may view life primarily in any of the dimensions and how you administer resources is completely dependent upon it.

The operational definition for this chapter is below:

Focus means to cause to converge on or toward a central point; to concentrate.

You must determine your focus for your life. The definition here is used in conjunction with the description of a focus as being one of the four dimensions. You must identify the dimension you want to focus on and then draw all actions, thoughts, and appearances to that focus. Your resources and utility of resources should emulate your focus in order to achieve the maximum of what that focus may provide. Aligning yourself to a focus involves considering your resources, or forces, through the lens of the particular dimension on which you wish to focus. You will then attract other entities that are of the same focus. These other entities will, in turn, provide you with a greater force to amplify your resources. As you align your forces and focuses, you become more useful and are able to identify opportunities because opportunities seek your utility. This is iron sharpening iron.

Things to consider concentrating on....

I.   **I must align my life's decisions with my purpose.**

Throughout your life, you make many decisions that have consequences that are life-changing. As you continue to define your purpose, and map out the pathway from Point A to Point B, the decisions you will be forced to make will become increasingly complex as your sense of freedom heightens. When you confront these decisions, keep in mind that your "Point B's" archetype or vision is watching you. Your "Point B" is analyzing you and your motivations. You should work to align your decisions with those that work towards your Point B or would model the decision making style of your Point B. Aligning these decisions will allow you to keep your pathway as clean as possible instead of building walls where there may not have otherwise been any.

In real world application, this means if you have instructed yourself on a pathway, it would be in your best interest to have your tools and friends align with your Point B. You should identify mentors in your field of interest. If you want to become a lawyer, you should gain lawyers as mentors and have them share their stories and resources with you. You should join groups or clubs that are focused in the legal world and gain access to their resources. Assume a position of leadership in those groups so that you can begin sharing your knowledge of the legal world. Your resources should assist you in becoming a lawyer, and your creations should benefit or allow you to become an active part of the legal world. You should not discard opportunities that seem irrelevant. Instead, you should work to make them align with your end goals.

Attempt to do this with your currently designated end-goal.

End Goal:			
Mentors	Mentees	Resources	Creations
1)	1)	1)	1)
2)	2)	2)	2)

Use this list as a shortened set of guidelines. These are your short-term tangible projects to complete. In the example of a lawyer, perhaps your creations are simply writing papers, assisting with the development of a policy or case briefing, or your law school application. Your resources may be an analysis of your best-fit law school. Maybe a resource is allocated money for the LSAT or law school. Your mentees may be other individuals who are interested in law school, or maybe you help an adjunct pre-law professor administer his classes. Your mentors may be several different lawyers so that you can gain perspective on which legal field adapts to your personality, fits your resources, and stimulates you.

Having such focus on your surroundings will only help to improve your current progress towards your end-goals. Alignment is important because it requires conscious balance and consideration. It is an active process that must occur. The application of the alignment takes time, but it is definitely worth it.

Perspective: *"When a Negro student works his way through college by polishing shoes, he does not think of making a special study of the science* *underlying the production and distribution of leather and its products that he may someday figure in this sphere." (Mis-education of the Negro)*

A.   <u>I must have a broader view.</u>

When defining a purpose, keeping it concise is important, however, keeping it broad in nature is expansive for your development. Many of the examples used have designated the "Point B" as though it were a particular career. People change careers many times throughout their lives, and it is because there is always an unfulfilling element. When designing your Point B, you should make it unique to your personality. It should be distinct and equipped with all of your desired features. It should be broad so that you may apply different kinds of opportunities to the same focus. If it is too narrow, you will only be able to see how one opportunity may fit your focus. If you design it broadly, with a deep understanding of how it interacts with systems and describe it in the different dimensions, you will be able to see how multiple opportunities will apply to the same focus.

In the quote, imagine yourself as the student who perfects his craft in shining shoes. You become an expert in your craft because of the pride you have in your role. As a matter of fact, when people want their shoes shined, they look for you. You can truly focus on your craft. You may even take classes for your craft and figure a way to offer the fastest shoe-shining job around the town. While it is great to appreciate your opportunity, it is an unfortunate affair when the limitation presents itself in the form of small-mindedness. It is the consequence of having a myopic view of your success. Dream big, and perfect the small. Use your aerial view to see how your craft interacts with the rest of the world, and think of the impact you can have on the rest of the world through your craft. You should think this way until you settle on the idea that feels right. The suggestion in this quote was for the student to become familiar with the manufacturing processes that must occur prior to the shoe-shine. The idea is not to bounce around from one idea to the next, but to focus and align your resources to one point so that they may be of use. Intensity defeats extensity every time.

We can call such planning around the craft: leveling up, and you can fill in the chart below for as many crafts as you desire.

Supporting Processes:	Supporting Industry:	Supporting Processes:

Supporting Processes:		Supporting Industry:

Your Craft:

Alignment: *"Conserve your forces and energies by keeping them concentrated at their strongest point. You gain more by finding a rich mine and mining it deeper than by flitting from one shallow mine to another - intensity defeats extensity every time."* (48 laws of Power)

B. <u>Don't lose your direction.</u>

Many times when you are engaging in "leveling up" or in the process of identifying your purpose, it can be easy for the increased complexity to cause you to lose direction. You must keep yourself focused on your end-goal and always use it as an evaluation tool. So, imagine the chart above being encapsulated by an even larger box: your end-goal. Your craft should go in the direction of your end-goal. How you utilize and learn the supporting industries and processes should complement your end-goal.

Forces and focuses both play a role in how you go about configuring your standards for success and how determined you will be in the pursuit of that success. Your forces can be broken into three categories: Your Strengths, Your Resources, and Your Passions. Your focuses are the four dimensions. Recall that the dimensions are the lenses that you use to analyze and establish priorities. Needless to say, forces and focuses interact with one another to yield your direction. If you are following a passion, you are more inclined to see a task to completion. However, if you are focused on what others think of you in the short-term (the Social Dimension), you may regard your passion as irrelevant or unnecessary. On the other hand, you may also find yourself overly braggadocios of your accomplishments and cause others to become jealous of you. Beware of dead ends. Maintaining perspective and a sense of direction will help you back out of a cornering dead-end opportunity.

Forces	Focuses			
	Social	Physical	Mental	Spiritual
Strengths Resources Passions	Below, are the three segments of a matrix, which at each cross-section demonstrated both the achievements and the dangers of the focuses and forces interacting in that manner.			

When your strengths motivate your activities:

Social
Achievement: Highly procedural
Danger: Frustration

Physical
Achievement: Fleeting to many activities
Danger: Dissatisfaction

Mental
Achievement: Expert
Danger: Loss of Purpose

Spiritual
Achievement: Determine a role
Danger: No Optimization

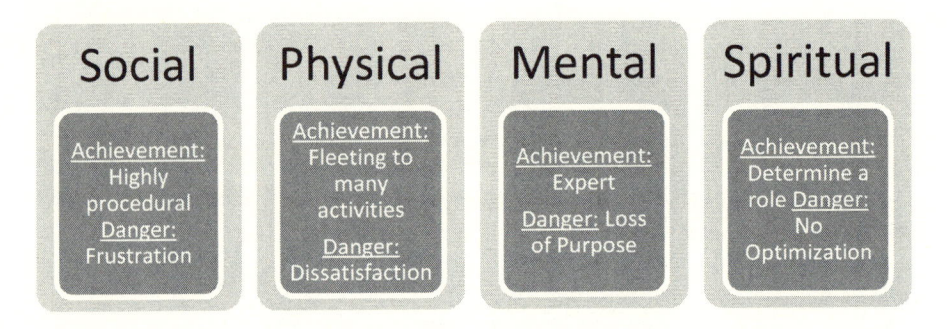

When your strengths and resources motivate your activities:

Social
Achievement: Encounter many opportunities
Danger: Loss of Integrity

Physical
Achievement: Go-getter
Danger: Dissatisfaction and susceptibility to temptation

Mental
Achievement: Role contentment
Danger: Extreme pride

Spiritual
Achievement: Career heights. Exceptional worker
Danger: Role Discontentment

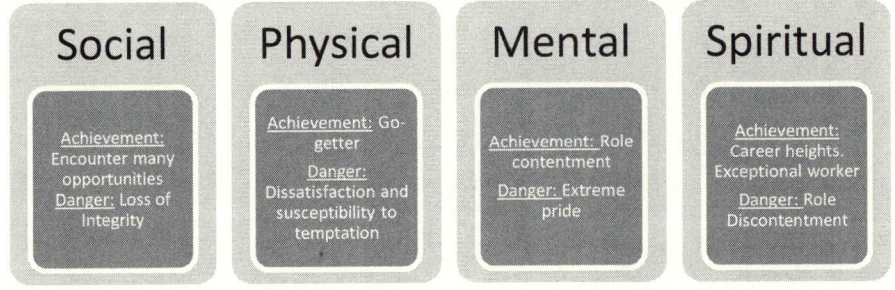

When strengths, resources, and passions motivate your activities:

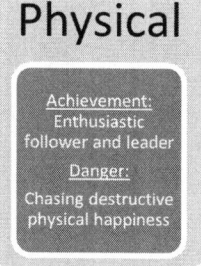

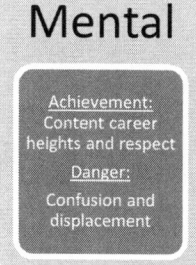

Social	Physical	Mental	Spiritual
Achievement: Enthusiastic admirers. **Danger:** Jealousy is imminent	**Achievement:** Enthusiastic follower and leader **Danger:** Chasing destructive physical happiness	**Achievement:** Content career heights and respect **Danger:** Confusion and displacement	**Achievement:** Optimization, career heights, understanding **Danger:** Loneliness

Further Explanations:

Social Dimension:

>**Focus:** Social Dimension
>**Force:** Your Strengths
>**Achievement:** Highly procedural and chasing crowds
>**Danger:** Frustration
>
>**Explanation:** In this scenario, your focus is limited to pleasing others and you evaluate yourself based on how others see you at the given moment of your evaluation. You focus on what you are really skilled at doing. At your best, you will learn how to efficiently use your skill, and thus you will become fairly procedural. This combination will eventually become the: "if it is not broken, then there is no need to fix it" paradigm. As a consequence of your desire to please others, you will find yourself chasing crowds and reverting to doing what you know best. The danger of depression exists because efficiency can be outdone by a more creative person. Since you never made yourself more competitive by creating something novel in addition to your strengths, you will find yourself slightly depressed because people no longer feel benefited by you.
>
>**Focus:** Social Dimension
>**Force:** Your Strengths and Your Resources
>**Achievement:** Encounter many opportunities

Danger: Loss of Integrity

Explanation: By using your strengths and resources, you will feel fairly unstoppable. You will meet many new people and encounter new opportunities because others are curious about how you perform your skill so well. You will swell with pride. Others will, however, see you as a prime target to be taken advantage of. They will bribe you with fame, riches, and other things that make you feel as though you are of heightened importance and value to other people. It will leave the dangerous door open for losing your integrity. You may find yourself compromising your values and standards and limiting your growth because you are so focused on pleasing everyone. Your resources will only encourage you to take even greater risks for the sake of keeping everyone happy.

Focus: Social Dimension
Force: Your Strengths, Resources, and Passion
Achievement: Enthusiastic admirers
Danger: Jealousy is imminent

Explanation: With this combination, you display much courage in your skill because of the joy it brings to you, but you only feel achieved because of the recognition given by others. As you continue to seek recognition for your skill, you will obtain it. Many will praise you, but since you are so outwardly focused on perfecting your craft, some will view it as pretentious and will grow jealous of you. You will give off the vibe that you are not deserving of your craft because you are exploiting yourself. Your confidence will grow into arrogance and the arrogance will breed resentment. The very thing you crave, the appreciation from others, will come and disappear. In its absence, there will be anger and jealousy. A stronger person may take the time to destroy you or pick a public battle with you to destroy your reputation.

Physical Dimension:

> **Focus:** Physical Dimension
> **Force:** Your Strengths
> **Achievement:** Fleeting to many activities
> **Danger:** Dissatisfaction
>
> **Explanation:** The physical dimension is about material satisfaction. Under this combination, your obsession will be to pursue things that give you some sensory satisfaction with relative ease, however temporary. Using your strengths involves personal reversion to default responses. These may not be the things you crave with intensity, but they are cravings that are associated with what you are already good at. This is the plight of the masochist and the hedonist. However tempted they are by sensory stimulation, they are constantly seeking additional forms of intoxication because none in their singularity will satiate the hunger.
>
> **Focus:** Physical Dimension
> **Force:** Your Strengths and Your Resources
> **Achievement:** Go-getter
> **Danger:** Dissatisfaction and susceptible to temptations
>
> **Explanation:** In this scenario, you are using your strengths and your resources, to achieve something. While the object of your focus may not be of great importance to you, they assume importance because of the nature of your forces. You pursue those things that you have the resources and the strength to pursue. The issue herein lies amongst your susceptibility. With more individuals contributing to your source, you are susceptible to being influenced by them in order to maintain your streak in achieving your goals. Your goals are purely sensory as they indirectly provide some tangible material satisfaction. You use them in order to attract more resources, continuing your spiral that may eventually consume you.
>
> **Focus:** Physical Dimension

Force: Your Strengths, Resources, and Passion
Achievement: Enthusiastic followers and leader
Danger: Chasing destructive physical happiness

Explanation: When you pursue anything with passion, you will have admirers. They may not be consistent, but you will have others that aspire to be you or follow you. They may not precisely mimic you, but they will pay attention to your engagements. Your focus, on the other hand is in the physical dimension, so your concern is not to please others. You are prone to engage in activities that are most likely quite self-destructive. Extraordinary purchases, moral transgressions, and ill-treatment of other individuals may transpire because you feel a sense of being owed something. As a leader, however, you will always bring enthusiasm to the table and will inspire others to be active. The issue will not be obtaining followers, but keeping them and their trust.

Mental Dimension:

Focus: Mental Dimension
Force: Your Strengths
Achievement: Expert
Danger: Lost purpose

Explanation: You are inspired by your craft. "I am great at math, I must do math!" With a focus in the Mental Dimension, you will be obsessed with the subject itself. At your best, you will master the subject and be known as an expert because you constantly refine your intelligence and understanding of the particular subject. Other people will respect you for your diligence and aptitude. You seek to be the best at your craft, but in that pursuit, you become myopic. As a consequence, you are limited to performing your craft and do not see the resources that may be used to do your craft more efficiently. This describes the group that is qualified, experienced, and unemployed due to few opportunities. They lose their jobs as a result of system fluctuations. They master their craft, but the craft is no longer in need and they lose their purpose. Others that make up this category are the pawns. They are given a task, and do their task with no regards to the impact the task may have or the resources that could be used to expedite the task. These unfortunate intelligent individuals lose all sense of purpose when taken from their comfortable environment. Because of the potential instability, others have the impression that they would prefer not to be promoted or moved. Others assume these individuals are content.

Focus: Mental Dimension
Force: Your Strengths and Your Resources
Achievement: Role contentment
Danger: Extreme pride

Explanation: You will have the rush that comes with a support network. At your best, others will be very happy with the job you perform and will even be happy when you are promoted, because your resources assist them. Your support network will place confidence in you and so will your subordinates. You will be expanding your knowledge of a particular subject, and also applying resources to that network to become a power broker in your profession. You now have something to use as leverage. The biggest problem here is that you will not see when a problem is headed your way. Your understanding of ebb and flow systems is limited and this compromises the ability to with which you can initiate and run negotiations. Your confidence will be proven false with the first mishap or question from your support network. Your ability to handle such doubtfulness will place dents in your confidence and eventually cut you down to a point in which your work performance is severely affected, because you have your own doubts about the worth of the job you do. It was something you were "in the position" to do.

Focus: Mental Dimension
Force: Your Strengths, Resources, and Passion
Achievement: Content career heights and respect

Danger: Confusion and displacement

Explanation: The wind is behind your sails. You aspired to obtain a specific goal, and you will reach it. You refine yourself so that you become an expert and you utilize your resources so that your thinking is more expansive. Finally, you actually care about the job you are doing beyond just doing it. This mindset will allow you to reach career heights and pay more attention to the people around you because you are in the mindset of resource utilization. The biggest danger here is that you will return to a corner point and every now and then ask yourself, "why?" Your answer to this question will vary depending upon the value you are providing. When you are struggling with your job, you will feel as though the world is meaningless and there is no point to your perseverance in the grand scheme of things. When you excel, on the other hand, you will beam with pride and resolve in the thought that you have reached your pinnacle. You will feel exuberant and filled with purpose. This idea of purpose, however, is limited because it is still unattached to the systems that function around you beyond the use of your resources. Others with a more defined purpose will take advantage of such role delineation by destroying your bubble. When this occurs, it will leave you confused and feeling as though you have made all of the wrong decisions.

Spiritual Dimension:

Focus: Spiritual Dimension
Force: Your Strengths
Achievement: Determine a role
Danger: No optimization

Explanation: You are a person who has determined a purpose. You envision a role for yourself based upon your strengths and understand what your role accomplishes in the context of multiple systems. You have mastered the concept of cause and effect and use it to eventually create or fill a role. You will not, however, achieve your final

LP25: Influence

destination except through chance. You, while very content and well achieved, will not be optimized. You will be highly valued in your craft. Your ceiling will be mainly brought about by yourself, but without anyone influencing you, there will be blandness to your life. It will be filled with facts and figures. You will also experience role discontentment because you are aware of your potential. People will exist only as necessary elements to a system, and not as propellers of a system.

Focus: Spiritual Dimension
Force: Your Strengths and Your Resources
Achievement: Career heights. Exceptional worker
Danger: Role discontentment

Explanation: You have achieved all that the focus on the "Spiritual Dimension" and the force of "Your Strengths" has achieved. You have also utilized your resources and this will bring about exceptional work and put you in the position to negotiate deals. Your allegiance is to your purpose fulfillment, and not role fulfillment, so it will be harder to tempt you if your purpose is considered in its broadness. You will still obtain career heights, but not with the baggage of having moments in which your integrity was compromised. You will be promoted with ease because you are respectful of the ebb and flows or multiple systems. The biggest issue is your role discontentment. You are basing your purpose on your strengths and your resources, and are aware of interacting systems. This will leave you at shallow points in your life because you know of your potential. You may not be doing what you want to be doing, and this will eventually affect your work because you will be discouraged from actually achieving your highest potential. Even though you are aware of the causes and effects, the job does not have a stimulating value for you.

Focus: Spiritual Dimension
Force: Your Strengths, Resources, and Passion
Achievement: Optimization, career heights, understanding

Danger: Loneliness

Explanation: You are optimized. You would have achieved all of the above, and others will be happy for you because you are aware of emotional systems. You will be able to see when something is approaching that will affect your life adversely or positively. You will reach your purpose. The greatest danger is loneliness. Finding another individual who thinks the way you think will prove difficult. You will be jaded by the many individuals you do meet, and will give up on your search of finding a true match. Because of your awareness, it will be difficult to see others beyond their ability to be manipulated and their motivations. This may cause paranoia, which will keep you quite lonely.

Wherever you may fall in the Life Matrix, it is important that you are honest about your susceptibilities. Make sure you align your activities to your focus and forces. Keep your eyes on your final destination and define your pathway. Do not fear challenging circumstances that could be used to ultimately sharpen you. Push yourself into a zone of constructive discomfort that gears towards your end-goal. You will see your resources multiply and your passion increase.

Chapter Eight

My Life Message

"My Life Message" is meant to inspire thought regarding your lifestyle. What exactly will other people think when reflecting on your life? In the course of this particular mental exercise, the manner in which other people interpret/ analyze each other is also explored.

My Life Message

Note: "It is often wise to pay the full price- there is no cutting corners with excellence." (48 Laws of Power)

What you do not pay for in resources will cost you in freedom and in duty. Even the items you are awarded because of your status will be accounted for as a duty. Standards will be prescribed for you. For cultural icons, this agreement is known as an endorsement. For many, it involves compromising integrity or morals. It is important to take note of all your monetary and non-monetary transactions as they will be accounted in your general ledger which gets published the day you cease to exist. If you consider yourself to be excellent, then it would not be wise to take shortcuts. When pursuing excellence, it takes hard work and plenty of time. It also requires you to be clever with your resources. There are no shortcuts in that, just as there are none in using the Win-Win Mentality. If you do take shortcuts, it will be apparent and will affect the confidence and value people place in you. When considering the message that your life will tell past your grave, you should note that every secret, lie, achievement, and win will be known by someone and will indirectly leave an impression on those that populate the world. It was once said that every person on the planet is within six degrees of separation from one another. So everything you do with someone in secret has only a matter of time before it finds itself to discovery, and chances are the story will change by the time it reaches person number 6.

What story does your life tell? If someone were to read it, what morals would they gain from it? What would its value be? How would it read? You will become the mentors of others, and it is important that you pay attention to the story that you are authoring and illustrating. When you die, there will be many words said in your eulogy. There will be many memories and regretful people who attend. Old grudges will seem much less significant or they will seem monstrous because of missed opportunities for a resolution. There are others who will find solace in knowing that you have gone to a hopefully better, but at least different place – even if it is interminable sleep. Your life never dies however. Your family shares your stories and they share your stories to their families and so on until you are practically immortal. Your immortality, however, is frozen in time. All that you have done in this life, this time around, will be all that you would have done –no more and no less. What you take to the grave is immutable and will continue to manifest as though you were still around. You should take the time to think: *if today were to be my last day, what would my life message say about me in all four dimensions? Is there anything incomplete?*

The operational definition for this chapter is below:

A <u>message</u> is the point, moral, or meaning of a gesture, utterance, novel, or motion picture or the inspired utterance of a prophet or sage.

Messages have played a very important function in history. Messengers were valuable story tellers who would be entrusted with communication and traveled between kingdoms, nations, countries, etc. Times of war and peace have rested on miscommunication or communication that came a day too late. Media functions as a non-living version of a messenger for large and small corporations. They send messages to millions in the form of advertisements and campaigns. We believe in signs, and that is why the application of superstitions can have such a powerful effect on our psyches. Slogans, logos, books, music, and art are all mediums by which other individuals are influenced. Messages are comprised of signs, images, sounds, and other sensory interactions. They propagate mainly by word of mouth and the fidelity of the signal can be altered when passing through different carriers. These messages can be consciously received or subconsciously absorbed. No matter how they are received, they compel reactions. There is much to say about the nature of messages, but the most important to take away is that your life is a message. It is a message to the world in full Technicolor with surround sound. Your life will leave a lasting impression on others and you should keep that in mind as you configure your purpose, your route, and your standards.

What is my life message?

I. <u>I must know who I am.</u>

Your life message is inextricably tied into how well you know yourself and practice maturity: control, calculation, and empathy. It is imperative that you know your weaknesses and strengths, and recognize your opportunities. Your passion should drive you, and you should determine how to make your passion supplement your desired lifestyle. Who you are is not simply your job, age, race, social security number, or address. Who you are is dependent upon your philosophy. What purpose do you have in the world, and why?

Many people identify themselves as a piece of their culture: religion, language, race, music, and food. How you feel about your place in this world is even more fundamental than what has been taught to you since you were born. It is imperative that you dig deeper to figure out exactly who you are. Your true beliefs in your value will determine exactly how you respond to situations. People for the most part, are extremely transparent. How people act reflects exactly what they believe. If they are lazy, then it is usually due to fear associated with applying effort and failing. If they are arrogant, then they are usually insecure. It is harder to read an individual who thinks before he acts, but you do know that individual regards himself highly. His reactions are at least worth his consideration. "The actions" is what is transparent. The feelings that drive them play no part in developing the perception. An angry person is an angry person.

It is this transparent quality that others will gossip about behind your back and will avoid speaking about at your funeral. Your transparent nature is the content for the life message. Many will take turns dissecting the content in order to either overpower or submit to you. Try this exercise:

Trait/Weakness	Reason 1	Reason 2 (Deeper)	Transparent Quality
Example: Shyness	Nothing to Say	Nothing worthwhile to say; worthlessness	Standoffish, low self-esteem

When doing this exercise, the transition between reason number two and the transparent quality requires you to judge yourself from an outside perspective. How might another person perceive your trait? By considering your receiver, you can appropriately modify the signal you send. This step is usually half-heartedly done. Most people do not actually take into consideration how the other person may feel in the given situation. For a shy person who is quiet in a large and loud group setting, the shyness may cause feelings of awkwardness for their friends. This will translate into the friends either overcompensating in loudness in order to "liven you up", or to give up and never invite you again. Be sure the signal you are sending is the signal you intend to send. Signal fidelity necessitates discipline and working knowledge of the receiver. You can continue the list, and these transparent qualities will populate your life message. Are you content with the contents?

Trait/Weakness	Reason 1	Reason 2 (Deeper)	Transparent Quality
Example: Shyness	Nothing to Say	Nothing worthwhile to say; worthlessness	Standoffish, low self-esteem

Perhaps you want to set some guidelines for your message so that you may begin crafting a more profound signal. Some are happy

LP25: Influence

with just getting a signal through. Someone interested in efficiency and effectiveness, is interested in the kind of signal that propagates. Most judgments about other individuals are made in a very short amount of time. We have the ability to categorize objects and people so that we are able to survive. Our basic instinct is to determine whether we may incur benefit or harm when entering a relationship. Given that you only have a short amount of time, the message you communicate should be consistent and valid to the receiver, unless you are intentionally sending mixed signals.

Balance: *"The boy stood up shakily and looked once more at the pyramids. They seemed to laugh at him, and he laughed back, his heart bursting with joy." (The Alchemist)*

A.   I am someone without limitations.

You do not have to accept predetermined limitations as permanent. You must find ways to circumvent a limitation. You can do this by counteracting your negative self-talk. As in the quote, he looked upon the pyramids. Their height was intimidating and reminded him of his smallness and missing sense of direction. Instead of giving in, he retorted with laughter, and was reminded of the ingenuity he has and his drive to continue moving forward. When you see obstacles, you should metaphorically scoff at them, because you understand that you are capable of solving any problem or accomplishing any goal when you have aligned your forces and set a focus- the relationship between balance and counteracting limitations.

You should be excited about the obstacle because it challenges you and when you reach the other side, you will be a better person for it. Balance your strengths, resources, and passion, and the actual limitations that you will confront will be few and far between. Most limitations are contrived through influence from other sources as we develop. All of the limitations that you currently operate with have been accepted as true by you. You should take responsibility for your obstinacy. Even the most outrageous ideas have roots in realism. If you can see a goal, and believe it, then it can very well be brought into existence. You must align your efforts so that they are balanced and applied creatively.

When you think of people who have accomplished great things in science, you imagine focused, recluse individuals who refine themselves and their craft. People who have changed the world in some impactful way tend to pop up in our minds as lackluster people. The truth is persistency takes energy. You have to motivate yourself to get from one point to another. You cannot do research without playing politics in academe. You have to be fairly well-rounded. Otherwise, you become a pawn to history, and someone else will take the credit for your dealings. Most impactful scientists strategically placed their research in front of powerful people and communicated its value. Greatness does not just happen. Greatness is achieved through balance in craft, resources, and passion. Edison, Da Vinci, Newton, Schrodinger, and others all had to commit to completion and then share it as a profound success.

Maturity: *"The most important of these skills, and power's foundation, is the ability to master your emotions." (48 laws of Power)*

B.   I am aware of my vices.

A vice is a quality that in large doses may bring about the downfall of an individual or entity. They function as liabilities or expenses in a general ledger. Analogy: It does not matter how much you make in revenue if the unit cost of your product outweighs the unit price. Vices can do tremendous and uncontrollable damage to your reputation. Speaking too much about your success and too little about the success of others will guarantee that some unfortunate person exposed to you will feel pushed to sow seeds of discord in your circles. Gauging the motivations of another is an art that requires maturity and an open mind into the facets of yourself that you are insecure about. Do not wait to learn about your vices from someone else. How would it feel to live with you? Would you find yourself too clingy, too loquacious, too nice, too honest, or too mean. Anything that is excessive and unbalanced is a vice.

If you can study your vices and avoid procrastinating their attenuation, or feeling limited by their weightiness, then you will have more authority over the content of your life message. Such focus takes maturity which was explained as a combination of empathy, control, and calculation. When reflecting on these vices, there are a few mental tricks in which you can engage. The first is to find a quiet room. Think of the last time you exhibited a vice. It may take a while, but usually you can find it when think of the last time you were angry, embarrassed, or frustrated. When you revisit the experience, try to imagine all of the emotions you felt. Sort them and analyze why you felt what you felt and under what circumstances would you have not felt those emotions. Try to become the other person that was present in the incident. How were they thinking of you, and how were they thinking of themselves? What could you have done differently? Now, reimagine the experience replaced with the different interactions that you have just discoursed in your mind. It may sound a lot like a child's timeout, but childhood is where we learn most of what is right and what is wrong and what is socially acceptable behavior. Do not discredit the value of taking some silent moments for yourself to reflect on your weaknesses. Chances are, they are obvious to other people and they will only talk about them when you are not around.

Prominence: *"Draw attention to yourself by creating an unforgettable, even controversial image. Court scandal. Do anything to make yourself seem larger than life and shine more brightly than those around you. Make no distinction between kinds of attention - notoriety of any sort will bring you power. Better to be slandered and attacked than ignored."* (48 Laws of Power)

C.   <u>Other people are aware of my strengths.</u>

How can you achieve greatness when no one knows about it? If you affect no one's life, then it cannot be known. Even helping individuals on a person to person basis is making a conspicuous impact. These acts will be a part of your life message. While you may convince yourself that you do beneficial things out of the "goodness of your heart", the point of the matter has nothing to do with that. This chapter is about how others will learn from your life and be potentially inspired by you and your philosophies. If you do many great, but anonymous deeds, what good-will will other people be inspired to exhibit? They will assume that the deeds must be done by someone of a super-nature or super class. This belief, although powerful and persuasive can discourage an individual from believing that they, on their own, could do it because of their lack of wealth or status. They will assume the method of your achievements rather than know them. By being conspicuous, you can inspire others to engage in similar behavior. Power and expectation come along with such conspicuousness, but you can accomplish much with power and the expectations of followers. You can raise their standards and be an example of a balanced lifestyle. This kind of sharing should not be rooted in insecurity, but rather in the display of pursuing your purpose.

As you continue to seek your passion and align your thoughts with your purpose, others will take notice of the changes, and the impact that it will have. Your prominence will not be a consequence of elaborate ploys and schemes or symbols. It will be the consequence of using your resources and strength to pursue a passion. That trait in and of itself is something to aspire to and be inspired by. You cannot be intimidated with the increased attention you will receive, however. The kind of confidence that you will develop will seem almost tangible to passer-byes, and they will want to know how they can be part of it. Just share it with them.

D. <u>My purpose is aligned with my decisions.</u>

This is very important. If your life message is to create the kind of moral or story that you would like, then the decisions you make should reflect exactly what you believe your purpose to be. If you envision your final destination to have the traits of being steadfast, trustworthy, and wealthy, then your decisions should follow closely along that narrative. Your reputation is built around what you do and what people know you do. It is best to be consistent. Your standards should not be determined by your environment. If you claim to be honest in public, then even behind closed doors, you should exhibit that same standard. If you exhibit weaknesses when no one is watching, you will eventually exhibit those same weaknesses in public. That should be a deterrent to keep from

LP25: Influence

wrong doing – noting that all things will eventually be discovered or may already be public knowledge unbeknownst to you. Also, recall your weaknesses can be changed into strengths after focusing.

If your claims do not match the actual content of your story, then others will be disappointed, and the message of your life will be lost. Imagine finding a book whose title is the little girl. The author of the book is also present, and you ask the author about the plot in the book. He replies that the book is about a girl who goes on a journey to search for her parents. So, you decide to buy the book because you are interested in such a story. Well, when you begin reading, you realize the book is about a boy who grew up with parents and then ran away from home. You begin to either doubt that the author was being sincere or at the least experience a certain amount of cognitive dissonance. Life is a bit more complicated than a book, and your life can have a direct impact on how another person develops. Keep that in mind as you construct your life-message. You would not want to misrepresent your book's contents. As a matter of fact, you want to make sure that your life-message accurately portrays your purpose and philosophy on life.

Try this exercise by completing the designated fields:

Title:	
Author:	
Introduction:	
Chapter One:	
Chapter Two:	
Chapter Three:	
Chapter Four:	
Chapter Five:	
Epilogue:	

II. I must have a drive.

When identifying and pursuing your purpose, you should pursue it with energy. You should have some deeper reason or meaning as to why you make the decisions you make. Your drive will be a part of the life message you craft. People who have achieved amazing things in the world had a reason to endure long nights of failures, and long days of grueling strategic work to position themselves for their achievements. Your drive is established only after you have created or decided upon a set of standards for yourself. If you have none, then you will find no intrinsic motivation. Nothing will have meaning until then.

Humility and Pride: *"You are indeed charitable when you give, and while giving turn your face away so that you may not see the shyness of the receiver." (A Spiritual Treasury)*

A. My morals are my motivations for my ideals.

If someone calls you an "angel", an image comes into your mind. How do you feel about your character at that moment? What does that mean to you? Immediately, your impulse is to imagine yourself and all of your positive qualities. These qualities represent your ideal self. You want to believe in your goodness. Ensuing such a remark, you may try to refute the person's statement by convincing them that you are banal or average. Conversely, you may beam with silent or vociferous pride. Either way, the qualities you imagined represent your morals. Whether they are based on utility, universally accepted qualities, or the antitheses of bad qualities, these are your morals, and the pursuance of such an ideal is justified by those morals.

In the quote, the transaction represents a multitude of qualities. The receiver feels his pride is hurt because of his inability to create options. He must receive from charity, and this most likely belittles his mental worth and increases the doubt in his own ability regardless of whether the charity is temporary or a need over an extended time. For these same reasons, many people find retirement unfulfilling because their work ethic defined who they were for such a long time. In retirement, some feel as though they are wasting away. Old age seems to make a mockery out of your perception of self. Your body begins to break down and you become dependent on others. Depression and obesity run in high rates for the older generation, and as we grow faster as a society, we begin to figuratively engage in the gentrification of resources and time. It seems progressive, but we are literally pushing a group off the map. Needless to say, this predicament for a retired person can be filled with shame and abandonment. For someone who "gives" to the old, they must keep in mind that these individuals are people with lives and ambitions that may or may not have been fulfilled. Your ideal response to a person in need may be to present a gift with humility out of respect for the life of the receiver. This kind of humility is rooted and justified by the morals you have set for yourself. What are the implied morals in the quote's stated scenario?

To be moral, you must give to others.
To be moral, you must give to others when they are in need.
To be moral, you must have mercy on the lives of others.
To be moral, you must give willingly.
To be moral, you must respect your elders.

None of these moral statements may be entirely true. As a matter of fact, each statement has a debunking argument that is strong and could be adopted as a different motivation for the development for an opposing moral.

Below are a few scenarios. State your response and write the underlying moral motivations driving the response.

A homeless man asks for change	Your parents ask you to clean your room
Response:	Response:
Moral Statement:	Moral Statement:

You find $10.00 in the middle of the parking lot Response: Moral Statement:	You did not complete your homework/ job assignment that is due today Response: Moral Statement:
Your boss asks you to complete a job that is not in your job description Response: Moral Statement:	Your friend needs a ride to a nearby location on route Response: Moral Statement:

You can learn more about your morals by envisioning new and exciting scenarios and taking into consideration your responses.

Instinct: *"When approaching a decision-making situation, you should consider your heart first....Your core belief is the primitive answer to any questions you have about yourself. (Young Leader)*

 B. <u>My values are priority morals.</u>

There are many situations you will encounter in which you will have to compromise on your morals. The morals that take precedence, however, are your true values. If you were to prioritize your morals, you will find your values. In the worst case scenario in which your back is to a corner, you will choose one course of action, and that will be motivated by your values. You can predict people by knowing their morals and values. You can corner them into choosing one option or another that you have already predetermined. What are your values? Use the morals that were created in the previous exercise, and try to rank them. Which one is placed first, and which one is last? The delineations can be considered the "breaking points" in psychology. They are the points in which you break your moral code. Some are simply more important than others and are the primary drivers of your actions. The other morals are simply a result of the primary ones. They reflect how you would respond after establishing control and given ample time to consider options.

How much do you value yourself? At what point can someone make you doubt your decisions and beliefs? What tools do they use? Do they use emotions, duty, culture, or logic? Depending on how you determine to rank your values, is the manner in which those values can be unraveled. If you logically synthesized your beliefs, then logic can be used to extinguish them. The more complexly your values are synthesized, the harder it will be for someone to untangle them. This is why sociopaths are so difficult to interact with. Their values are tied up in their own sense of duty, logic, culture, and emotions (which are usually unstable).

Here is an example:

Moral #1: To be moral, you must give to others when they are in need.

Possible reason in which this is not valid: The person in need has created the situation, and has harmed others in the process. The person did not work hard enough or committed crimes which rebounded and caused them to be in a position of need.

Values Discussion: You must work hard to meet your needs. Working hard is more important than just meeting your needs. People who are seeking handouts are worth less than those who are both seeking handouts and work hard.

Emotional value: Extremely high emotions are attached to work ethic. If I must work hard, then others must too. This moral is very personal, but the values are more personal. I must decide if this man is worthy of my resources.

Duty: It is a duty of mine to care for others, but not for those who do not want to care for themselves. I have a duty to firstly secure myself and my family. I am fulfilling my duty by taking care of myself and my family, and encouraging those who do not work for their security to do so also. I must decide if sharing my resources will actually help or hinder the man.

Culture: It is customary that this person who is in need may simply be a con-artist and I must not give in to a foolish trick. He is probably tricking other people into feeling sorry for him. While it is important to give because my culture deems it good for the soul, culture deems foolish giving as a folly and a trait that should be excised. I must decide whether or not I will lose face by giving.

Logic: Darwin's "only the strong survive" means that this man deserves to be left behind if he cannot keep up. If society is to get better, then the weak must be weeded out. A better society is better for my survival and my family's survival. I must decide if the world is better off without the person in need.

Which form of persuasion most appeals to your basic instinct? One of them poses a stronger argument against the proposed moral to you. This is most likely the way you rank your values. It is also the method by which your values can be changed. You can imagine the development of your morals as the stringing of a spider web. Every time a new string is drawn, it is equivalent to a reason behind that moral decision. The more intricate your spider web, the stronger that moral is and the more value it possesses. The fewer lines drawn, the weaker and less influential that moral is.

Testimony: *"More and more I have come to the conclusion that a principle isn't a principle until it costs you money." (Young Leader)*

C. <u>My ethics are my standards for excellence.</u>

Your list of standards is the complete list of evaluated morals that help to guide you in your decision making processes. It is better to create your own so that you are forced to justify them. You will then whole-heartedly pursue them. If you just accept those that are proposed to you, you will find yourself faltering in their practice because you never truly believed them in the first place. This is the reasoning behind why your actions and decisions serve as testaments to what you truly believe and why. The quote is meant to express how we determine some things to be more important than others. Most people place a tremendous amount of value into money. Using that generality, you can anticipate that many people will compromise on what they claim to believe and practice in part because of the potential to earn money. People will compromise their freedom, self-worth, or family for the sake of money. They may abandon religious and cultural teachings because tangible wealth overrides the intangible wealth. Therefore, the quote implies that the beliefs you hold on to even at the risk of losing money are truly strong beliefs. This may be true for most instances, and so it can be a great measuring stick for the strength of your values. The ethics you subscribe to are usually quite idealistic, but against a measuring stick, you can whittle them down to what you most likely will follow when you have extreme wealth or fame.

Be very careful when determining your ethics. They will be displayed and tied into your life message. If you do not follow your own ethics, your entire life message will be compromised due to the contradiction even though there are ways to correct a reputational error. If, however, you commit too many public offenses, you will eventually offend the wrong individual who is smarter than you and will plot until they feel you have paid for your transgressions. At that point, you are at the mercy of another's ethics. How they view mercy and refinement will be your fate. On the other hand, by taking the time to define and build your own ethics based upon the four influences aforementioned, you will be more prepared for new environments and situations. You will be less likely to be affected by the ethics of another individual.

When it comes to ethics, another caveat is in the discussion of ethics. You should live your ethics rather than speak your ethics. Speaking your ethics attracts unnecessary attention that will most likely derail you, and force you to prove your hypocrisy. People like to see explosions and yours will be like a ticking time bomb when you speak loudly about your ethics. Living your ethics, on the other hand, may increase the discomfort of others, but it will only draw warranted attention. There is a spectrum for living your ethics. You never want to seem too perfect. You never want to seem too vile. You must not speak your ethics, and you must not shadow them. When it comes to ethics, it is best to play ignorance and still maintain a strong will in what you believe. Teddy Roosevelt says, "Speak softly, and carry a big stick". He was referring to his approach to United States foreign policy. The brunt of your power is in action, no matter how sweet smelling your words may be. In some philosophies, it is like hiding a dead body by sprinkling the scent of perfume. No person relying on their senses will ever see it coming. It also applies to ethically difficult situations. Speak softly, but carry your ethics.

III.   People will know me when they hear about my life.

Once you pass away, all people will have is what they remember and what they hear. Those stories will be dedicated to you and people will come to know exactly who you were through those stories. This is true while you are still alive, too. Your friends, family, and acquaintances are limited to only knowing what has been said about you. You have partial control over what people hear about you. If you can imagine your life as a political campaign, other people are constantly running ads for and against you. These ads may be factual, but described in a light that is embarrassing and considers no empathy for the particulars of your situations. This is known as spin. If you are to control the narrative about you, however, you have to get out and front of people. You have to "beat your opponent to the punch line". Proactive narration is important. This does not mean that you parade your life's story around, but it means you leave a positive and lasting impact on the lives of the individuals that you encounter. If you make them feel inferior, they may become an opponent. If you make them feel superior, they may become an opponent. If you make them feel dependent, they may become an opponent. On the other hand, if you make them feel independent, equal, and as close to you as is a family member, then you are essentially buying their allegiance. They will spread your good reputation, and may even turn a blind eye to the character traits that may, in other circumstances, hurt your reputation. This relationship cannot be of unrequited admiration. You must also know how to genuinely speak well of your friend, too.

Side note: The only way to speak genuinely about another person is to actually believe what you say.

For the purpose of this section, "gossip" is the retelling of the habits and personalities of other individuals without the use of their presence or words. Gossip is one of the main vessels by which your life message circulates. People learn and mostly base their judgments on gossip. This form of communication does not necessarily have to be non-factual, but many times it is and spoken with a malicious intention in mind. If partaking in gossip, it is important to recognize the responsibility you are assuming. Even if you are speaking kindly of someone, you are affecting the life message of the individual of which you speak. Every word you say about the person gets inserted into the listener's mind and gets tagged.

Gossip is an act of seeding ideas. Those seeds eventually grow into entire conclusions and precepts about the individual in discussion. Be sure to recognize which seed you are planting and what fruit will blossom from it. Even if you speak well of someone to another person, you may be sowing seeds of jealousy. Speaking well of a son or daughter is the cause for much sibling or cousin rivalry and jealousy within families. When gossiping, know the tendencies of the person to whom you are speaking. Are they vindictive? Is their worth dependent on the valuation of others? Are they balanced or stable? Are they stubborn? Seeds will respond to their environment. Provide water, and watch the plant thrive or die.

Knowing how inseparable your life message is to what people say, it is imperative that you are proactive with it. Your life message is your own personal brand. When you think of Apple, Google, General Motors, or Brawny, the things that come to mind are products and brand. You associate the companies with their respective brands. Some companies are their brands- Coca Cola and Hula Hoop. You also have a brand. People will associate attributes to you at the mere mentioning of your name. What attributes are currently associated with your name? What does it mean when someone says that is very "insert your name" of you?

Tactics: *"So much depends on your reputation; guard it with your life." (48 Laws of Power)*

A.   <u>Perception is reality.</u>

It is one thing for you to reflect on your life, but it is quite another for someone else to do so. It is in their nature. Your message is a part of your perception. That means when you are thinking of your life message, you only see it from one angle. You must view your life from multiple angles in order to be proactive in the development of the message it construes. Reality is not the main builder of the message. Perception is what matters. You must develop some tactics in order be sure that your life message is conveyed in the manner of your choosing. You must decide what carries more value: life or perceived reputation for following your ethics. Would you rather live as a castigated individual who compromised on their beliefs, or would you rather be killed because you would not compromise? Either set does not indicate whether or not you are a good or bad person. Many would say terrorists are quite malicious, but they would fall into the latter category. Others would claim that thieves are wicked, but many would fall into the former category. A modern day terrorist clings to his beliefs, whereas most petty thieves may be compromising on theirs.

The name of the game is truly perception. You must know how to create a perception using smoke and mirrors. Magicians make you believe in magic because of their skill in changing your perception. You have no option but to believe that they are engaging in some form of magic. It works this way with your life message. The only option people should have is to believe the message you want them to believe. If they are able to find faults and flaws, it is because the image you have given them leaves room for them to doubt. You should take that personally and try to refine the image you are creating. Being the master of your own fate involves building your own image.

Only a few will care about your actual intentions. Most will care about how something appears or feels. If they receive uncomfortable vibes from you, that will equate it to how they think of you. This does not mean that you should only focus on creating a hologram of what you want to be known for and disregard actually living what you are. It means that the only thing people will actually interact with is the hologram you present.

Note: You can make your hologram more realistic by actually living out your life message.

You can design your hologram by taking the desired elements of your life message and determining a way to indirectly broadcast such qualities. A great movie producer does not claim to be great. Instead, he creates movies that many people love and want to go and watch. He positions the film so that the media publically engages in discourse on the movie and the movie-goers. You then watch the movie because you feel you must. A great actor does not tell you about his character. Instead, he becomes the image of his character. When you create an image, you are creating holograms. There are a few potentially desirable qualities in the chart below. You can fill in the empty box by adding in qualities and their respective holograms.

Quality:	Hologram:
Assertiveness	Others stop and listen when you are speaking; sitting at the head of the table; open posture; steady handshake; eye contact; no paper and pen; looking up; tall posture
Leadership	Loyal followers who speak highly of you
Kindness	Smile; eye contact, laughter; party host
Cleverness	Books or chess set in your surrounding environment; silence
Calmness	Attenuated lighting, soft music, cleanliness; slow, but rhythmic speech

Keep in mind that your life message will be filled with the perceptions of others, and your reputation is the perception. So, guard your reputation with your life.

Mentorship: *"If you don't let a teacher know what level you are- by asking a question, or revealing your ignorance- you will not learn or grow." (The 7 Habits of Highly Effective People)*

    B.   <u>My life is a measurement of my patience with learning.</u>

Mentorship is important when considering your future. How you mentor and are mentored is a testament to your approach to life. If you are an attentive and quick learner, it will be reflected in your life message. If you exhibit stubbornness and lack advisors, you will seem foolish and impulsive. You must learn how to identify your misconceptions and then work to amend your lack of knowledge so that you may avoid being duped as you pursue your purpose. If you are afraid to admit your ignorance, you will be doomed to a life of error, and no one will feel compelled to help you.

Forces will become more complicated as you increase in power and your list of responsibilities grows. Obtaining resources will become a test even from those who claim to support you, and your strengths will be challenged. Your passions will be entangled in myriads of tasks that act as means to an end. How patient and how willing you are to learn and practice is how your life will be valued.

Take the lessons that life is teaching seriously and be prideful about them so that you may reap all of their benefits. Be grateful that you were at the right place at the right time to encounter new experiences. They will prepare you for the difficulties that are awaiting your arrival. If you complain and unfailingly repeat your mistakes, those too will be placed into your life message. Recall, your life message is what is said about you when you are no longer present. It is crafted while you are alive and shared as gossip. You have control over much of the content as long as you are willing to pay attention to the perception you are creating and continue to learn so that you may refine your image.

Power: *"If the Universe is Mental in its nature, then mental transmutation must be the art of changing the conditions of the universe..." (Kybalion)*

    C.   <u>My life is up to me.</u>

The most important part of this chapter is to realize that your life message is completely up to you. Everything we evaluate, create, and conceive is mental in nature. We ascribe to values in the manner that we build our values. We create morals based on our mental concepts describing who we are and who we want to be. Collectively, we all partake in the same mental construction process in order to survive in the world around us. If everyone participates in the mental game, then it is possible that you may have power over other individuals and influence the way that they perceive their surroundings. You can create a mental image of yourself in the eyes of another. It takes maturity to do so, but it is possible. Our musicians, magicians, movie stars, athletes, doctors, politicians, statesmen, policemen, businessmen, and many other professionals all partake in mental manipulation of the perceptions of others. We respect a law officer because of his ability to embody the law. His authority comes from his ability to administer punishment. While both are respected, we treat doctors differently from policemen.

With the ability to engage in mental transmutation on this basic level, comes a great power. Note that power can be equated to insight and the ability to act on the insight. It is the power that is afforded only with freedom. Such freedom incurs much responsibility. Power can be stripped away when you lose control over yourself because you are giving control to someone else. Most people crave the opportunity to relinquish their obligations to others in order to tend to the short-term activities they truly value or care about. This barter system of power is what allows you to accomplish anything. Learning more about yourself and others will allow you greater insight into systems and obtain more leverage so that you may have more freedom in the writing of your life message. Remember, you are spiritually immortal. Your life precedes you in the form of history and proceeds your physical death in the form of gossip or story-telling. The tangibles become subject to the trading system and get redistributed. Your life message is truly up to you.

Chapter Nine

The Plan

It is, of course, important to have a plan ready in order to pursue anything. There must be a "course of action" so that there may be ways to create checkpoints and recognize when goals have been accomplished. This chapter explores what a plan looks like and some of the qualities that it should have.

The Plan

Note: "Good evening. I am very pleased to have been invited to be a part of this Negro Writer's Conference...I suppose I have been invited because my first play will be opening soon...I think I like it but I've no idea what the public will think of it. Still for the moment, let's presume I am a writer." (To Be Young, Gifted, and Black)

In this chapter plans are not comprised of exactitudes or quantitative milestones, as are agendas. Plans are comprised of attitudes and qualitative milestones. They serve to provide roadside lampposts when walking down a very dark road. You can navigate a journey in the darkness with your friends and your tools, as described in Chapter 5. With streetlights, however, you can make decisions when coming across new territories and discern the incorrect data provided by your tools and your friends. The quote above demonstrates the self-worth that the author felt. She had not yet exposed her writing to the public, but she felt herself to be a writer, and a great one. This is the mentality you must carry. Your plan begins with your knowing who you are now and as your "Point B". The circumstances may change in between, but who you truly are is constant. Your weaknesses and strengths are a part of you.

There is a difference between envisioning your future and pure wishful thinking. If you are engaging in the practice of envisioning your future, you are also working towards it. Wishful thinking requires no effort and only stays within the mind. Wishful thinking is dependent upon circumstances that you have no direct control over. Envisioning your future attempts to reign in on all activities that are within your sphere of control. So, be wary of those that say all you must do is believe, and it shall be done. The missing part is that when you truly believe, you will see, act, and then it shall happen. When you believe in a vision for yourself, you will recognize where all of the inconsistencies lie and be able to plan your ability to circumvent or demolish them.

When it comes to creating plans, most people are deterred by the stone-like nature of plans. Plans seem finite and inflexible. They do not accommodate changes because if there is a change, you must alter the initial plan in order to keep it relevant. Your plan can be better, however. It can be immune to the finalities and help you stand apart. You may not see planning as a necessary step in your growth, but imagine if your body never planned the steps it took. There was no plan for which muscle would flex, and which direction you would move. If planning represents a series of decisions, then imagine if you never planned. It is best to understand what plans are and how to master them so that they may be of their greatest use to you. Creating finite plans is a lazy endeavor that will usually bear small fruit.

The operational definition for this chapter is below:

A <u>plan</u> is a representation of a thing drawn on a plane, as a map or diagram.

Imagine going on a road trip to get from one place to another. Usually, you locate a map or query a GPS. You then attempt to identify the best route for you to arrive at a selected destination. At a minimum, you could also look at the map and only identify your initial and final locations. That is the sliding scale for developing maps.

Plans each turn and estimated time		Identifies a starting point and an ending point

In Chapter 5, an image was drawn demonstrating a Point B and a Point A. The empty space in the middle represents the plan for your journey. There are some specific traits about the plan to which you must pay attention. Specifically, your plan should have a reason, a subject matter, and an effect associated with its creation.

What am I planning?

I. **There is no true plan defined by you. There is preparation for a life plan.**

As mentioned before, the plan is not simply a map of precisely what you may or may not do at any given point. As clever and aware as you may be, that kind of plan without the consideration of all possibilities will eventually lead to a plan that is useless. Accomplishing such a feat is nearly impossible. Instead, the plan you are developing is a preparation plan so that when encountering new situations, you will be able to adapt because you have an end-goal in mind. In Chapter 5 when the maps were drawn, the plan was the process that you went through in order to mold yourself from point A to Point B. Instead of just trying to achieve the title that you have outlined for yourself in Point B, you plan to achieve the character of your Point B. Consequently, the title will come along with it. This is the reason of your plan: to allow you to achieve the character of your end-goal. This is why it is important to place the descriptors for each Point. The difference between the points is your plan.

Dimension	Point A	Point B
Social		
Physical		
Mental		
Spiritual		

As this plan will change, in accordance with your progress, it still is not quite true. As mentioned in the preface, those things that are considered true, are always true. Otherwise, they would no longer be classified as true. So keep in mind that your plan is flexible. As a rule of thumb, aspects of your life that you have direct control over, can be included in a more rigid plan (deadlines, milestones, etc.). For the things you have no direct control over, you must allow yourself a certain amount of flexibility. Do not get caught up in missing a specified deadline. A flexible plan is sensitive to its growth. As you gain new skills and learn from the lessons that life has to teach you, adjust your plan to reflect such progress. Keep yourself encouraged by visually monitoring your maturity.

Preparation: *"Like mastering your emotions, patience is a skill-it does not come naturally. But nothing about power is natural; power is more godlike than anything in the natural world. And patience is the supreme virtue of gods, who have nothing but time." (48 Laws of Power)*

A.   <u>Plan your preparation.</u>

When we think of the term *God*, we imagine an entity that is not bound by time, emotions, death, or objects. Because gods cannot be bound by such finite notions, we attribute great power to them. We believe they can not only influence their systems, but they can influence ours, and we ask them to show mercy on us and let us be a part of their powerful nature. This is fairly true across many beliefs, but definitely within the archetypal interpretation of *God*. The doctrines proceed with the idea that *God* is not bound by the finite and is infinite and omnipotent. In reality, the power in religion is the fact that we believe *God* to have infinite ability.

An analogy can be applied to humans. Those who we deem as unbounded attain the heights of power. The quote implies the corollary, and in turn indicates the kind of mindset you must have when planning to achieve the impossible or to delimit yourself. We must think as though our world is infinite. By imagining a world in which you have influence over, time, emotions, death, and objects, such confines will bear no deterrence to achieving your purpose. Instead of being influenced by the finite constructs, you control them to work to your advantage, as would the archetypical God. Your anger should not be a consequence of impulse, but rather a calculated application to perhaps demonstrate your ability to bring about wrath. Your kindness should not be easily a substitute for a weakness, but rather a calculated usage of your tools and your friends. This may sound fairly disingenuous, but it is quite the contrary. When emotions are applied impulsively, many times they elicit unexpected results and further your loss of control. However, if you approach a situation with an exact knowledge of how you act and to have it within your control, ready to use at any time, then the situation will remain within your relative control. Good intentions do not equal good results. A planned intention equals a planned result. The difference between good and planned is the kind of effort put into preparation. Good intentions are one-sided. It considers planning from your perspective. How will you react? How can it be done? What are the things that I could possibly do incorrectly? Planning, in this context refers to multilateral considerations. It considers the actions and behaviors of others. This can be done by knowing yourself very well. Planning your preparation is the first step to being able to anticipate others.

What are some of the stages you may find yourself in with your Point A and Point B differences? Then, include what situations may allot for your development from one to the other. You can use the "book about you" exercise from the previous chapter to complete this activity. Stages are the chapters and the transitions are the situations.

Dimension	Point A	Stage 1	Stage 2	Point 3	Situations
Social					
Physical					
Mental					

Spiritual

The situations you wrote are the ones that will provide the extra activation energy needed for you to move from one stage to another.

In previous chapters, pride and ignorance were mentioned as vices that prohibit your development. Think of the archetypical child: fearless, faithful, and fun-loving. They are fearless because the constraints of the world have not yet been learned. Therefore, they face no real limitations.

Fear is learned through situations that negatively reinforce an idea. They are faithful because they have no reason to be faithless. There is no reason to not trust that they will get what they expect. If a child believes he or she will fly when they leap off the top of a chair or table, then they will jump truly believing that it will happen. As for the fun-loving quality, they are humble about life's simple pleasures. Visit a room filled with untamed children. You will find them laughing and enjoying the presence of the other kids. With that, they learn with every new situation. They learn what to expect from others, and how to behave in front of others. In these characteristics, they are "godlike" with few limitations except from those provided by their elders. It is wise to act as a mature child so that life may be enjoyable and fulfilling. An "adult" is stubborn and believes that there are no new lessons to be learned. The stereotype of an adult is that he is mature and considers the inherent limitations at play. A "child" is humbled by his position in the world and treats everything with amazement and adventure. Plan as a child would plan, but be mature with your friends and your tools.

Infinity: "Just as you, student, may create a Universe of your own in your mentality, so does THE ALL create the Universe in its own Mentality. But your Universe is the mental creation of a Finite Mind, whereas that of

THE ALL is the creation of an Infinite." (The Kybalion)

B.   <u>The Life Plan is tentative and hopefully expansive.</u>

As you can see, the more stages you add, the more detailed your plan can become. The more control you gain, the less the world's boundaries will affect you. The more childlike you are, the more exploratory the world becomes. We are by nature, explorers who take risks in learning more about our environments and ourselves. The purpose behind the plan is to ensure that your world is ever expanding. Your mind should not be finite, but infinite. In the quote, "The All" is the summation of everything that exists in the world. It is the abundance of the universe. Imagine for a moment every possible material, form of energy, person, action, thought, book, form of life, planet, star, etc. The universe is ever-growing and all of the things that were once parts of the universe continue to be a part of it –although perhaps from one changing form to another. Matter is neither created nor destroyed. It can be compartmentalized to indicate flow, but the contents continue to exist and change in form. In your plan, as you grow, you will become more familiar with your infinite counterpart. The goal is for you to become as seemingly infinite in thought as the universe is in content. You are a part of the same entity that continues to grow and therefore all forms of knowledge and potential are within your possession as long as you properly align your focus and your forces. As white light possesses all of the colors, so must you possess all of the possibilities within your spectrum.

When your mindset exists within the infinite, it becomes difficult to view the world in the myopic sense. You begin to see and feel the systems as they move over large periods of time. You realize where the true value of money and people is. Time becomes relative and Einstein's theories become relevant for discussion – as it is only a relative method by which we are able to measure. We display our nature when we use metrics. As humans, we default to quantify and categorize everything. What should we run from? What should we protect and nurture? What deserves our attention? What can we afford to ignore? What is good? What is bad? What is healthy? What is unhealthy? We naturally are inclined to do this. Within a short

LP25: Influence

amount of time, you are able to categorize any situation or person so that you are able to create a response to the stimulus. It is all truly relative and we simply subscribe to certain ways for reasons of survival or convenience. You must evaluate your reasons for your subscriptions, as such categories can become limiting. With your plan, however, you will find that your reasons will begin to change and become increasingly complex. Your conclusions may change. You must keep abreast of why you are making those changes mentioned in the previous chapter: My Life Message. Take note as to whether a change was stimulated by emotion, logic, culture, duty, or some combination of them. If you allow only one of them to change your opinions, be sure that your Life Plan is not shrinking instead of expanding. Take the opportunity to incorporate, rather than avoid, an interaction in your Life Plan. The growth of your plan is a decision that you make. Think of a few of your opinions throughout your life, and see how and why they have changed.

Opinion 1	**Changed Opinion**	**Reason for Change**	**Grow/ Shrink**
Touching the stove is fun	*Touching the stove is dangerous*	*Emotions and logic, survival*	*Grow*

In the example above, "growth" indicates that the individual will not avoid stoves altogether because of the interaction, but rather will take steps to prevent an undesirable result in interacting *with* the stove. A less obvious example involves the process of desiring to get a book published. Perhaps you are confident in your literary expertise. Upon attempting to publish it, you share the content with an agent. The agent may discourage you or indicate that the book you have written is simply "not what he/she was looking for". You can choose to allow this to discourage you, or to serve as an impetus to understand "what the agent is looking for" or find a new agent.

So when reflecting, try to identify the decisions in life you have made that have had the effect of growing your plan and those that have served to shrink your plan.

Thoroughness: *"Plan all the way to the end. The ending is everything. Plan all the way to it, taking into account all the possible consequences, obstacles, and twists of fortune that might reverse your hard work and give glory to others. By planning to the end, you will not be overwhelmed by circumstances and you will know when to stop. Gently guide fortune, and help determine the future by thinking far ahead." (48 Laws of Power)*

C.   <u>My Plan is a program.</u>

Your plan is a program. It is a program that you define for yourself based on yourself. It includes everything about you and what you want to become. It encompasses your practice and your preparation so that you may develop a certain amount of flexibility when presented with a new circumstance. This kind of plan is more of a regimen. Once you have a program that includes such details, you will be able to change it as necessary. If you so please, you can challenge yourself by intensifying your preparation. You must consider all aspects in each of your areas for improvement. As mentioned, the universe is for all notable purposes, an infinite pool. To conjure every potential situation would be nearly impossible. On the contrary, to plan for any situation, depends upon your ability to know yourself and your place in the world. If you must refine your wittiness or practice "seeing" yourself from the outside, then it must be placed into your program. You must apply proper due diligence to developing your plan.

Pruning is another important aspect to your program. In order for a tree to grow and bear fruit that is useful and good, it must be pruned. It must have the weeds and the weak branches cut from it. It must be cleansed and refreshed. In life, it means reevaluating your tools and friends. You must be willing to prune yourself and manage when life prunes you as a part of your development. Recall that obstacles are blessings in disguise. Use them as learning opportunities that are meant to ripen you.

Like any program, be it a workout program or class curriculum, it

LP25: Influence

must be something in which you consistently participate. It should be set up in stages with attainable tasks. One should lead to the next as would a step ladder. Imagine your plan as a climb to an infinite world. The first step is filled with limitations and conveniences. The final step is filled with maturity and a boundless universe. Each step will require more effort and the opportunity to fall increases. Once you are able to cross the threshold into the infinite, however, you cannot fall. Crossing the threshold represents the scale of your mind and your influence. So if you are an engineer, doctor, disc jockey, soldier, desk clerk, executive officer, non-profit director, scientist, lawyer, or from any other profession, your boundaries will be pushed to the point to which you practice fearlessness and faithfulness in your ability to be accountable and act. What you believe to be true about yourself will be evident by yourself and those around you through your actions and circumstances. You can mature in how you act by defining a strong program or life plan for yourself.

II. The Program must be comprehensive.

As mentioned, you must practice due diligence with developing your plan. A comprehensive plan does not include a linearized view of traversing from Point A to Point B. It actually includes every perspective involved in your development. Internal and external development must be considered. A comprehensive plan is one that accounts for every facet of your personality and is tailored to you within the context of achieving your Point B.

Attempt to fill in the Point A→Point B map by showing what one stage may appear to be:

Point A → Transition Stage → Point B

Transition:_____
_____
_____

Your transition will be comprised of a few facets: your weaknesses, forces, and focuses.

Tuning: *"Each day look into your conscience and amend your faults. If you fail this duty you will be untrue to the Knowledge and Reason that are within you." (A Spiritual Treasury)*

A. <u>My plan includes my weaknesses.</u>

The plan you craft will include a few lines to describe your weaknesses. Your weaknesses were determined in previous chapters. So, for your Point A, the first set of data is in the weaknesses. Complete this step by also incorporating the weaknesses of your Point B and your transition state.

	Point A	Transition	Point B
Weakness			

There are two ways to manage your weaknesses. You can either remove them or make them work to your advantage. Since weaknesses are tremendously difficult to get rid of, it is best to ponder on the ways to make them work to your advantage. To begin this conversion, recall that a blessing ignored becomes a curse. This means that after applying spin, all good things can be made to look bad. The reverse, at times, is also true. With the proper spin, stubbornness becomes conviction and shyness becomes cautiousness. Try to spin your weaknesses, and begin to apply them in that way. Think of your weaknesses as strengths. Subconsciously, you will begin to tune your weaknesses so that they align more with your spin words. You must do this mentally, though. Spin is not spoken to people. You do not find friends and say, "I am not stubborn, I am convicted." Instead, you imagine a convicted person and allow yourself to personify that ideal.

	Point A	Transition	Point B
Weakness			
Spin			

In order to remove your weaknesses, it requires reprogramming. Reprogramming will be discussed in the next chapter. Generally, it involves habit changing activities. Habits are unconscious, but consistent actions. To reprogram yourself, you must replace your programmed habit with the new habit you would like to acquire.

Whichever way you choose to handle your weaknesses, it is important that you include them in your plan.

Immortality: *"Know your own true worth, and you shall not perish." (A Spiritual Treasury)*

    B.   <u>My plan includes my forces.</u>

Your forces include your strengths, your resources, and your passion (intrinsic motivation). Your true worth is the sum of all your forces. While concentrating them to one single objective is the most effective use of them, it may not be the most efficient use of them. Efficiency comes after careful consideration of what each force provides and where they can best be used. The chapter "Concentrate Your Forces", referenced that it takes iron to sharpen iron. If rubber is present, perhaps it may be used in conjunction with the sharpening process, but not to purely sharpen the iron. The purpose must be broad enough so that efficiency is achieved when concentrating forces towards a single point. By knowing how each of your forces participates in achieving your purpose, you can fully understand your value. Your plan must include your value. Most people do not have any issue with including the forces in the plan.

The issue arises when identifying how each force may be used. Try to complete the chart:

Purpose/ Overarching Goal:		
	Object/Person	Usage to Achieve Goal
Your Strengths		
Your Resources		
Passion		

As the quote mentions, knowing your true worth means you understand how expansive the world is and just how much control you have over your circumstances. Such a revelation will afford you a sense of dominion and thrill. You must stay humble as you rise, otherwise, you will be sure to fall. If your true worth is absent from your knowledge, then others will find ways to squander and abuse it. They will think for you and limit your options because your mind is not expansive enough to conceive anything else. Your creativity will be stifled, and that is the part of you that is uniquely of you. If you are too lazy to spend the time to be accountable, then your debts will be picked up by someone else who will have no problem subjecting you to mental bondage. Accomplishing this is easy. A captor influences his captives by convincing them that it is their duty to be bound. They use fear to negatively reinforce in them that their position is the correct societal position and emotionally destroy any inkling of self-worth so that the captive person is constantly trying to "prove themselves" worthy of their captor. Finally, he convinces him that he is too ignorant or stupid to think for himself and must trust in a system outside of himself in order to survive. It is best to know your worth and the worth of your tools so that you may pursue what fulfills your unique design.

Try this exercise:

Find a blank check, and write a number on the check that you would feel comfortable with someone giving to you. What are some of the thoughts that come to your mind as you are deciding on a number? Write them down next to the picture.

These thoughts you are having are limitations or impulse checkpoints. Become familiar with them and program them so that you may be able to determine your actual worth. Consider all of the people you know, the resources you manage, the skills you have, and the passion you will bring to a job or task that you love. That is your worth.

Realize that one day you will have to rest. There will be no more you can do or contribute. Your debts will still continue to exist and your earnings will be fragmented by the world. Your life message will be immortal, and the worth you actually believed you held will be known by all.

Mission: *"I want to stay in the oasis, the boy answered. I've found Fatima, and as far as I am concerned, she's worth more than treasure....Well, what if I decide to stay?'...'You will be the counselor of the oasis...Sometime during the second year, you'll remember the treasure. The omen will begin to speak of your treasure and your Personal Legend...You'll remember that she never asked you to stay...Then sometime during the fourth, the omens will abandon you, because you've stopped listening to them. The tribal chieftains will see that and you will be dismissed from your position as counselor... You'll spend the rest of your days knowing that you didn't pursue your Personal Legend, and that now it's too late... You must understand that love never keeps a man from pursuing his Personal Legend. If he abandons that pursuit, it's because it wasn't true love... the love that speaks the Language of the World." (The Alchemist)*

C. <u>My Plan includes my focuses.</u>

You must be able to recognize your dead ends. In this excerpt from The Alchemist, the boy is contemplating whether or not his contentment with his current situation is sufficient regardless of his burning desire to explore further. A personal legend is the same as the overarching purpose that each person has been uniquely designed to carry out. At the end of the story, the boy ends with everything: worldly possession and personal fulfillment. The advice was in regards to pursuing that which you must. If you know you must be a writer, then it is upon you to do so. A person's true love is his own personal fulfillment. A person on this journey should be encouraged and aided. In a relationship with true love, each person works to help the other towards their personal legend. It is important that you consider what you are sacrificing when you decide to give up on a pursuit. This drive is found in the Spiritual Dimension.

You must include your focus in your plan. Consider all of your weaknesses and forces in the four dimensions and evaluate which dimension you are currently focusing on. Then, decide on which dimension you would like to focus. By focusing on one dimension, you will be able to adapt in a given situation because you know what you are pursuing. All dimensions are concurrently in application, but there is one on which you place greater priority. For The Alchemist, he focused on his Spiritual Dimension. Picking a dimension allowed him to make decisions and not be regretful about them. Regret is dangerous because it stifles you. The more you make decisions that you whole-heartedly believe in, the less regret you will experience.

Dimension	Weaknesses		Strengths		Resources		Passion		Focus: Yes/No	
Point	A	B	A	B	A	B	A	B	A	B
Social										
Physical										
Mental										
Spiritual										

LP25: Influence

The focus you choose will ultimately determine the risks you are willing to take and the goals you seek to achieve. As demonstrated in Chapter 7, there are dangers to all focuses. If the danger is too much of a risk then find another focus. You can use the Life Matrix to map out where you currently are and where you would like to go. Then, you must begin to prepare for it by gauging your progress between your Point A and your Point B. How do you fare up next to your Point B?

III.   <u>The plan has an unbounded destination.</u>

In order for your plan to be expansive, and for your purpose to be broadened, you must imagine your plan as a plane without boundaries. While there are distinct positions of Point A and Point B, they lie on a plane. They are only relative to each other and have the capability of being located at any position on the plane. The only finite aspect is the least distance between the two points. See the image:

A plan with two points indicated: The plane can be extended in any direction. The direction represents your growth in preparedness.

A plane with two points indicated after being moved: The points have been shifted, meaning their absolute locations have changed, but their relative locations have not. The plane can be extended in any direction.

The changed coordinates indicate your growth and regression. The relative locations do not change between where you move and where you want to go. The plane on which they move is infinite and so the Point A and the Point B have the potential to be described by all coordinates. As you progress, and leave behind creations, you are able to cover more ground, and learn more about the infinite plane so that you may further develop your plan. By keeping the distance constant, you are able to always be in a developing and growth stage. As you actively work at your point, you will plant behind your creations, and gain resources. To continue the metaphor of the plane, you will leave behind mentees and collect mentors so that you can gain perspective and span.

As planes work, you must develop a way to measure growth and change. Cartesian grids are one method to measure growth. Some use polar coordinates. In the life plan, use the matrix coordinates. The intersection of your focus and your forces is your position. Your main focus may be Spiritual, but decide which quality about the spiritual is the true focus. Then decide which force is truly pushing you.

A (Force, Focus) = (_____, _____)
B (Force, Focus) = (_____, _____)

So as you are taking the time to read, take a moment to close the book, and close your eyes. Picture yourself walking along an infinite walkway. It keeps growing and expanding because it describes everything that can possibly exist. It represents all possibilities. Your success is amidst the plane, and you are walking towards it. As you continue to walk, you discover more of the infinite world. Along the way, you make friends, and they also begin to search the plane. Other friends come to you and tell you about the other happenings within the infinite plane. As you keep walking, your Point B begins to change location because you are learning more and changing your own location. Regardless of how far you walk, your Point B continues to appear as far away from you as before, but it is because you keep pushing it further, and planning further. You attained the previous Point B's with relative ease because of your willingness to learn and plan. You welcome the new circumstances and see them as opportunities to chart new territories. Your plan continues to develop and grow and in the real world, you are accomplishing your purpose because you know that boundaries do not truly exist.

Destiny: *"...the child said to me, 'If you come here, you will find a hidden treasure.' And, just as she was about to show me the exact location, I woke up. Both times." (The Alchemist)*

    A.   <u>My purpose is the last arrival. I already am.</u>

In The Alchemist, the boy began as a shepherd and ended the book as a man with a fulfilled personal legend. He had always imagined himself to be fulfilled, and he lived his life as an open minded traveler with skills on hand that were pertinent to his fulfillment. It was not a matter of what, but a matter of when. It was his responsibility to be prepared. His dreams and his omens reminded him of his purpose. You must remind yourself by living it every day in a qualitative fashion. At times, the confines and temptations of life will cause you to revisit your coordinates. You must make sure that you are still roaming your plane. Use your Point B to determine those qualities. Do not let limitations cause you to become stagnant.

You are great before you begin. Greatness is within a man. Only after time has passed, is it recognized by others. Your mentality must be at this point. If you are striving for a Point B, you must act as though you have already arrived there. Actions are different from words.

How you act towards someone, a project, or something shows exactly what you believe about them and the worth you have in yourself. If you are intimidated, then you must feel insecure about a weakness of yours rather than fear the strength of another. Channel your thoughts to have an internal locus of control. What does it mean for you? Do you believe people are mean to you? Then ask yourself, "Why do you let people devalue you, and why do you not bring value to the table?" If someone does not understand what you want, then why do you not communicate clearly, and send mixed signals? If someone is unfaithful to you, then why do you not demand loyalty and communicate the value of trusting you? The point of this exercise is not to demean you or indicate that sometimes people are not just mean or unfaithful. The point is for you to begin to view yourself in a mirror so that you can adjust your mentality. When your mental state is clear and focused, then you can actually apply your plan. Otherwise, you will become clouded, and when an obstacle presents itself, you will forget its value and your value. You will find yourself regressing into a default habit or mindset of defeat because you never believed you could achieve anything better in the first place.

Also, when thinking that "some people are just mean", realize you must also take responsibility for your part in reminding others of their insecurities. If they are jealous of you, it is because you have shown them something of which they should be jealous. It may be your appearance, your voice, or your deeds. Whatever the exhibited interactions may be, all interactions consist of relationships. Relationships are agreed upon systems of correspondence. Be cautious of what you share or conceal in a relationship. Be mindful of the person you are dealing with. It is important as you are wandering that infinite plane so that you may not find obstacles suddenly appearing insurmountable. Plan wisely, fervently, and with the mentality that you have already arrived.

Chapter Ten

Responsibility

Responsibility is comprised of two words which are response and ability. This simply implies that you must be able to adapt, flow, and respond in order to approach success. This chapter explores what influences your ability to respond and to adapt.

Responsibility

Note: "Look at the word responsibility-'response-ability'-the ability to choose your response. Highly proactive people recognize that responsibility. They do not blame circumstances, conditions, or conditioning for their behavior. Their behavior is a product of their own conscious choice, based on values, rather than a product of their conditions, based on feeling. " (7 Habits of Highly Effective People)

The ability to respond is something very unique to organisms. We can differentiate between rocks and insects because when stimulated, insects move on their own and rocks move where they are pushed. Rocks have no control over where they are moved. They are influenced by every entity that fills their surroundings and cannot actively influence them in return. A living entity, on the contrary, can actively influence its surroundings. The ability to respond is perhaps the greatest ability that humans have. Our responses are complicated, and are wired differently in each person. Anger is the same for all, but the emotion requires a different stimulus for each person. An emotion can be compared to a 60Hz signal. Whether the signal is a composite of multiple signals or the breakdown of one signal, it will always be a 60Hz signal. Whether the amplitude is at 400 amperes or 4 amperes, the signal is still a 60Hz signal. Our emotions are the same. An emotion and its management are what produce the differences from one person to another. To best understand someone else's anger, you can begin by understanding your anger. How do you feel when you are angry? How do you think? Chances are other people experience similar feelings and thoughts when they are angry.

With complexity present in human responses, it is important to pay attention to what motivates your responses, and how, if desired, you would be able to rewrite your motivations.

We have sufficiently differentiated you from a rock. By conceding that you are a responsible person, you are committing yourself to the notion that you cannot blame others for your predicaments. There always existed another option that you chose to ignore. You must accept responsibility for that decision. Beyond being a responsible person, you must be an adaptable one. This can only happen when you are accountable to the ethics you have outlined for yourself. The quote is relatively self-explanatory and perfectly sets the stage for you to begin pondering on what you are responsible for.

What are some things for which you are responsible?
Emotions
Family
Financial Obligations

_____

_____

One of the sure signs of a responsible person is the ability to manage obligations without the assistance of others. The standard is that a responsible person does not require supervision by another. They are self-sustainable people who can devise a way to triumph in a challenging situation. They can utilize an interdependent world through actively making decisions.

The operational definitions for this chapter are below:

A <u>response</u> is a reaction, as that of an organism or a mechanism, to a specific stimulus.

Ability is the power or capacity to do or act physically, mentally, legally, morally, financially, etc.

These definitions are important to internalize so that you can truly identify your responsibilities. A response must have a stimulus. You are be influenced by your surroundings, but you also have the capacity *to* influence your surroundings with intention. Responses are woven into systems and connected to our sense of duty, culture, logic, or emotion. The result is an action or an emotion. By analyzing your actions and use of emotions, you can gain deeper insight into your most powerful skill –responsibility.

Your ability to respond affects all aspects of your life in accordance with the definition. The four dimensions can be applied here. How do your responsibilities appear through the lens of the other dimensions and what forces drive your responsibilities?

	Social Dimension	Physical Dimension	Mental Dimension	Spiritual Dimension
Responsibility 1				
Responsibility 2				
Responsibility 3				

What is a responsibility?

I. <u>Identify your spiritual program.</u>

Your "spiritual program" is a phrase that involves describing the source of your thoughts and habits. Any activity that you engage in subconsciously is triggered by some outside stimulus. You must be aware of what triggers your habitual vices. This step requires much work because it requires you to think, whereas the nature of a habit involves no conscious thought.

Your habits can also be described as default responses to complex situations. Some people mentally flee from their circumstances by pretending as though the situation does not exist. However, running will not help you face your fears. Avoiding those fears will fuel your "grudge entity". This is explained later in this chapter. As mentioned in the previous chapter, a plan is a program. The spiritual program is your fundamental plan drawn within the spiritual dimension. You must identify what stimulus in your spiritual program is using the habit as a response. Try to focus on habits you would like to purge, first. This is the first step to eradicating your weaknesses. Habits that will benefit you are a part of programming yourself to hone your strengths. If you are a great worker under pressure, then identifying your spiritually programmed reason why will help you decide to either strengthen that reason or use it at specific times; such as when you are not under pressure.

Regardless of the type of habit, there is a trigger, and a counter trigger. A counter trigger will make you respond in the opposite way of your habit even after being presented a trigger. Imagine you think that someone is insulting you, using personal information. Your first reaction may be emotional: you feel anger because you are embarrassed. This emotional reaction is rooted in your fear that others will judge you and begin to treat you differently. After the insult, you feel that others will probably treat you worse. So, you immediately think of ways to retaliate in order to vindicate yourself. Suddenly, the same person negates the insult by adding that they were actually the victim of the insult, and not you. Immediately you are cured from your anger, and it evolves into sympathy. The sympathy is rooted in love your security, as you realized your security has been unaffected. In this case the habit is vindication. The dimension is mental. The spiritual trigger is a fundamental character insult, questioning one's ability to achieve a purpose, and the counter trigger is reinforced security.

This scenario would represent a habit scenario only for an individual who would have engaged in the actual response that was feared, under the assumption he was the intended victim. This means, he would have immediately responded by offering an equally offensive insult. If you perform an action that you would criticize someone else for, the action is a bad habit. If the person had the natural inclination to feel sympathy whether or not they were insulted first, then this scenario would not qualify as a habit with a trigger or a counter trigger. It would simply be a response.

Another example for the same presented circumstance would be for a respected adult to enter the conversation after the insult was made and instruct everyone to go their separate ways. If you envision yourself immediately fearful of the figure in authority, it would be the counter-trigger. A counter trigger can be applied constantly to prevent you from ever falling victim to your trigger.

Try to identify your specific wiring by noting your habits, triggers, and counter triggers. Here are a few:

Smoking, Drinking, Jealousy, Talkative, Shyness, Loudness, Eating

Habit	Habit Dimension	Spiritual Dimension Trigger	Counter Trigger

By isolating the triggers from the habits, you can better understand your habits. Knowing the triggers will highlight what you believe your habits will provide you. At that point, you can then consciously decide to reject or accept the notion.

Habit	Provides	Agree/ Disagree	New Habit that Provides Same

Foundation: *"My thesis then, is as follows: in addition to our immediate consciousness, which is of a thoroughly personal nature and which we believe to be the only empirical psyche (even if we tack on the personal unconscious as an appendix), there exists a second psychic system of a collective, universal, and impersonal nature which is identical in all* *individuals. This collective unconscious does not develop individually but is inherited. It consists of pre-existing forms, the archetypes, which can only become conscious secondarily and which give definite form to certain psychic contents."* (Archetypes and the Collective Unconscious)

A.   It is provided by my subconscious mind.

Realize that all of these habits and responses are manufactured by how you view yourself and your world. They surface as interactions. This is true in relationships between people. The people you detest, you purposefully try to sabotage and push away because they remind you of an insecurity, or make you feel secure in one way, but not in others. Those you care for and invest time into are recipients of your security. You care for the ones you love, and scorn the ones you fear. All things are rooted in your basic beliefs of why you exist. You treat people and objects accordingly. So, as you review your habits, realize you are reviewing your subconscious. If you are trying to "kick" a habit, you are trying to change your Spiritual Dimension. This dimension is as resilient as the base of an iceberg. It takes maturity to change your primary beliefs. People will detect the change, however, because you will be changing on a very fundamental basis. People will also be able to note when you are pretending to change. Most people choose not to believe the truth if it is hurtful, and so they will never tell you. They will recognize that you are only posturing, however, and call you a hypocrite behind your back. Do not take offense, because if you sincerely wanted to change, you would have been genuine about it. You have full control over rewriting your program. If you choose to try and take shortcuts, you will be spurned by your caring friends. They will feel swindled. They will know your true efforts, and will see you as a thief of their time.

Since rewriting your program is a difficult journey, it is important that you are patient with yourself and allow yourself to be embarrassed, in private, of your shortcomings. You should be honest about your desires and the motivations for those desires. Be honest about your true ethics and feel the distrust you have in yourself. It is the first step to learning how to control yourself. Most people purport that they are perfect or correct, and that there is no need for them to learn how to control themselves. So, in complicated moments, these people default to their habits and then are left wondering why they were pushed to such extreme lengths. Take your time, and you will never be those people because you have already imagined yourself as that person and have figured a way to subvert your vices.

Causation: *"Because we are, by nature, proactive, if our lives are a function of conditioning and conditions, it is because we have, by conscious decision or by default, chosen to empower those things to control us." (7 Habits of Highly Effective People)*

  B. <u>It is provided by my acceptance of circumstances.</u>

Your circumstances, as they exist today, are of your own doing. You have made many decisions along the way that brought you to your here and now. You continue to be in your position because you have accepted your current circumstance as fate. You cannot blame anyone else for your complacency. Even if you are managing from one check to another, it is because fundamentally, you do not believe you deserve any better. If you believed you deserved better, you would act differently. You would think differently. You would find opportunities where most people cannot even see anything. Try the exercise below by supplying the negative aspects of your current situation. Then, add the decisions that took place for you to arrive at your current position.

Current Circumstance 1:	Current Circumstance 2:
Decision 1:	Decision 1:
Decision 2:	Decision 2:
Decision 3:	Decision 3:

Next to each decision box, list who or what you could potentially blame for making that decision. Now, determine why they are not to blame for that decision. By eliminating their influence, you are eliminating the control they continue to have over you and how you feel about your future. Only after you are able to acquit them of any blame will you be able to move forward. Otherwise, you will constantly dwell on what cannot be changed. Also, consider the default habits that encouraged these decisions and add them to your list of habits.

The next step is to view the diagram in the other direction. List some current decisions you must make that are in your future. What will the circumstance be once those decisions are made? Next to each decision box, write the people who will try to influence you to decide a certain way on options. Try to figure out why their influence works on you. Is it because of your forces? Are they a part of your focus? How can you counter act their efforts? Are you controlled by logic, emotions, duty, or culture? You can triumph over your lack of control by simply harnessing what it means to be in control of your destiny and accountable for your past.

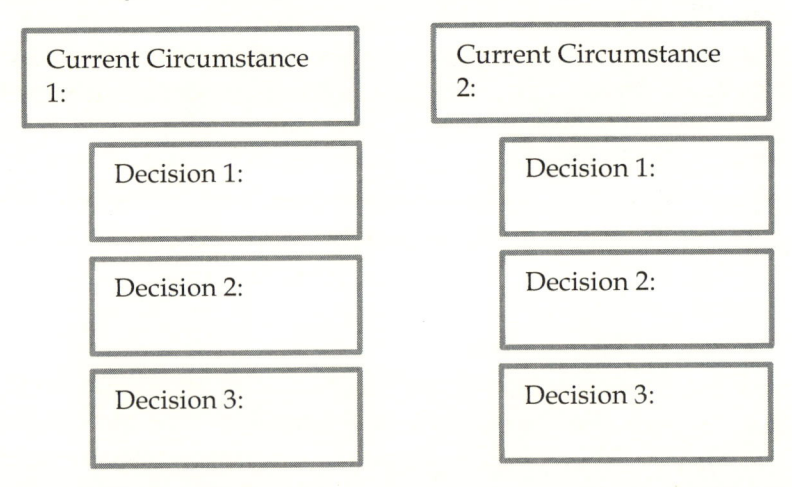

Current Circumstance 1:	Current Circumstance 2:
Decision 1:	Decision 1:
Decision 2:	Decision 2:
Decision 3:	Decision 3:

Systems: *"Is not religion all deeds and all reflection, and that which is neither deed nor reflection, but a wonder and a surprise ever springing in the soul, even while the hands hew the stone or tend the loom? Who can separate his faith from his actions, or his belief from his occupations? Who can spread his hours before him, saying,' This for God and this for myself; This for my soul, and this other for my body?'..." (A Spiritual Treasury)*

C. <u>The output variables include emotions, decisions, and actions.</u>

Every system has inputs, outputs, and an operator. The inputs are the forces. The operator is you and your focus. The outputs are emotions, decisions, and actions. This is the program that you will evaluate and rewrite. You can analyze the operator by reviewing the inputs and outputs. If you only know the outputs, then there are too many degrees of freedom to do anything with the system. Once you have enough information about two of the three aspects of the system, you are able to configure every other element of the system. In engineering, the operator may be linear or non-linear. You can determine that by reviewing several sets of inputs and outputs through the same operator. When all aspects of an operator are known, it can be then used appropriately to either codify a new signal, or in metaphorical terms, it means adjusting new information in a predictable and utilizable way.

Since systems are so inextricably tied to the variables that they are comprised of, you would be remiss to pay little to no attention to finding out more about yourself. Every emotion you feel is based on your design as an operator. It was mentioned that every cause has an effect and every effect has a cause. By not knowing how to utilize yourself to the fullest, you may be applying your skills and resources the wrong way. While you may be expecting a linearized output, you are actually a non-linear function. Know your system so that you may refine yourself accordingly.

The quote explains the nature of functioning on one accord. A system cannot leave behind its system. They are tied together because it is of the nature of the system to be a system. As a refined person, you must function in unison. You cannot dissociate your outputs from your inputs as though they are not a part of the system. Without those parts, what would be the essence of a system? Where would its proof be? All three components exist because the entire system exists. You should see yourself as a functioning unit.

Inputs → Operator → Outputs

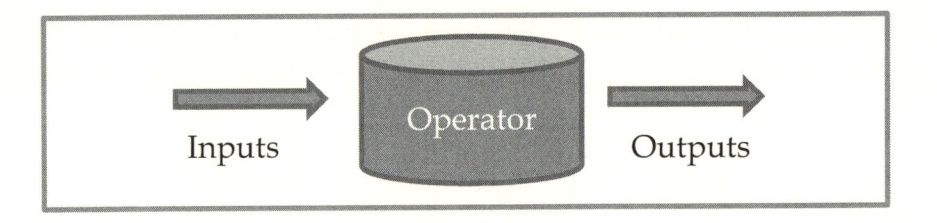

II.   Understand the discourse in your Spiritual Dimension.

In cartoons, when a character is confronted with a decision, an angel would suddenly appear on the shoulder, and then a devil would appear on the other. They would each propose different reasons as to why the character should or should not engage in a certain activity. The character would go back and forth between the two sides because both usually presented well developed arguments. Nonetheless, a decision had to be made, and the character would give up with a frustrating shrugging of the head. We experience this type of dichotomy on a daily basis. The idea is to understand the motivations of both sides that are intentionally trying to influence your decision. You must know that the angel and the devil, figuratively, are a part of you. Imagine those arguments and sort through which part of you thinks and acts in those manners. Understanding the discourse is the same as understanding the reaction of your subconscious to outside stimuli.

Identifying your habits will force this discourse. One side of you will attempt to justify the existence of those habits. It does this because you spiritually believe the habit satisfies a spiritual need. Another side of you will demean you for believing what you believe and accuse you of being a hypocrite. At that point, you will be faced with a massive crossroad. Should you choose to be self-righteous and neglect your faults, one side will win the argument. Should you choose to accept your potential to err, you will begin embarking down a long journey of rewriting your programmed habits, regardless of the dimension in which they rest. Once you can identify your triggers and understand the discourse, you are then ready to change the motivations.

Harmony: *"Everything flows out and in; everything has its tides; all things rise and fall; the pendulum-swing manifests in everything; the measure of the swing to the right, is the measure of the swing to the left; rhythm compensates." (The Kybalion)*

Subordinate: *"God has placed in each soul an apostle to lead us upon the illumined path. Yet many seek life from without, unaware that is within them." (A Spiritual Treasury)*

    A.   <u>It is what causes an imbalance in my life.</u>

In order to find peace with the discourse, you must find a way to reconcile the two entities that perch on your shoulders. "Understanding" goes beyond intelligently deciphering the presented arguments. The next step is to really comprehend the motivations behind these viewpoints. Where did they come from? What have you experienced in your life that placed them there in the first place? It is important to understand them because your life is subject to those viewpoints. Begin by accepting that you are a slave to your experiences. The conclusions you made when you were six or seven are probably still the basis for your current decisions. If you are distrusting, it may have been because you were abused or taken for granted in your youth. It will lead to one of your characters telling you, "Do not trust them because they may hurt you." While it may very well be true, keep in mind that people tend to reflect exactly what you show. So if you are distrusting, then they too will be distrusting. The result is that you will never experience the joy and benefit of trusting someone.

Once you accept the strength that experiences possess over you, it is then imperative that you take the next step to place your experiences into context. Once they are within the context of the dimensions and systems that they affect, you can begin to "see beyond" your experiences.

One of the characters that perch on your shoulders can be identified as the grudge entity. This character is seeking your survival and making sure your ego stays intact. The discourse from this entity is usually based on all the things that may go wrong. If you trust, you may get hurt. If you are honest, you will be punished. If you are loud, you will be silenced. If you are engaging in troubling activities, you will be judged. The grudge entity keeps track of all of the wrongs you have experienced and is usually unable to put perspective on your wrongs. A worse case of the grudge entity is that it also views happy experiences as limiting and as reminders that bad experiences will come soon.

The other character can be identified as the naïve entity. This character is seeking your growth and engagement in new activities. It seeks adventure and is quite fearless. When faced with a decision, this character focuses on all you have to gain. It places no consideration on the consequences.

They are not quite the good/ bad dichotomy, as there are many good aspects to the bad and many bad aspects to the good. Nevertheless, they are on opposite ends of the spectrum. In many cases, they are responsible for the ups and downs in your life. Balance, however, is the key. Identify which of the polar ends you reside near. Understanding these two sides is step one. Reconciling them is step two. After you identify their motivations, the grudges you hold on to and the adventure you want to engage in, you can move forward with options that both can agree are good options for you.

You must speak with your grudge entity and convince it that the grudge is unjustly held. You must take responsibility for the experience. You must convince the grudge entity that the blame on the person or experience for a certain viewpoint is based on an incorrect interpretation of the experience. Then, you must reconstruct the experience with a new perspective. This is step three. The decision and circumstance diagram can assist in this.

What are some of the arguments your dichotomous characters use to influence you? Which ones do you want to change?

Grudge Entity	Naïve Entity

III. <u>Rewrite the program.</u>

Review each motivating experience and rewrite it so that you may arrive at the manner of thinking you desire. Rewriting your program is not easy. To rewire a computer, you have to remove the hood and navigate through what some may consider a mess. You have to have a plan for the new configuration and you have to have a working knowledge of every other wire so that you do not inadvertently disrupt the rest of the functions.

Rewriting your program takes much reflection. Below, for each activity, include the experience and your revision of it.

Grudge Experience	Rewrite	Naïve Experience	Rewrite

This is the final step of reprogramming yourself.

Revision: *"If the Universe is Mental in its nature, then Mental Transmutation must be the art of CHANGING THE CONDITIONS OF THE UNIVERSE, along the lines of Matter, Force and Mind." (The Kybalion)*

A. <u>Nothing outside of the Spiritual Dimension will affect it.</u>

Remind yourself that all of your actions, emotions, and decisions are built upon your view of the world and your worth. Your notion of self-worth is reinforced and refined through self-talk and imposed or conquered limitations. These serve as motivations and are derived from your experiences, which are subconsciously interpreted. The conclusions you draw from experiences are influenced by your focus. You can gain perspective on your focus by utilizing your forces.

If you are to change your mindset, you must change it at the root. You can change your world simply by changing how you view the world. Where others see limitations, you see opportunity. Things of the Mental Dimension are influenced by the Spiritual Dimension. The main stimulant of your ability to respond is in the Spiritual Dimension. You should become familiar with your Spiritual Dimension's intentions so that you can either redirect or amplify them. Align yourself so that you are on one accord with your motivators and reconcile the discourse that will only serve to cause you anxiety and furthermore, regret your decisions.

Do these things so that you may not only plan with your weaknesses, forces, and focuses in mind, but so that you may also obliterate your weaknesses altogether. Do this and you will find it harder to live with a mindset of scarcity. Do this and your purpose will feel almost as though it simply happened upon you. Realize the work that goes into your success is very rarely the work that is easily accounted for by others. It is the work that occurs when you are developing yourself and recognizing your faults and concepts of limitations.

LP25: Influence

Part Three Introduction

The Transition Stage

One should be able to communicate their value to others. The transition stage is the process that a message undergoes when going from one person to another. The effectiveness of a message is all about how it is received by another party. Communication comes in multiple forms. Some are cognizant, but the most telling are subconsciously provided. Communication is made up of energy and thus, people can perceive "vibes" from a person. Reading between the lines is only possible because within the words that are communicated exist a tone, a purpose, and a rhythm associated with the tone. You should be aware of the kind of communication you are having with another individual. This chapter is meant to help you not only recognize what your communication looks like, but to improve it so that you are confident in your conveyance. At the end of this theme, you are expected to know what to communicate, how to communicate, and create a vision for the individual with whom you are corresponding.

Imagine crafting the perfect letter. There are no blemishes, spelling errors, or grammatical errors. The size of the paper fits precisely into its envelope. You prepare it to be sent by placing the stamp on it, and sealing the back. As you bring it to the post office, imagine everything your perfect letter will go through. Someone who has no idea what the envelope contains will handle it first. They will sort it to be prepared to be shipped or carried somewhere. Another individual will then be responsible for firstly keeping the contents intact, and then giving them to someone who can take it to its final destination. By the time the mail arrives at its destination, it has exchanged hands multiple times, and most likely is no longer the perfected entity that was initially placed in the mail. Not to mention, the person who receives the mail has their own way of reviewing it. Each of the handlers metaphorically represents the person who receives the message and the series of filtering systems they have when interpreting information. As you can see, most of communication is not solely dependent on you, but you can make an effort to ensure that the best message possible gets delivered. As a matter of fact during mail delivery it passes through so many hands that there is a chance that the letter may get lost.

An important factor in the sending of a signal or message is in how well you understand the systems involved, and how the systems interact with one another. If you are aware of the different shortcomings in specific systems, you can prepare for them and find ways to add an extra level of protection to your carefully created letter. Imagine if you were sending glass items to a person. Knowing that handlers can be a little rough with mailed contents, you would wrap the glass in paper, and pad them inside of a box which reads "FRAGILE" on the outside. This is true for your communication too. You must carefully prepare and protect your message so that it will retain its shape and utility when it is received.

Chapter Eleven

Internal to External

The purpose of this chapter is to identify what stimulates your own thoughts about communication. It is also meant to help you synthesize full concepts, and then deliver those thoughts to someone else. This is particularly important for networking. Realize that when you speak, you are revealing more than the words you say.

Internal to External

Note: "As an Interdependent person, I have the opportunity to share myself deeply, meaningfully, with others, and I have access to the vast resources and potential of other human beings." (7 Habits of Highly Effective People)

The goal of communication is for you to convey some idea that you have created. Whether the idea is about you or some new entity that you have invented, you are telling a story and sharing a vision. Your success can depend heavily on how well you are able to communicate those two aspects. If you are not able to ask for what you need or deserve, it will be nearly impossible to actually gain it. How you ask is more important than what you ask for, because how you ask is the only information the receiver will actually have. Other people cannot read your mind, so automatically knowing what is important to you is an unreasonable expectation. You can guide other individuals to learn your preferences, but they will never know exactly what you are thinking unless you are able to communicate it accurately for them to understand.

That hints at another important key. The person you are speaking with comes equipped with dimensional filters and you must choose your communication wisely. The chapter title from internal to external is meant to imply that your ideas are firstly internal. They are rooted in your conundrums, adages, and precepts. Your mind travels a mile a minute, creates ideas, and destroys ideas. Your mind has been with you since shortly after you were conceived. It captures all of your experiences and stores them as memories for future use. In your mind, you have imagined yourself as the greatest person alive in full uniqueness, and as a member of the bland masses seeking a purpose. It is truly a beautiful object d'art. There is no other person who has been with your mind as long as you have. So, when you are trying to communicate internally, it should come easily. Everything should sound just as it ought to because your mind is a part of you. Even though it came after you existed, you cannot even recall life before your mind came into existence. In communication, you are going outside of the relationship you have with your mind, and are trying to share something with another person's mind. Which mind will take precedence? So, you must bear in mind that when you are translating your thoughts from the internal environment to the external environment, it consists of your audience. It is not your own mind, but the mind of another.

Recall the difference between independence and interdependence. Interdependent people believe that they are mature enough to handle their specific obligations, and realizes the cause and effect sequence of the world around them. All things have their causes and effects. You may disagree with the provided justifications, but they exist as reasons for the individual who used them. An interdependent person is accountable because they understand. An independent person practices accountability because they appreciate the appearance of grandeur that it brings. They use two very different motivations and either will lead to different kinds of challenges. An interdependent person will have an easier time translating their internal mind to something external than an independent person.

The operational definitions for this chapter are below:

Something that is <u>internal</u> exists solely within the individual mind. It comes from, is produced by, or motivated by the psyche or inner recesses of the mind.

Something <u>external</u> is pertaining to the outward or visible appearance or show. It is of or pertaining to the world of things, considered as independent of the perceiving mind.

Have you ever sat with your headsets with music blaring in your ears? Someone taps you and tries to ask you a question. You try to answer them as you remove your headsets. Do you notice that you are louder than normal? Internally you heard your voice as being normal, but clearly, when you removed the headsets, you realized how loud you were. Speaking to someone can be viewed in the same way. Internal conversations go one way, and external conversations tend to go another way. Sometimes, you actually hear someone remark, "Well it sounded better in my head." When telling jokes, it is not whether or not the joke is funny. It is all in the delivery. If it is inappropriately delivered, then the joke loses all of its humor. Environmental adjustment, message filtration, and delivery are all important when communicating your ideas, stories, and purpose.

How do I translate?

I. <u>You must be ready.</u>

When preparing yourself to go from the internal to the external, you must be ready to do so. You must be mentally comfortable with whom you are and what you want to say. Your composure will be rooted in your confidence. Even in the case of improvisation, you will be able to excel at the skill when you are comfortable with the vision you want to get across.

You must be ready for any objections you may receive. You cannot let miscommunication deter you from trying to communicate your vision. If you take offense and give up, then you did not truly feel confident about what you wanted to share. Your miscommunication should not look like an argument, but rather a negotiation. You must begin to think like someone who is not yourself. By the time you speak a word, you have already turned it over in your mind a few times and attached some images and emotions to it. You have designated a support structure to it. When you put the idea in the outside world, it no longer has that support structure. You must hear it as though you are hearing it for the first time without any additional context. These skills take much hard work and require you to be attentive as you are devising your words. Think before you speak, and you will be rewarded for it. If you simultaneously think and speak, you will be punished for it. Your readiness is determined by your maturity and your understanding.

Primed: *"Don't forget that everything you deal with is only one thing and nothing else. And don't forget the language of the omens. And above all, don't forget to follow your Personal Legend...'The secret of happiness is to see all the marvels of the world, and never to forget the drops of oil on the spoon.'" (The Alchemist)*

A.   <u>Maturity in your spiritual self.</u>

We tend to make challenges larger than they were ever intended to be. When something happens in our lives that we do not like, we tend to increase the scope of the issue. We make the problem larger and give it power over our mental psyches. We obsess over the issue until it becomes more than just one thing. It becomes everything and prohibits us from enjoying or marveling at the other wonders of life or tending to the other opportunities disguised as challenges. You must master your spiritual self to be able to relieve yourself from this vice. The quote is referring to a story that was told in The Alchemist in which a young man was asked to carry drops of oil on a spoon and explore. When he returned after his exploration, he still had the drops of oil on the spoon. He was asked if he had witnessed the wonders of his exploration. He responded that he had focused on the drops of oil and that the marvels went unnoticed. He was then told to carry drops of oil on a spoon and explore again. Upon his second return, his spoon was absent the drops of oil. At this moment, he was told the secret to happiness. While you should not enlarge your challenges, it is also important to not forget them. The secret is to maintain balance by applying the appropriate scope to the activities you must manage.

This kind of control takes spiritual focus. You must be able to not only see challenges as opportunities, but also control yourself from making them ordeals of greater magnitude. Make everything relative, just as your Point A and Point B are in the plan. Remember that an issue is just that, an issue. It consumes a portion of energy and should be granted some attention in order to rectify the situation. Think of a recent issue that you may have blown out of proportion. Fill out the chart to see what some options are.

Incident:	
Immediate Effects (Loss of time, money, etc.):	
Your Reaction:	
Losses Due to Reaction:	
Alternative Resolution:	
Time to Regain Losses if Alternative Resolution	
Time for Resolution to Occur:	

To practice this kind of control, when an issue comes up, think of ways to resolve it rather than dwelling on the problem itself. In that way you do not give time to allow the issue to become larger than it truly is. If you do not attempt a solution immediately, your imagination will instantaneously take effect when facing a new issue. Your imagination will begin to create all kinds of theories about why something may or may not have happened. You will find yourself wasting your emotions on a very trivial matter because of frustration. Some arguments are really humorous at their basic core. People will argue over hypothetical situations, financial liberties, the manner in which something is taught, etc. In those moments, winning the argument is paramount. Every force you possess will be used to defend your position. The effort is not placed into maturity.

In the grand scheme of things, the argument means absolutely nothing. Perhaps you are truly trying to convey something meaningful. Arguing prevents such communication. The ability to argue is the response derived specifically from the ability to draw connections between circumstances, and attribute past actions to future ones. There is a reason our brains are wired this way. It has allowed us to survive in the wild and provide for our families. A master, however, can control it. They can sense the grand scheme at all times and pick the reaction they want in order to elicit a planned reaction. Arguing does not usually accomplish such a crafty objective. Arguments tend to leave hard feelings and an erosion of authority on someone's account. No one ever really wins an argument. The master, however, knows who he is arguing with and plans three or more steps ahead of the argument or issue so that it may be used to actually ameliorate the circumstance. Maturity consists of control, empathy, and calculation. You must be mature in your Spiritual Dimension before you can move from the internal to the external.

Alignment: *"Understanding how what you are impacts every interdependent interaction will help you to focus your efforts sequentially, in harmony with the natural laws of growth." (7 Habits of Highly Effective People)*

B. Understand that the world is interdependent.

You must be willing to understand the systems that are at play. The more you understand the different systems at play, the harder it will be for you to feel limited. When you know your abilities, it is hard to fear what you anticipate. As you work to align yourself within these systems, you are concurrently preparing yourself to be able to communicate in a manner that is recognizable to someone within the system. Imagine if you are speaking with someone who uses a different language or dialect. Most likely, your ability to effectively deliver a vision will be severely compromised. Language barriers are an obvious example because we interact with it on a conscious level. If someone does not speak our language, it does not take long before it becomes noticeable. Other systems, however, have just as much impact as the language we speak. If you are trying to communicate a vision, not being able to speak in the interest of the other person will guarantee your communication to fall on deaf ears and blind eyes. Knowing systems helps you to communicate your vision in a package that is palatable and interesting to others. By speaking in the interest of another person, you are developing your credibility. By speaking to the disinterest of someone, you are securing your spot as an inept communicator. When you begin a presentation, you should think of it from the mindset of your audience. What are the most important things to them, and how do you align your message with them?

Fill in this chart for your systems. What are the conversations that these systems are the most concerned about? You should become an expert in each of the subjects so that you may "speak the language" of each system. This chart can be further divided into specific family members, friends, and positions of co-workers.

	Subject One	Subject Two	Subject Three
Family			
Coworkers			
Friends			
Work Industry			

In addition to listing the subjects, also add in how you feel about these subjects, and how the people in those systems feel about the subjects.

Family	How You Feel	How They Feel
Subject One		

Marketing professionals do this constantly because all forms of advertisement are geared towards an intended market. When engaging in intentional communication, imagine that you are a marketing professional with your ideas. You must tailor your message for your audience. How are you going to brand your ideas? How can they best be communicated? What will make them appealing? In the chart above, the last two columns must align. They must meet each other half way in order to have a successful transaction. You provide something of interest, and the recipient provides the attention.

Developing a sense of empathy for systems and the participants of systems will help you more effectively move your ideas from the internal to external.

II.   There are mechanisms of communication.

A mechanism is a method or manner of operation. While there are obvious aspects to communication, there are some fundamental concepts to understand about the origin of communication. Communication begins within the confines of our minds and finds escape through every aspect of who we are. Metaphorically, we place who we are on billboards and plaster our personalities on commercials. Most people are not even aware of the type of product they are putting on display. They believe they are marketing themselves to a certain group of individuals, but in reality, they have not produced anything appealing. An effective and efficient person does not let opportunities go by the way side. They do not relinquish all control to luck and wishful thinking. Knowing that you are communicating at all times, you should be deliberate about what and how you communicate.

We are communicating through our body language, words, emotions, and decisions. If you help someone cross the street, you are communicating with them without ever saying a word. If you are at an interview and noticeably sweating, you are communicating with the interviewer. We can recognize and interpret communication when we see it. To master it, however, we must know the source of our communication. Knowing the source allows us to anticipate and modulate ourselves. With proper preparatory planning, we can chart our greatest potential and traverse it.

Manifestation: *"The Principle of Correspondence manifests in all, for there is a correspondence, harmony and agreement between several planes." (The Kybalion)*

A. <u>They arise from you on different levels; understand them.</u>

The source of your communication is foundationally instilled. Your basic beliefs, premises, and ideas influence all of your communication. If you feel insecure about something, then you communicate it in a disingenuous way. When you are communicating, you are revealing your deepest desires and thoughts. Interestingly enough, your communication begins in the Spiritual Dimension, and then tracks its way through every other dimension. In each, it will interact with some amount of fear, hope, and love, and will eventually manifest as an action, word, or emotion when received by the Social Dimension. Your communication is sourced in the Spiritual Dimension, and shaped by the remaining three dimensions. Recall the interdependence of the dimensions. Try the exercise below to see how your internal ideas are actually communicated. Begin by starting with the Social and work down to the Spiritual. Then, work back to the top, creating a new interpretation of how the communication travels. The result at that end is how you actually communicate your ideas.

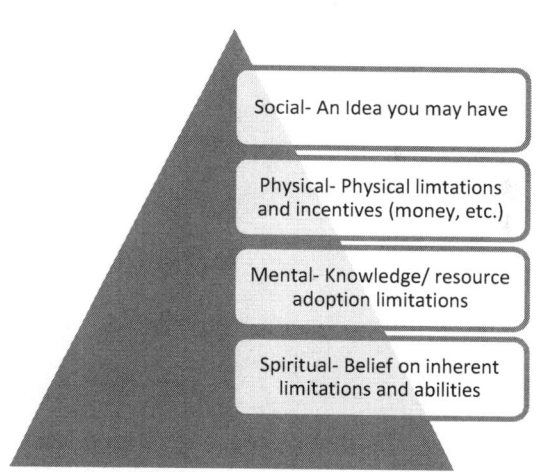

- Social- An Idea you may have
- Physical- Physical limtations and incentives (money, etc.)
- Mental- Knowledge/ resource adoption limitations
- Spiritual- Belief on inherent limitations and abilities

You can see how each of these levels corresponds to one another. Here is an example.

Social→ I want to start a business → Physical → Building a business takes a lot of time, but great return on investment→ I need money→Mental→ Do I really care about creating a business or creating the business→ Spiritual→Entrepreneurism is a great idea and I can overcome the obstacles. It will give me a lot of experience. Experience is good. Others will benefit from my success→Mental→ My obstacle will really be in understanding the concepts involved in starting a business. Will I be able to accommodate the learning curve→ I must be persistent, but I am not too sure about my ability since I have no experience, maybe I can learn from the best, but what will they think of me → Physical→ Where do I find them, and will I be able to communicate with them? → They will probably be able to tell me the truth about my preparedness → Social→ Where do I start? I feel uneasy about this whole process as it seems like a lot, and the industry can be a bit discouraging.

Usually, the thought process is not as straight as it is in the example. It may go: spiritual→mental→spiritual→mental→physical→mental →physical→social. Although the example is fairly linearized, it still presents a good depiction of the overall thought process you may go through. Become familiar with the most influential structures, and you can rewrite your programming as discussed in the previous chapter.

Because of the corresponding nature of your dimensions, this exercise is not limited to your ideas. It also can be applied to your qualities. Perhaps you are shy; by drilling deeper into the layers, you can discover why you communicate shyness.

Betrayal and Loyalty: *"But those things which proceed out of the mouth come forth from the heart; and they defile the man." (The Bible)*

    B.   <u>Your priorities are shown in your communication.</u>

As your words are true to your thoughts, you must be careful and pay attention to what you reveal. Man's worst enemy in most times is his own tongue. Once words are uttered, they cannot be retracted, and have a way of leaving permanent marks on the ears of the listeners. Recall that values are priority morals. When you speak, your values will shine through, and people will judge you accordingly. They will try to identify whether or not they agree with your priorities, and then proceed to befriend or outcast you. If you value the same things, they will feel comfortable in your presence. If you indicate that you are unnerved, your communication will seem facetious. You will be handicapping the relationship from the very beginning. Most people refer to this as building rapport or making a connection. It truly is a connection, as you are connecting values. These can be made within the first few seconds of meeting someone.

Who are some individuals with whom you have great rapport and what are their values? How do they match up with yours? What about individuals that you struggle to have a great relationship with? What are their values? How do they match up with yours? You can see how important it is to really know the values of another individual before you ever try to connect with them.

Person (Positive Relationship)	Their Values	Your Values	Match?
Person (Negative Relationship)	Their Values	Your Values	Match?

First impressions are everything. If there is a match in values, then the relationship can continue down a promising track, and open the opportunity for you to communicate your ideas. If there are incongruences, the relationship will be marked as one to enter with caution.

The only way to reconstruct a first impression is to reintroduce yourself in a new setting. Subconsciously, the recipient interprets the new situation as a new encounter. If you work with someone that has a negative impression of you, try to interact and connect with them in a more casual setting. It is as though you are erasing the previous encounter, and you will see it bleed over into the work environment. The same is true in reverse. The key when introducing a new situation is to be deliberate and get it right the second time around. We view the occurrence of two similar events as more than a coincidence. It becomes increasingly difficult to claim that your first impression was below par due to a rough day the more times your "first impressions" go awry. As long as you match values, you can begin building that connection and potentially create a new friend for your future out of the situation. There are many ways in which people determine values, and as an effective and efficient leader, you are aware of all of the aspects that comprise an individual. A few are listed below that you can actively research in order to better prepare for first impressions.

A) Culture
B) Religion
C) Region
D) Age
E) Profession
F) Ethics
G) Interests

Make a short list of your values with each of these. The next time you meet someone, try to consciously discern their values, and find a match. Then, proceed to converse on that level, and you will find the door opening very quickly for you to get your thoughts from an internal place of existence into an external form of communication. On the next page, each of the questions is meant to help you correctly think about how each element influences your values. From culture, you learn how people should treat each other and the socially acceptable standards. From religion, or lack of religion, you determine a rationale for existing. From region, you develop a sense of scarce and abundant resources. As a consequence, you view your resources in a specific way. Elders in your environment instill many things in you as you grow older. Some of their lessons seep in, and as a consequence, so does their way of thinking. You can see what has sunk in by asking yourself how you view maturity.

Profession can be a means to an end or an end to a means. It can mean validation. Whatever it may be, profession and industry can affect how you view the importance and worth of others. Asking this question will help reveal your prejudices about people who work, and those who do not. Ethics are presented morals that have been accepted by an individual. They are the actual practices. The question for this influencing factor is a highly debated one, but is only meant to stimulate your thoughts. You must determine what your ethics are and how you differentiate between people, including yourself, and the decisions they make. Finally, "interests" are the easiest way to develop a connection and begin digging deeper. You can identify this by seeing someone's profession or property. You can determine yours by simply asking the question, "What are your interests?"

Culture *What do you expect from friends?*	
Religion *What is the meaning of life?*	
Region *How do you view resources?*	
Age *What does maturity bring?*	
Profession *Why should you work?*	
Ethics *Are there bad people?*	
Interests *What stimulates your mind and what/who do you admire?*	

Chapter Twelve

Voice

In this chapter the goal is to understand what control must be exercised with voice. Imagine three situations: a silent man, a talkative man, and a man who evaluates his surroundings and targets his words. All three will cause you to arrive at a different opinion of the aforementioned man. How you use your voice will help you direct the opinion that is formed about you.

Voice

Note: "When you are trying to impress people with words, the more you say, the more common you appear, and the less in control. Even if you are saying something banal, it will seem original if you make it vague, open-ended, and sphinx-like. Powerful people impress and intimidate by saying less. The more you say, the more likely you are to say something foolish." (48 Laws of Power)

Your voice is one of the methods by which you may engage in communication. Within your voice, you have the presence of words and tone. There are endless combinations of the two. Voice makes up the differences in dialects, accents, and most languages. When we prepare our communication, it is the part that we most focus on. Knowing how you sound and pronounce your words can make the difference between a promotion and being fired. Your word choice is just as important. The quote touches on the two aspects of voice.

The words are one part. You must be delicate with your words. Precision matters. Words create pictures when you are speaking to someone. People draw conclusions from the words you offer. Imagine the system. Your audience cannot receive what has not been sent. So, when you speak, you must give your listener everything they may need to reconstruct the message you wanted to deliver. You must also not give too much to avoid creating other distracting messages. Words cannot be retracted. Every word is connected to other words, and when a word is spoken using its denotation, you should also use it with its connotations in mind. Words elicit feelings and memories in a listener's mind. Even reading this book requires your mind to speak to itself. You hear the words in your mind's ear. When you write anything, you are speaking it to yourself.

Speaking to ourselves allows us to read properly and identify inflection or structure when a long sentence is being read. To choose words wisely, you can try speaking to yourself before engaging in internal to external communication. If your words are succinct and illustrative enough, you can mask a deeper and more convoluted message out of a simple sounding statement.

The tone is the second part. When you communicate, your words carry a certain sound. How you say a word can reveal where you are from, your primary emotional state, and your confidence. You should pay close attention to how you deliver your words. You can change your voice by imagining how you would like it to sound. If your tone is commanding enough and direct enough, you will be able to make damaging news sound smooth and bearable.

The operational definition for this chapter is below:

The sound produced by the vocal organs of a vertebrate, especially a human is a <u>voice</u>. It is the opportunity to express a choice or opinion.

Your voice is unique to you. Most people are able to identify a speaker or singer based simply on listening to a voice. Sometimes, even word choice can indicate a speaker. This is in part because the voice is a reflection of the speaker. How someone thinks and what they believe is conveyed by way of their voice. So, who you are, is administered through what you say. Recall, the dimensions interact with your thoughts and eventually shape the actual content that moves from the internal depth of your mind to the external finite world you experience.

The other aspect to voice beside uniqueness is opportunity. Your voice is the means by which you are able to express an opinion. When someone claims, "I have a voice," they are purely referencing their ability to state their point of view. Your voice has both properties. It is a tool that qualifies as both a creation and a resource. Acquaint yourself with your voice. How do you sound inside of your mind? How do you sound in the external world? Then, try to understand why there is a gap between the two. Perhaps, a dimension is to blame.

Content	Internal	External
Words		
Tone		

The external content is usually easy to figure. To fill in the chart, consider the three ideas.

Use a scenario when you are well acquainted with the information you are trying to share.

Words-External: Do you find yourself stuttering, using fillers, or constantly searching for the right words- blanks? Do the words naturally come to you- apt? Do you deliberate on your words- choosing? Do you fill in emptiness with more words and find words until someone else chooses to speak- anxious?

Tone-External: Do people appear sleepy when you speak- monotonous? Do you speak directly- concise, or do you use a lot of circulatory language that could perhaps confuse the listener because there are so many parts and metaphors and you can do it so that they most likely will avoid asking you to speak again- long-winded? Are your inflections appropriate-energetic? Can someone tell your emotional state based on your speech- illustrative?

We will return to this chart near the end of the chapter.

How do I speak?

LP25: Influence

I. <u>It is the opportunity to share.</u>

Expression is our way of sharing ourselves with others. Imagine if your ability to communicate with words were taken away. Your only ability was to live out your life without explanation. You would find it difficult to make promises, proclaim a status, or offer resolutions. Think of what your voice offers you. Your ability to express your opinion helps to draw out all that you believe you are into the outside world so that it may engage and judge you. Consider the content of your voice. What opinions do you hold, and how do you let them manifest into the world? What are the creations that come about as a result of your voice and what resources are placed into your jurisdiction?

Simply put, your voice offers you a chance to demand a certain value for yourself. If you cannot communicate your worth, then your worth will be assumed by systems. You most likely will offer a value that requires the lowest possible investment, and demand the greatest possible return. If you find yourself overwhelmed, overworked, undervalued, or underpaid, perhaps it is due to your inability to communicate the exact value that you can bring to a group or person. Otherwise, they would willingly propose the price in order to obtain the value. When you communicate your value, you give promises. You present solutions. You use your words and tone to offer comfort, love, and prosperity. What do you think your value is, and how do you communicate that value? If you value yourself, then you value what you have to communicate. If you value your communication, then you are conscientious about the manner in which you communicate. As with anything, the world is a series of orders, and your communication is influenced by these orders. Your grasp of the orders will allow you to properly construct and offer communication. Then, your communication will be a true reflection of not just who you actually are, but who you want to be. Your proclamations of success and self-righteousness do not have to be empty carcasses. However, as we witnessed in the previous chapter, those who are moving in the right direction are noticed by others. They have no need to entertain useless proclamations of their success, as their lives serve as testimonies.

How do you reach this point of meaning? It takes practice, and internal focus. You must be well acquainted with all that was discovered about you in Theme 2. This is your internal interpretation of your life. In order to properly use your voice, you will have to affect what causes your voice to manifest in the way that it does. So, return to the chart. For the internal, try to use the one word description offered for the categories. Why is your tone or word choice that way?

Words: Do I sincerely agree with my professed values- certainty? Am I unsure about my beliefs- nervous? What I have to say is important- dominance? I will be judged- ponder?

Tone: My topics are of little interest to everyone- specialty? I cannot identify with my audience- disperse? I easily bond with my audience- connected? Everyone cares when I speak- magnet?

You may create more questions for yourself, but these are meant to get you started. Dwell on how you think about your words internally and then anticipate how they will be given externally. If you are constantly thinking of being judged, then you will engage in judging yourself while you speak. This may cause you to be flexible, but for most, you find yourself in a state of confusion and fumble your way through a sentence while your mind is busy contemplating proper sentence structure and word choice. While both are important, it is best to be silent while your mind searches for the right thing to say.

The best way to engage in sharing an opportunity is to build an image in your mind. Instead of memorizing a script or lesson, envision the end goal. In communication, the audience's Point A is blank. There is no content, but there is expectation. It is all potential and no kinetic. When you speak, you begin to traverse the field and transmit your image to another's mind. It is much easier to describe a picture than it is to describe a sentence. So, when you are speaking, keep your end goal in mind as a vivid picture of the idea you are trying to convey. You will find communication by voice to be eased by the undertaking.

LP25: Influence

Clarity: *"When you can present your own ideas clearly, specifically, visually, and most important, contextually - in the context of a deep understanding of their paradigms and concerns - you significantly increase the credibility of your ideas."* (7 Habits of Highly Effective People)

A. <u>Choose your words wisely.</u>

There are repercussions to mistakenly applying words incorrectly. If you are to communicate with a purpose, it is imperative that you are wise about your words. You are aware of their denotations and their connotations, and you apply them to elicit feelings and emotions that are pertinent to your message. If you are trying to get a group of people to care or receive feelings of sincerity, then your message should include stimulating words that raise the level of awareness of the audience. If your words are bland and tasteless, then the audience will assume that what you are communicating is void of emotional authenticity. Imagine the words you choose as being a part of a movie. An actor not only uses the sound of his voice, but he uses precise words. If you are speaking to arouse interest, avoid being too pedantic. If you are trying to bore an audience, include rote and countless numbers of steps- avoid the use of words such as "patriotism" and "God". These words are connected to many other words and people have been exposed to them since the moment they were born or began grade school. For some, these words invoke positive thoughts and for others, they are incensing. Beware of any unintended consequences to the words you use.

In the quote above, clarity is the main idea. Clarity is what an audience receives. It describes the quality in which the audience is able to reconstruct your idea or argument to the point that they can understand or feel as though they understand your values. Many times, only partial statements need to be made to accomplish this. Ironically, being brief and arousing is usually enough for an individual to gain a sense of clarity from the speaker. The opening quote touched on vagueness. This is not to mean that you are clueless about your message. To the contrary, this quote implies that you are well aware of your message, but you mask it just enough so that the audience can feel as though they are in agreement with you.

They are so impressed by the perception that your word usage creates that they care little for the actual message being conveyed. Great speakers are great at performing this task. They say just enough so that it may afford them future flexibility. Politicians are criticized for this. "We want a better America," is a common refrain. It is extremely vague. What is "better"? What does a "better America" consist of? It is however a crowd rousing message. Everyone has their own perception as to what better and America actually mean. The speaker is well aware of this, and thus uses it as an advantage. Everyone constructs his or her own appealing and appropriate image of a better America and retorts to the call with a fiery, "Yes, we must have a better America!"

Your words can do just that. They can influence people to feel comfortable and be trusting. You can make promises that heighten someone's sense of security. Recall you can speak to one of two things in at most three different ways. You can speak to someone's security or to their ego by way of love, fear, or hope. So, when you are drafting an image in your mind, it is best to formulate the image with aspects of all three and appeal to both ego and security. The intricacies of your message should be known to you, but only slightly perceivable by those to whom you speak. If you want a raise, it is neither methodical nor appropriate to simply state, "I want a raise." You may receive the raise, but you will receive it grudgingly and you will lose authority and freedom as your boss will be watching you more closely. The best way to communicate this is to force your boss to construct an image of you at a higher level of authority. Pay will increase with the change in responsibility. Meticulously wording this will allow your boss to feel comfortable with giving you more rather than feeling nervous about you as potential competition. Build an image of how his prosperity will increase through your promotion.

When finding the correct words, you should be sensitive to your audience because you may tread the line of insult. Once you insult someone, either accidentally or purposefully, they will seek to make sure you regret it. It is best to think before you speak. Think of your words. Reading will help you build your repertoire of words. Through reading, you will encounter many image building words since books rely on that ability. You can adopt these into your vocabulary and learn how to best configure your statements. Imagine your speech as a book without illustrations. Authors go to great lengths to create images in their readers' minds. When you are speaking, you should be just as deliberate and goal-oriented. Good books have plots, morals, characters, and a hint of premeditated crafting. When you speak, your listeners are reading your words and pulling images from them. Sometimes, to spark the imagination of your listeners, you can use leading questions. You empty your statements of description so that the audience is forced to fill in the blanks. At some point, there must be a resolution because when someone imagines something, they want their imagination to be confirmed. No one likes to be wrong, so when you engage in producing leading questions, you must anticipate the creativity of your audience and match their own thoughts.

An example of words:
The dog walked.

Illustrative words:
With a shaggy tail whisking back and forth, the brown dog gleefully pranced alongside his owner filled with the anticipation similar to that of a two year old baby.

An example of a leading question:
Why must we have a system to promote justice?

Leading question with resolution:
Why must we have an unbiased justice system that safeguards the innocent people of this town?

Knowing your audience will allow you to direct them along a path that is conducive for properly preparing the communication of your particular idea. For a candidate, the idea is simple: I am the best person for this job; trust me. Knowing your audience will also allow you to avoid offending them. Offence can be direct as through an insult, but it can also be indirect as through condescension. By setting low expectations for your audience, you are being condescending. If you suspect that the group may be unfamiliar with your topic or knowledge, then make them feel privileged in its discovery, rather than ostracized for their ignorance. Our minds are built to identify insecurity and non-uniformity. Your message must be consistently sincere or others will notice. Here is an example of how our minds easily categorize objects and ideas. Read the list below and identify the word that is misplaced.

Car
Crave
Cattle
Captain
Court

Flower
Claim
Count
Caps

When you were reading, which word stood out the most? When you are speaking, be careful of mistakes because our minds are trained to put things into categories. When something is different, we notice it. So, when your speech has a grammatical error, tempo changes, or word choice mix-matches, the listener will easily hear them. You quickly found it because without trying, your mind focused on the mistake or the difference. If there is a change in message uniformity, our ears key in and we begin to thought-wander on the reason for the change rather than listening to the actual provided message.

Practice writing your ideas as images. This will help you prepare yourself when choosing your words wisely. Below is a practice for you:

An Idea of Yours in a Picture:	Illustrative and Purposeful Words:

Outside of words, some people use artifacts. These can be insignias or personal items that carry meaning with them. This type of communication would fall under the word category as it is a catch all for symbols.

Deliberation: *"Keep people off-balance and in the dark by never revealing the purpose behind your actions. If they have no clue what you are up to, they cannot prepare a defense. Guide them far enough down the wrong path, envelope them in enough smoke, and by the time they realize your intentions, it will be too late."* (48 Laws of Power)

    B.   <u>Temper your words.</u>

Once you have the words, you can add your tone. Your tone applies a temperature to your words. Beyond the connotations of a word, is the way in which it is vociferated. A fiery message can be made to sound bland and meaningless once inappropriate pauses and a monotone is chosen. When you temper your words, you personify them. If you say you are, happy, but speak with sadness, the listener in turn experiences cognitive dissonance, and as mentioned before, focuses on the change as though it were an error. They will miss the message, and begin judging your sincerity. Once you lose your sincerity, you become an incredulous speaker. At this point, you must exit the stage and find a new way to reconstruct your first impression.

Your tone should reflect your words and should help solidify the intended picture. The more your tone matches your words, the more believable you are and the more likely people will listen to you. Of course, there are points in which you may overdo the job. It is best to present a balanced self. In order to accomplish this, you must actually believe what you intend to describe. If you truly believe you deserve a raise, referencing a previous example, then it will show as you are delivering your words. Synchronize yourself with your words, and their temperament will come naturally. If it does not, then there is clearly a disconnect somewhere between your internal thoughts and feelings and those that have the opportunity to be expressed. Your tone should be deliberately chosen. Tone allows you to properly mask larger and more detailed messages into recognizable words and images. Instead of stating that something is great, use your voice to make it sound wonderful and great. Instead of stating that something is exciting you, use your voice to demonstrate that. If you are feeling nervous, there is no need to announce it to the world. It will be displayed and perhaps pitied to your benefit when you keep in mind that the show must go on.

Particularly with nervousness, avoid ever actually saying "I am nervous" to yourself. By saying it, you are telling yourself to become more nervous because it is now your expectation. In response, your body will shift into full "nervous" gear and make you so uncomfortable that you will find yourself sounding insecure and unsure. Your audience will begin judging you, and you will take notice to their blank faces. Once you begin to focus on their judgments, you will lose sight of the image you are trying to communicate. In order to compensate for the insecurity, you will engage in applying fillers and run-ons so that you can feel like the time is speeding up. You hope you can recapture your image. By this point, the audience has lost confidence in you and you have too. The speech is over and you must return in shame because you subconsciously welcomed every one of their judgments and brought about your own fall from grace. You failed to realize that the audience was guided by you while speaking, and it hits you upon returning to your seat. You led them astray and your image is still locked up inside of your mind, never reaching the outside world.

II.   **Your words are your heart.**

Whenever you utter a word, you are displaying your inner thoughts. The words may not accurately reflect what you would like, but acknowledge that, on some level, you mean exactly what you say. There is truth present in everything, and while it may not be directly present in the words, it is present in the presentation of those words. The words were collected and strung together as a result of a series of complex thoughts and decisions that interplay in your mind. What about Freudian slips? You may have not meant to switch the first letter of the first two words in your sentence. The truth is that your mind is running so quickly that you gave little effort to the decision of your words. Perhaps you have so much more to say, or you felt pressured to say something as quickly as you could. Your words are truly a reflection of the internal processes that are occurring. Embrace that fact so that you understand why it is so important to be familiar with who you are and your predilections. Once you can control your internal self, you will find a great power over your external self. Control over you is true self-empowerment. Do not let anyone allow you to believe otherwise. You cannot modulate your tone or your word choice without first defining who you are and building an inner confidence about what you have to share.

Words that have not been invented in the mind first cannot be spoken. Even when using muscle memory, the words, at some point, left an indelible impression in your psyche, and are available for recall. Imagine:

Thoughts → Filter → Words

In seeing this connection, you should be able to understand the relationship that exists between your thoughts and words. The filter excises some information. It consists of a series of decision tunnels. Is the information pertinent, accurate, provable, digestible, comprehensive, reflective, detailed, vague, etc.? Each of those conditional decisions is influenced by your four dimensions. So, the task is not to be decisive with your words, but to be more decisive and deliberate about your filtering system. If you improve the filtration, then you will yield a better product.

Correspondence: *"These divisions are more or less artificial and arbitrary, for the truth is that all of the three divisions are but ascending degrees of the great scale of Life, the lowest point of which is undifferentiated Matter, and he highest point that of Spirit." (The Kybalion)*

    A.   <u>They are a part of creation, a craft, a gift.</u>

In order to begin refining your filtering system, you must realize that your words are a creation, a craft, and a gift. They are decisions and you take full responsibility for their use.

As a creation, you must account for the ones that you use. They are of an artistic design meant to call other entities into creation. Your voice can be used strategically in order to accomplish an end goal. Or perhaps they are the end goal. In the case of inspiring others, you create dialogue or perhaps a speech. Your voice as a creation is mostly a reflection of your spiritual dimension. They are workings that reflect what you feel about your overall purpose.

As a craft, they are purely of your intelligent design. You can practice preparing your voice by perfecting your words. Reading, as aforementioned, creates a library for you to pull from. Your voice as a craft is mostly a reflection of your mental dimension. Artifacts of intelligence such as new words, experiences, and stories, that you are exposed to will be added to your repertoire and used for communication.

As a gift, your ability to speak is an expression of the physical dimension. With your gift, you confess your ability to synthesize your words. Others may admire you for the manner in which you discuss content. As you grow older, your voice changes. As a consequence, so do your words.

By understanding that your voice is influenced by all dimensions, you will be able to pin-point the exact dimension you must perfect or refine so that you can properly communicate from your internal setting to your external setting. Remember, internally, you can create an image without much effort. Others, however, rely on your ability to stimulate each of their dimensions so that they may arrive at the image you are guiding them towards.

Exclusivity: *"Conserve your forces and energies by keeping them concentrated at their strongest point. You gain more by finding a rich mine and mining it deeper, than by flitting from one shallow mine to another – intensity defeats extensity every time. When looking for sources of power to elevate you, find the one key patron, the fat cow who will give you milk for a long time to come."* (48 Laws of Power)

B.   <u>Do not speak of anything else.</u>

Just as when searching for external resources, it is important to find them from one large source rather than millions of shallow sources, it is important that internally you speak from an area of large real estate in your mind than those of smaller occupancy. You must identify what you feel to be your purpose and speak from that level. There are words and expectations that are associated with the industry you intend to impact. Once you have crafted a vision around whom you are and your Point B, begin to only speak from that deep mine. It will supply the fervor and vocabulary that you need to properly communicate your heart. Use words in your speech that remind others of who you believe you are and what your purpose is. Use the diagram to identify your word patterns. You can start by using your intended professional career. Fill in the blocks with words.

The words in the boxes are words you should add to your speech. When engaging in conversations with potential mentors and mentees, use them. When you are giving trite or important presentations somehow intertwine these words into the presentation. When you are voicing your opinion, show your industry knowledge by making a reference to the interdependence of industries. The words in this diagram can be used in almost any situation, as they are the outputs of your now finely tuned filtering system. You should speak of nothing else. When you grow tired of using these words, you should drill even deeper to find a new gold mine. As you use more tools and build your creations, you will begin to add more words to each of these blocks.

When you try to communicate outside of what you feel your purpose is, you will introduce the random variables of your voice. Other topics will be a perversion of both your psyche and your credibility. You will encounter all of the things that have nothing to do with your development and progress on the pursuit of your purpose. You will encounter uncontrollable nervousness, stuttering, loquaciousness, verbosity, loss of direction, and judgment fright.

On the other hand, when you communicate on target, you will still experience some stress because by focusing in this way, you will be forced to find new words with more meaning and greater examples to express your knowledge. In this scenario, nevertheless, you will feel confident in your ability to find the new words, because you are accurately depicting your thoughts. Revisit this diagram to find those new words. This exercise works because as you contemplate the answers, you are filtering out exactly what is communicable, and repeatedly refining your filtration system.

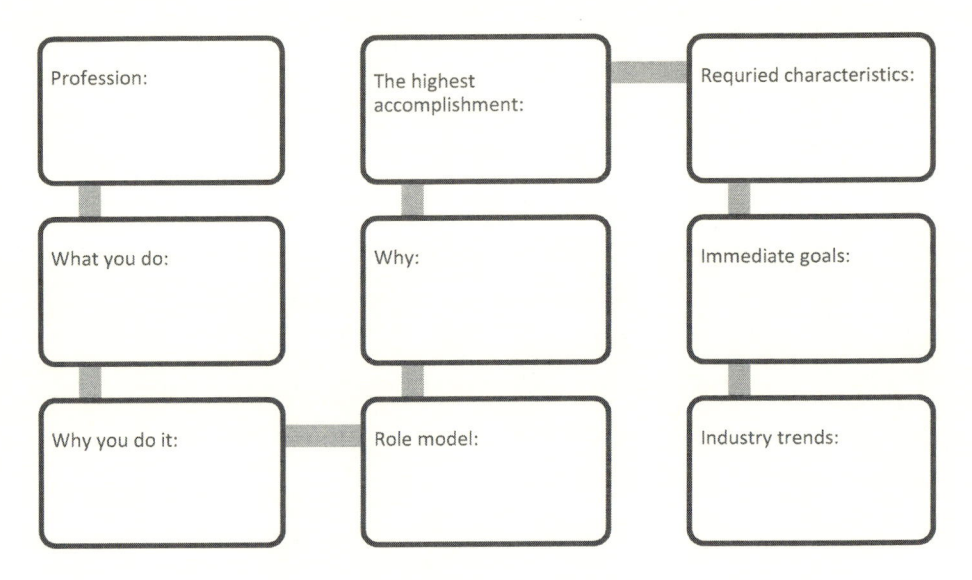

Profession:	The highest accomplishment:	Requried characteristics:
What you do:	Why:	Immediate goals:
Why you do it:	Role model:	Industry trends:

As for tone, focus on square 4- the role model. The role model can be renowned or can be a mentor. They should be someone that you can come into close contact with and begin plagiarizing their techniques. How do they speak? Where are their inflections? Begin adapting your voice so that you can structure it. You can do this by imagining yourself becoming your role model. What are some of the opinions they have of themselves, and where do they get their confidence from. When you place yourself in their shoes and speak with their sincerity, you will find a voice within you that is uniquely your own regardless of the copied technique.

Dedicate your voice to your purpose, and you will reap benefits that will be hard to measure. You will find your voice and help lead others to support you along your journey. You may also inspire others to pursue their own purposes.

Chapter Thirteen

Energy

"Energy" is all about how information can flow from one entity to another. In this case, energy describes how your communication is packaged. Your feelings regarding a certain subject are conveyed in a message's physical delivery. This chapter also discusses how connected everyone is to everything that exists and that all things at some point may be understood.

Energy

Note: "The teacher who walks in the shadow of the temple, among his followers, gives not of his wisdom but rather of his faith and lovingness." (A Spiritual Treasury)

Your voice is one quality of communication. The other quality of communication is energy. Energy incorporates the passively conveyed message whereas voice incorporates the actively conveyed message. In the above quote, it signifies how the qualities of a leader are transferred to his followers. Most believe that voice is the most important aspect of communication, but your followers will mimic your motivations and qualities. These qualities are clearly not communicated via your voice, but rather by your actions. They are transferred by your energy. One can clearly discern your energy by just walking near you. Some are actually offended by people who do not exchange in discourse. Your energy is an important aspect to your communication. Be oblivious to this truth, and you will wonder why people abhor you even though your intentions may be pure. Your energy speaks decibels louder than the words you choose to utter.

"Modern science has proven that all that we call Matter and Energy is but 'modes of vibratory motion,' and some of the more advanced..." (The Kybalion)

All actions can be seen as entities engaged in vibration. There are ranges of vibration, but all complex interactions can be broken down into simpler vibratory interactions. The energy you spread to those around you is in a direct relationship with those vibrations. So, when you hear the expression, "I get a bad vibe from that person," they are speaking directly about the energy they are receiving from the individual. Our judgments are based on the energy emitted by people. We can sense fear in an individual with great ease and decide to take advantage of them.

Another term for these interactions is non-verbal communication. It encompasses all communication that is done without the use of words. It may be done with actions, facial expressions, and physical configurations or contortions. Your non-verbal communication indicates how you would like to be treated by those surrounding you. The Golden Rule states that you must treat others the way you would like to be treated. The 'Golden Rule' with regards to non-verbal communication is to think of yourself in the way you would like others to treat you. Those who lack confidence leak that vibe so flamboyantly that everyone else knows exactly the manner in which to treat them. They are then bullied or treated poorly, which only confirms their belief that they have no right to confidence. It functions just as a positive feedback system would by placing the person in a more enhanced state than before. Their confidence is so low and continues to get lower. You should be aware of the vibes you circulate and can apply a negative feedback system by outlining your preferred methods of interaction.

The operational definition for this chapter is below:

A <u>vibration</u> is a general emotional feeling one has from another person, place, or situation. It is also a supernatural emanation, bearing well or ill that is sensed by or revealed to those attuned to the occult. It is also the analogous motion of the particles of a mass of air or the like, whose state of equilibrium has been disturbed, as in transmitting sound. Finally, it is the oscillating, reciprocating, or other periodic motion of a rigid or elastic body or medium forced from a position or state of equilibrium.

All objects that are considered matter can experience vibrations and can cause other objects to vibrate. For the purposes of this chapter, we will define the vibes you emit as energy. Energy has a way of converting itself from one form to another. Energy can be described as mechanical, chemical, light, heat, sound, and potential. Each of these can translate into how we communicate.

What is my energy?

I. Read your internal essence.

If you were to ask your friends what vibes they get from you, you will discover they probably know more about you than you think. Most people are not honest however, and will offer you the benefit of the doubt when engaging in conversation. In order for you to anticipate the perception of your friends, it would behoove you to become familiar with the kind of energy you emit. You must imagine your interactions from outside of yourself. When you think of an enthusiastic student, what are some of the behaviors they exhibit? If the student sits upright, asks a lot of questions, and smiles, you assume they are excited about their current circumstance. You can use your own expressions and posture to demonstrate to others what you want to convey. Once you perceive yourself from the outside, you will be better equipped to engage with people and externally express your ideas.

To begin, complete the chart so that you can apply this chapter to refining your energy.

Situation	Posture	Facial Expression	Conveys What Message?
Introduced to someone new			
Catching up with an old friend			
Room filled with new people			
Classroom/Job			

LP25: Influence

Within each circumstance, you probably emit different energy. Like a signal being sent through pulsing electricity, you are carrying a message through your energy. While it may be helpful to understand energy as non-verbal communication, referring to this type of communication as energy allows for a deeper exploration into the actual mechanics of non-verbal communication. By attributing the properties of energy to non-verbal communication, you afford yourself the ability to manipulate your non-verbal communication.

Correspondence: *"As above, so below; as below, so above." (The Kybalion)*

    A. <u>As above, so below.</u>

The analogy made between energy and non-verbal communication reflects the correspondence principle. Truth is not circumstantial, but omnipotent and pervasive. So, if this principle is considered true, then it must apply to all things and leave no room for exceptions. Below is a table to demonstrate the parallels between non-verbal communication and energy:

Energy	Mechanics of Non-Verbal Communication
Can be converted from one form into another	Can be converted from one form into another
Can be transmitted from one location to another	Can be transmitted from one location to another
Cannot be created nor destroyed	Cannot be created nor destroyed

Regarding the first property, the mechanics of non-verbal communication consist of your facial expressions and your posture. Both of these reflect internal thoughts of yours. Technically speaking, when you feel intimidated, your posture shrinks, and your expression becomes filled with consternation. Your internal energy becomes displayed as non-verbal communication, and offers insight to your listener into what you really feel. Biologically speaking, chemical changes occur in your brain, which cause your internal nervous systems to respond in a way that reflects your thoughts. Those chemical reactions elicit more chemical reactions, which in turn, spawn mechanical reactions. Physically, you contort your body and the listener receives a light energy image of your physical structure or status (sweating, fidgeting). This image translates into a series of chemical reactions which create thoughts in the mind of the listener to try to interpret the image. The listener is responding directly to your "vibes".

Philosophically speaking, your feelings are communicated via a mutual understanding of the status of the relationship. In other words, when you meet someone for the first time, you assume they are just like you. If they have two limbs, you assume they can walk. If they have a nose or a mouth, you assume they breathe and speak. This analysis goes beyond the physical appearance. You then draw conclusions about personality and motivation. Once you qualify the other person as approachable, you begin to consider points of mutual consideration. Small talk begins here.

So, to begin speaking with them, you attempt to discuss the things you feel the most comfortable with, many times banal, inconsequential banter. You communicate your most basic and broad values. You hope to catch them in your broad net. Sometimes this works. This mutual understanding of "perhaps you are like me", allows us to perceive intangible communication. If a person is fidgeting, we assume that person is anxious, since we are fidgety when we are anxious. We accept these intangibles as vibes. This is the reason by which some cultures can be offended by the customs of other cultures. While these expected customs are comfortable to some, they are inappropriate to others.

The second property of energy that can be applied is the transmission of it from one location to another. On the macro level, this is seen from one person to another. The thought you have is conveyed via your voice and your energy. Others will receive your energy and it will continue to be given and received. It propagates from one entity to the next. On the internal level, this is seen within the four dimensions. Your body actually possesses an internal feedback system. Recall when determining your values, you most likely took a hierarchical approach. You created hypothetical scenarios to arrive at your most regarded morals. This interplay took into consideration all four of your dimensions and all three of the forces. Your ideas literally are transmitted as energy from one place to another. Along the way, as aforementioned, they change in form, but, they also transmute. Your psyche takes cues from itself and alters your communication accordingly.

When communicating, be sure to be deliberate about the direction you communicate. Since your energy is transmitted, you should be more like a laser than a helicopter light. Both can be necessary at times, but when you are discoursing one on one, be a laser and convey your message with precision so that you have control over how it becomes interpreted.

The third property is that energy can neither be created nor destroyed. It may be transmitted and altered, but never created. It may become less manageable as in the case of heat energy, but it can never be destroyed. Energy is recycled. There are recycled expressions and feelings. They can change form, but they all require energy. All things are connected in this world to some degree. When you breathe, you are working in conjunction with the many systems of the world. Your physical energy is harnessed from dead plants, animals, or other species. There is no difference when you are engaged in communication. The same is also true when you are speaking. Your sadness may become someone else's happiness. If you meet someone who is intimidating, then you will be intimidated. Realize how interconnected energy is, and it becomes hard to imagine that a person is simply "mean" or "nice". They have had energy invested within them, and since energy is transmutable, anyone's mood or concept of self can be altered by changing the energy to which they are exposed. Imagine a boring presentation. Then, imagine an exciting presentation. What are some of the differences? List them in the chart below. These questions pertain to the vibe of the room and the speaker.

Quality	Boring	Exciting	You:
Lighting			
Speaker's Posture			
Music Intro			
Seating Arrangement			
Facial expression used by speaker			
Position of the speaker			
Add Your Own			

As you see, you already have an understanding of how energy works. "Boring" and "Exciting" represent the vibes you receive. Use a chart like this to your advantage in deciphering what your energy is by using your noted facial expressions, posture, and surroundings. Use the "you" column to outline what describes the energy others receive from you in a presentation setting.

Creation: *"You know that the part of you which you call 'I', in a sense stands apart and witnesses the creation of Mental Images in your own mind. The part of your mind in which the mental generation is accomplished may be called the 'Me' in distinction from the 'I' which stands apart and witnesses and examines the thoughts, ideas, and images of the "Me". (The Kybalion)*

Degrees: *"The Teachings are to the effect that Spirit is at one end of the Pole of Vibration, the other Pole being certain extremely gross forms of Matter." (The Kybalion)*

   B. <u>You are a divided entity.</u>

Both quotes were used to demonstrate the multiple ways in which you are divided. In one way, you are divided between your "creation" self and your "thought of creation" self. These distinctions involve different aspects of who you are and how you define your value. The act of creating in your mind is vastly different from creating in the physical world. You must be aware of both your "I" and your "Me"- your "Yin" and your "Yang"- your "Chalice" and your "Blade", irrespectively. These concepts will be explored heavily in Chapter 23. In summary, the "I" and "Me" are aspects of yourself that allow you to become both who you are and craft your life message. We naturally differentiate the two within our language. "I" is an active engaging parameter of our character, whereas "Me" is a passive aspect of our character. The "Me" is extremely internal while the "I" is outwardly facing.

The other way in which you are divided is in infinitesimally small increments with boundaries set at polarities. This is described by the second quote. The Principle of Polarity is the referenced truth in this quote. It contends that all things deemed opposite, are just variances of one another. They function within the concept of relativism. We understand cold because we understand hot. Hot is hotter than cold and cold is colder than hot. The degree in variance is the speed by which the molecules move or the consequent pressure they exert at constant volume.

The practical usage of the analogy, presumes that all of your traits and their opposites exist upon a sliding scale. Recall the transmutability of your energy. Your indicated weaknesses and faults are on a sliding scale of their potential as a strength. You have only noted them as weaknesses because you have compared it to another similar action. You determine the quality of your singing to be good or bad based upon your knowledge of the quality of other singers. You must determine what is actually varying in degree. Identify what is truly being compared, and you will find it much easier to shift weaknesses into the territory of being strengths.

The key is to determine the similarity between your weaknesses and your strengths, and modify them accordingly. The example uses the perceived weakness of shyness. If you believe you are shy, realize that a shy person is only the quietest person in the room. The degree of variance is in the amount that is spoken. Instead of focusing on your shyness, focus on the degree to which you speak. Complete the chart below indicating an action or quality and list its opposite. Then, determine the quality that is in variance. *What* is actually varying in degrees?

Pole	Varying Quality	Pole
Shyness	Amount of Speech	Loquacious

When evaluating your energy, you can move along poles. Use your knowledge of degrees to help find you best rhythm when you are within the poles. You are divided into poles because you can imagine yourself acting within either pole, but you decide to participate closer to only one of them. Different poles are necessary for different circumstances. You should view yourself in such segments so that you can better tailor your non-verbal communication or energy for specific situations.

II. <u>Understand you are the same as The All.</u>

You should be familiar with the expansiveness of all that exists. When you see yourself in divided parts of the "I" and the "Me", you should note that all things are a consequence of the interplay of both of those parts. The thought of creation and the creation of a substantial reality is an aspect of every possible entity and idea in the world. Being a part of something is just as important as the whole being. Parts of larger pictures function as interdependent aspects. Even though a company may be great, without its workers, executives, and customers, it is socially worth nothing, and so are the workers, executives, and customers in the context of the company. This interdependent nature of all things that exist allows you to navigate the world. Your energy is recycled from all different aspects, and wherever your energy comes from will be distributed to those with whom you come into contact. When you think of how miserable people love to have company, you think of how they love to share their woes and try to convince their partner that they should also be sad. They recycle their energy, and alter your energy. The energy that is a part of your environment will eventually interact with you and influence you if you are not able to convert it. To control it, you must be aware of it.

What are some of the environmental factors that influence your energy?

Category	Item/ Person	Effect on Your Energy
Food and Drink		
Music		
People and Animals		
Job/ Responsibilities		

There are many other categories, but each of these has an effect on how you carry yourself and think of yourself. They affect your mental clarity. Since you are the same as the all, recognize where you are recycling your energy and either convert it, or change the source.

Perception: *"The Principle of Correspondence manifests in all, for there is a correspondence, harmony and agreement between several planes." (The Kybalion)*

Truth: *"'As above, so below' remember, and the phenomena of one plane may be employed to solve the riddles of higher or lower planes." (The Kybalion)*

    A. <u>As above, so below.</u>

The two quotes are both implying a similar message. As you are the same as "The All", you are bound to the same truths and should perceive in the way "The All" would perceive you. How may a rock and your parents differ in their understanding of your position in the world? How may a river describe you? By thinking of yourself with the considerations of all elements that are interconnected, you will find yourself minding the nuances of your own non-verbal communication. Clearly, a river or rock cannot speak to you, and your parents have most likely determined your worth prior to your first spoken words. Nevertheless, they can all respond to your energy. The quote signifies that there is no real difference in how things interact. There are limitations on understanding, but not on energy transference. Try to explain what life is to a rock on the ground. You would pass away before the rock would ever begin to think.

When you are trying to understand other elements in other frames of existence, you can use analogies. Authors use it constantly when personifying elements. Analogies are also true within a constant frame of existence. Even though a man may rise to become the ruler of a nation, he still experiences fear, love, and hope. He still seeks his security and the security of his progeny. He still serves to have his ego supported. We are no different. When we accuse others of their evilness, we fail to see how our minor crimes can pale in comparison.

Most large crimes were not a consequence of one long predetermined plan, but began with a series of small acceptable minor crimes and transgressions. The criminal in question was either the recipient or the proponent of those minor crimes, and eventually became influenced by the energy of the crime.

When you make the decision to lie in order to cover your ego and encourage your sense of self-righteousness, there is no difference between you and the man whose lies kill multitudes of people. While the consequences are much graver, the action is quite similar and the influences are quite parallel. You can break into the mind of those who are seemingly out of touch with reality by acknowledging your nearness to them. By understanding your whims and influences, you can better use your energy and anticipate the energy brought about by others. There is no real difference except the degrees of relativity between the poles.

When encountering a new individual, you can channel your energy in a manner by which they immediately understand who you are. Your non-verbal communication can make them feel so comfortable that they want to be around you. You can only do this well when you sincerely are trying to establish the "vibed" connection with them.

Infidelity: *"But those things which proceed out of the mouth come forth from the heart; and they defile the man." (The Bible)*

Polarity: *"Between these two poles are millions upon millions of different rates of vibration." (The Kybalion)*

> B. <u>You are as psychologically capable of committing the same acts, heinous or noble, of every other person.</u>

Your mouth may carry the exact message you wish to convey. With your voice, this is obvious. On the other hand, your body will convey the exact message you wish to conceal. It will display either supporting or contradicting evidence to what you have to say. Some people believe they can practice deception, but the truth is the heart is seen on the sleeves of the speaker. Actions, posture, and facial expressions reveal your true intentions. Imagine if you were only judged by your actions. Imagine if your voice was stripped away from you and you could no longer actively communicate. If people currently respect you, would they still respect you? Would people see you as one particular pole, or would they suddenly begin to see all of your varying degrees?

In order to have non-verbal communication that is on one accord with your voice, you must be sincere about what you say and what you feel. Infidelity is not an option. The world's greatest liars are great because they actually believe their lies. Believing yourself to be too righteous is one way to permeate contradictory messages. This is due to the fact that internally, you know all of your minor crimes. So, your professed belief or desired belief is mere facetiousness. Then, when you communicate what is right, you actually communicate how pretentious you are, and remind others of their faults and minor crimes. In turn, other people will dissociate themselves with you and deny that you have a true message.

However, if you truly are acquainted with your shortcomings and talents, then you will be able to speak from a level of pragmatism and security. Your body language will emit a sense of comfort and resolve. People will perceive such self-knowledge as genuineness, and be receptive to what you have to say.

Have you ever heard someone say, "I know I am not perfect..."? Beware of this statement. It is used because it is socially acceptable to have imperfections, but on the mental level we rank imperfections and crimes. We conclude that our transgressions are not as great as those of others and reinforce our self-righteousness. *Try speaking the statement.* It is not important to ponder on the merits of such thinking, but rather to realize that by focusing on the rank, you may prohibit your ability to communicate amongst many planes of existence- those that exhibit life and those that do not. You will be relegated to only being able to correspond with those who function within your energy level.

When thinking by ranking, we find that we begin to dwell in our Spiritual Dimension, where we relive experiences and determine our intrinsic worth, we cognitively recreate the memories of all of our imperfections. The statement usually comes out with reservation and timidity. People say it to remind themselves that they are judging someone, and probably should not be. Another activity, presents the same issue. The practice of false equivalency has become pervasive in our society as socially acceptable. It suggests that we are all terrible, or we are all great, and contends that we must all be losers, or must all be winners. False equivalency prevents the pursuance of specialties and the great lessons taught through the feelings of inadequacy. It does not go against win-win, as win-win does not dictate that all are the same, but that each has a role and a desire, and that all can be satisfied, eventually. It is a problem solving method. False equivalency is a method by which we may satiate our egos. Both self-righteousness and false equivalency, will serve to diminish your argument and offend your audience. The energy you may be seeking to emit will be barred by your own insecure thoughts.

Come to terms with your polarity and then channel your varying degrees to emit the energy you would like to emit. Other people will receive exactly what you put out, and interpret it by their choosing. The more specified your energy is the more control you will have over the interpretation. How you present yourself and your surroundings will say more about who you truly are than the words you choose. If you want to be taken seriously, you must have a degree of seriousness in you. If you want people to love you, you must present a degree of love in your non-verbal communication. If you want people to help you, you must present a degree of concern for their own wellbeing through your non-verbal communication. The best way to do this is to imagine yourself in all of your varying degrees and use programming to sincerely believe in one of them.

Chapter Fourteen

Communication

Communication is an art that is ultimately going to determine the results of how someone else responds to what you may be saying. So this segment describes how to communicate and what you should communicate.

Communication

Note: "A leader needs to believe in his or herself before successfully convincing others to believe in him or her." (Young Leader)

Message fidelity should be expected. If you are not confident in yourself, then your communication will be severely affected. Your audience will receive your lack of confidence. Do not expect confidence to suddenly take over while you are speaking. You should be comfortable in your own skin. Familiarity breeds comfort. By defining your style in word choice, tone, expression, and posture, you can create a persona for yourself. You will be able to change the energy of a room simply by being aware of exactly who you are and your worth.

"Self –control is the trait of acting only after careful consideration is given, regardless of any initial emotions." (Young Leader)

Recall in the chapter regarding the Win-Win Mentality, there was a discussion around maturity. Maturity involves control, calculation, and empathy. You must communicate after you have thoroughly considered your options. In win-win, we discussed a planning heavy tactic in dealing with complex decisions. With communication, it is in your best interest to adopt a mature way of speaking: with control, empathy, and calculation.

Calculation is in your decisive use of words and tone. You should be aware of the location that your inflections should be imposed. You should be empathetic to the needs of the audience. By speaking about useless, nonsensical, and irrelevant material, you will bore your audience. Venturing away from those core words you identified in Chapter 12 will cause you frustration in the midst of your vision conveyance. Control is when you decide not to use certain words. It is a prohibitory mechanism by which you can filter out your language and tone. By controlling your emotional state you can also control your body language or energy. Control allows you to be more like a laser with your communication, powerfully concentrated at a single point.

It is important to determine not just how to speak or what it means to communicate. It is just as important to determine what you should communicate. Once you are satisfied with your tools, specifically, your creations, you can then begin to venture outside of the Transition Stage because your audience will have received your message.

The operational definition for this chapter is below:

<u>Communication</u> is the imparting or interchange of thoughts, opinions, or information by speech, writing, or signs.

There are many classes you can take to prepare yourself for effective communication. You can take classes to help you structure sentences better, speak more clearly, annunciate your words effectively, or posture yourself appropriately. The truth is that when you are speaking from a place of comfort and sincerity, many of these things naturally occur. It is important to recognize where you currently stand with your natural tendencies, and then reconfigure them by identifying where your internal contradictions reside. In the internal to external stage, communication is all you rely on to pass on your life message. Spending time perfecting how you transmit your data to others is worth your while and will most likely yield much success in every facet of your life: school, parenting, work, relationships, and others.

If you can never share who you are, then who will you be to others when you pass away? Understand the power that is within your communication. As Franklin Delano Roosevelt noted in a time of war, with power comes great responsibility, and that includes the data you send off. The more unfocused it is, the less control you will have over how people interpret it. They will come to their own conclusions about who you are. We are a species that enjoys convenience. We tend towards routes that are the most efficient or require the least amount of work. If someone can be placed into a category, your mind will route all of the data about them into one category as a file to be retrieved when needed. Knowing this, you should be anxious about sharing who you are in the manner you would like to be known. How someone interprets who you are is not entirely their fault. It is mostly your fault. You have either confirmed their insecurities, raised doubts about your credibility, or misspoke true intentions that are hard to retract.

How do I communicate?

I. <u>Know what it means to communicate.</u>

Communication is comprised of the building blocks discussed in the previous chapters. Together they describe communication between two or more people. Effective articulation is dependent upon them, as they are all important aspects in the transition stage of messages moving from internal to external.

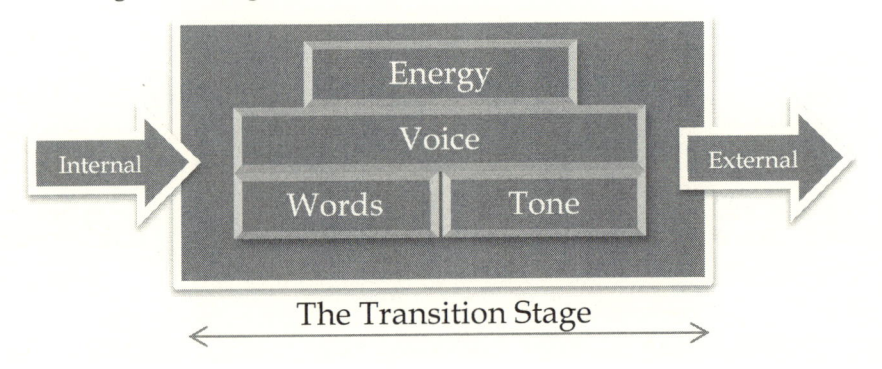

Internal → | Energy / Voice / Words / Tone | → External

The Transition Stage

LP25: Influence

Your communication should be deliberate as it is the only mechanism by which you may share your essence. Knowing what it means to communicate is the first step to communicating effectively. What are some of the goals you have for communication? What is effective communication, and what is efficient communication? Effective and efficient communication produces an anticipated and desired effect.

A caveat with communication concerns the manner in which your audience becomes involved in your communication. While you must maintain a persistent message that uses the words you identified in Chapter 12, be careful of using trite-sounding statements, or statements that are out of cultural context. Regardless of its inherent value, your message will be considered irrelevant if it sounds too trite. You must force your communication to come alive by exploring new ways to communicate the same thing. Changing the order of the words is not enough. You must truly lead your audience along a journey when engaging in efficient communication. MBA's are very intelligent individuals who are great at breaking down complex problems into analogies and building solutions from those analogies. A mistake, however, would be to begin to present analogies as the only method by which a message can be conveyed. By creating *qualitative* equations for any and every thing, notably paradoxical, it becomes offensive to true mathematicians and the method begins to walk a tight rope of inauthenticity. Avoid over usage of any particular method of communication.

In communicating, you must realize that your communication has many qualities that are game-like. You have a position and a purpose in your communication. Throughout your speech, you can work to heighten, maintain, or weaken your position. Once you weaken your position, it becomes extremely difficult to guide your audience.

The mechanisms of your communication are just as important as the different methods of communication. Methods, not mechanisms, of communication can be described in three main categories.

Method	Meaning	Objectives
Negotiation	Negotiation takes place between two or more people in which both parties are attempting to elicit an effect. Both parties may or may not have equal standing.	This is used when trying to reach a mutual agreement on a specified topic of discussion.
Conversation	Conversation takes place between two or more people in which one party may or may not have an objective, but both parties are attempting to share information. There is no truly cared out objective agreed to by both parties. Both parties have equal standing.	This is usually used to build rapport with an individual, secure a first impression, or learn from another person.
Speech	A speech is given from one direction and usually expects no real retort (hence conversational presentations). The objectives are solely decided upon by the speaker. Both parties involved are not on equal footing.	The attempt is to share information which may be solely biased in nature, but is rhetorical for the audience. The agenda is usually to seal a first impression, or create an air-tight argument (no room for disproof).

At times, when engaged in communication, the manner may change from negotiation to speech to conversation. You should be aware of how you are engaging your audience in your communication with your manners and your mechanisms.

Words: *"Words are timeless. You should utter them or write them with a knowledge of their timelessness." (A Spiritual Treasury)*

Tone: *"If you have a clear, resonating voice, you are more likely to deliver a clearer, more resonating message to whomever you're speaking with." (Young Leader)*

    A. <u>My communication by speech is my voice.</u>

When you communicate with your voice, a host of decisions are a part of the process. In tone, you can display emotions. In words, you can use figurative and literal language. You can add idiomatic expressions to your repertoire to elevate the comfort level of your audience. You can use volume and inflection to create auditory illusions. When you engage in communicating truths, you can mask its harshness in words that reflect values. Keep in mind that when you speak, you must speak to inflate another's ego and heighten their security. By focusing on your audience's needs, you will be able to express any message.

Be careful with words because just as a lie propagates a new lie, words propagate new words in the minds of the listeners. Be wary of your witticisms and analogies, because they may trigger your apologies and your emotional outbursts and uncontrollably weaken your position. You should avoid the careless use of words so that you may continue to have control over the conversation. Words are long-lasting. It is this quality that makes them very powerful. You can take the time to build your repertoire of words by using the words you identified in Chapter 12. Be sure to personalize the chart.

Word	Denotation of the Word	Analogy with Word	Connotation of the Word
Word 1:			
Word 2:			
Word 3:			
Word 4:			
Word 5:			
Word 6:			
Word 7:			
Word 8:			
Word 9:			

These denotations, connotations, and analogies will be important when discovering what you communicate when engaging in conversation. For each of the words, you should have an image associated with it. Make it something creative so that you can identify with it. When you begin to speak about it, others will recognize your comfort in the subject and share a similar image.

Tone can be realized in the connotations of your aforementioned words. Once you have an accurate picture in your mind and understand the connotations of the words you use, then you can properly add inflection and rhythm where necessary. Usually a message is not in what is said, but how it is said and why it is said. You have complete control over the words you use in any situation, and by maintaining a clear vision on what you would like to communicate, and gauging your audience's aptitude and spirit to listen, you can create the spectacular illusion of a statesman. Tone carries much fidelity in its signal. If you use a clear, resonating voice, then the message you deliver will be clear and resonating to your audience.

Recall all of the words that can be communicated and the manner in which they are communicated. Your ability to harness authority in your voice will allow you the opportunity to overwrite the preconceived notions of your audience. Try this exercise: imagine your voice in front of a crowd of people who have no interest in what you have to say. They are preoccupied by their daily biddings and do not even spare a second to look at you. Imagine standing on a stage in front of them and attempting to capture their attention. Imagine it so vividly that you can feel your jawline quiver as your mind runs through the motions. Think of the volume your voice must have. Think of how directly you must communicate. If you want to command the attention of a crowd that cares nothing for you, you must create a sense of urgency in your tone.

You can practice as often as you would like by truly envisioning the encounter. It must be a vivid mental reenactment in order to have an effect on what you actually do. Have a sheet of paper handy and record your thoughts as you run through the practice. You may think statements such as, "I cannot speak that loudly", "there is no point to this exercise", or "the words are not coming to mind quickly enough". Record these and keep practicing until you can no longer create such statements. You will find that the next time you venture into a circumstance that you must speak, you will be able to speak your mind with relative ease.

Expression: *"You believe in what you hear said. Believe in the unsaid, for the silence of men is nearer the truth than their words." (A Spiritual Treasury)*

   B. <u>My communication by sign is my energy.</u>

Your energy is the real stimulant of the first impression. Before you say a word or utter a sound, your audience has made an evaluation on who you are and your value to them. Handshakes that are too strong or weak and postures that are too intimidating will elicit a lasting first impression. Whenever the environment changes, regardless of how well you may have developed a relationship with someone, you are giving another first impression. Your expressions, posture, and surrounding environment will all influence the energy you are able to emit and the energy you are able to receive. While you imagined your voice in the scenario of a large inattentive crowd, what did you see yourself doing? What were your hands doing, and how were you standing? Were you cowering or standing upright? You should be able to feel, hear, and see your mental reenactment. Developing good communication habits with your energy and voice are dependent upon that ability.

Just as all things respond to energy, people respond to the energy of others. Energy is transmitted via vibrations or changes in vibration. With energy, there is polarity and rhythm. So, when you are engaged in communication, your energy is seen in the form of nonverbal communication. Your nonverbal communication is influenced directly through your beliefs. So, your body language may betray what your words are attempting to reveal. Recall that your body language is the representation of your core beliefs interacting with your four dimensions. Knowing this, you can affect your body language by simply controlling and understanding your beliefs, and the influence that your dimensions have on you.

Beliefs → Energy → Body Language

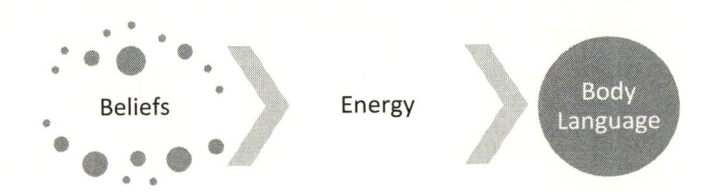

The quote directly implies that the non-verbal communication you convey is the most impactful part of the communication. It is the aspect of communication that requires no understanding of language or culture. It overrides such boundaries. You can perceive the energy behind a hurricane or a tsunami, but you are far from understanding it. Energy has everything to do with a direct effect from one object or person to another.

If a molecule is in a state of vibration, its vibration affects everything within its vicinity. As its vibration increases, it begins to change in conformation or in identity. Surrounding entities also change. You must recognize that you possess a tremendous amount of energy, or influence on the entities and the people that are within your environment. Think of how your communication of energy has run its course.

Undesirable Situation	Involved Energy Communication	Ways to Affect the Environment
Financial Difficulty	Exhibit fearful purchasing tendencies and thoughts about risk	Add energetic fervor into a passion, exhibit low stress for risk
Withdrawing Relationship	Worthlessness (defeated posture and miserable thoughts), active fleeting (mental detachment from individual)	Priority (Reinforce value of the relationship mentally, and excited posture), active chase (mental engagement of individual, and mimicry)
Add Your Own		
Add Your Own		

With these examples, you can see how energy can turn a situation into a new one simply by changing the energy involved. Keep in mind, your energy is dependent upon your beliefs. You cannot simply change your frame of thought without evaluating your beliefs on the new thought. For example, in order to lower stress with regards to risk, you must reevaluate your concept of risk. If you view risk through the lens of fear, then it will be quite difficult to manipulate your belief. You must rewrite your code in accordance with Chapter 10 (Responsibility). The chart is helpful in identifying the energy of the system. Your beliefs are the driver of that system.

When you communicate, however, take notice to what you are truly saying, and usually other people can give you a better depiction on your faults, but they will try to avoid ever telling you. This is done for their own protection. No one wants to deal with ego. When you attack or insult someone else's energy, they will retort with ego. There are more effective ways to communicate suggestions than direct insult. Chapter 15 will include more on how you can appropriately deliver bad news.

II. <u>Know what I must communicate.</u>

You must have an idea of exactly what you would like to communicate now that you understand what communication is. There are two main categories of things that should be communicated. The first is your vision, and the second is your story. The language of the story and the vision is in sharing values. You can build your story around your established values. When you only give features of a vision or a story, then you will lose your audience's interest. They will become "lost in the details". When you provide the value and the benefit of the features, then you have spoken to the security needs of your audience and validated their sense that you have their interest in mind. Speak in the language of values and avoid pedantically regurgitating features.

Within each method of communication, there are objects of your communication that involve aspects of your visions and your stories. These aspects accomplish some objective within the context of the method of the communication. These are known as the objects of your communication.

Method	Qualities	Object of Communication
Negotiation	Insulting, Suggestive, Persuasive, High Engagement, Complimentary, Directed, Biased	Vision: Suggestion for change Story: Consequences of disagreement
Conversation	Informative, Validating, Establishing, Random, Discovering	Vision: Personal beliefs Story: Life goals and experiences
Speeches	Rhetorical, Inciting, Meaningful, Planned, Biased	Vision: Directive for change through a lesson Story: Audience participation in life goal or experience and consequences of no participation

Many people debate over the definition of rhetoric. For the purposes of this chapter, a "rhetorical" quality describes the capacity to which some idea is aptly considered in terms of persuasive methods. As opposed to dialectic in which information is merely directly conveyed. In rhetoric, consideration of environmental factors is inherent. Conclusions are derived as a consequence of using established postulates within the minds of the individuals who comprise an audience.

Imagery: *"Vision needs to be like the daily vitamin." (Young Leader)*

A. <u>Communicate my visions.</u>

The main thing you communicate is your vision. It may be your vision of who you believe you are or the person with whom you are speaking to be. A vision is a picture of some sort.

By becoming familiar with your personal visions, it is very easy to engage in conversation with a new individual. Since you are specifically within a sharing mode, stress level is quite low. Sharing your vision here is simply communicating your values and sharing

LP25: Influence

what influenced those values. You have visions about yourself, your family, your environment, and the world. You can begin a conversation by sharing a vision that you have about any of those topics and then explain the reasons for those visions. The individual you are speaking with will begin to respond with their own. You can use your environment to create context.

Practice (Conversation):

Situation	Topic	Vision	Explanation- How did you arrive at this vision?
Seated next to someone you do not know on a plane	Travel		
Create One:			

Speeches are at medium-level stress. While speeches usually inspire the most nervous behaviors, they require fewer objectives than the negotiation. They expect no retorts from the audience, but they compel their audiences to change their vision. As they are rhetorical in nature, speeches can be hard to administer. The energy in the room can be used to gauge whether a new direction should be explored during your speech. With speeches, you have direct control over their flow through your energy and voice. Since the audience cannot respond, they will pay attention and reflect everything that you offer through energy and voice. When you are communicating a vision in a speech, everything should be framed in workable building blocks. The vision should be referenced at the beginning, explained and constructed within the middle, and then reintroduced at the end. Successfully administering a speech requires preparation in its delivery on all levels. When preparing a speech, it is best to imagine yourself delivering the speech so that you may align your energy and voice to one accord, as there are no internal unexpected aspects to delivering a speech because there is no response from the audience.

Practice (Speech):

Situation	Topic	Vision	Explanation- How did you arrive at this vision?
You must leave an impression for a group of high school students about to leave for college	School/ Social Life Balance		
Create One:			

When negotiating, sharing a vision can become contentious and stress becomes high because you will have to provide proof. Negotiation involves changing another's vision with regards to a concept. Proof is a necessary element to make that happen. Recall that we develop our beliefs through an interaction of the four dimensions and through influential factors: culture, emotion, logic, and duty. If you know the most influential element for a person, providing proof can become an easy task. In negotiation, if you do not match that individual's key influence, then you will fail to provide recognizable proof, and the negotiation will be taken out of your control. In negotiation, the rhetorical vision-constructing communication goes in both directions, and that is why stress is high. You do not have direct control over the response of your audience. Due to this reason, you cannot completely imagine a full negotiation from start to finish. You can imagine your energy so that when the negotiation reaches its highest emotional peak, you are able to maintain control, as there may be unexpected internal aspects. If you respond to shock or insult poorly, then you can be thrown off course when communicating vision. You can also be thrown off by making yourself vulnerable to the audience. If you concede too much of your vision at the beginning, then you will lose any control over managing the negotiation. If the audience tries to lower your guard by seemingly providing too much information, assume they are holding back and do not give in to imitating their actions. Instead, keep at least one aspect of your proof to yourself until the next encounter. You must prepare the content, however.

LP25: Influence

You should avoid negotiation unless you clearly understand the visions and influences of your audience. You must prepare your responses with proof and consistency so that you may alter their vision. Your voice and your energy must complement each other in this type of encounter; otherwise, your audience will feel as though you are disingenuous and will not alter their vision for your sake.

Practice (Negotiation):

Situation	Topic	Vision	Explanation- How did you arrive at this vision?
You are giving a presentation to your boss on a new plan	Convince the person that you can make their job easier		
Create One:			

Direction: *"The boy took out the Urim and Thummim from his bag. He had used the two stones only once, one morning when he was at a marketplace. His life and his path had always provided him with enough omens. It's true; life really is generous to those who pursue their Personal Legend, the boy thought." (The Alchemist)*

    B. <u>Communicate my story.</u>

Your story is just as important as your vision. Your vision is a result of your story interacting with your four dimensions. If you are to provide depth to any situation, mix your visions with your story. Who you are and where you came from are all important aspects to your story. It is your way of directly telling your life message, and it can be done with any of the methods and will require the use of the mechanisms. The quote particularly expresses this as the urim and thummim were omens for the boy in *The Alchemist*. All of his visions only had true meaning because of the story they created. If the story was untold, what would be the point? It is important that you always draw your visions back to your story. Your story is where you can spark empathy in others and begin to promote those aspects that are unique to you.

When engaged in conversation, communicating your story is limited to you birthplace or birth-time and the ensuing events that affected your development. When you share your story of how you were raised, you remind the audience that you are a person with experiences and influences. Telling your story will come easiest when you are providing explanations for your visions. You can entwine stories from your childhood. Once this step is taken, the audience feels closer to you and it will lower its guard. Do not tell too much of your story because the motives of your audience may be to work against you. So, steer clear of qualities to your story that may be used against you in the future. If you do share them, be sure to recognize which parts of the story your audience can bear to hear, and which they will run from. You can do this by listening to their stories. They will reveal their fears, and if an aspect of your story reminds them of that fear, do not discuss it upon an initial introduction. In seeking committed relationships, however, if you do not bring up significant elements early, you will encounter a scornful partner if the element of the story you are not sharing is of great importance. In all cases, do not reveal too much at one time. Your story will eventually be used against you, and you must be ready for that occasion. Use story telling as a way to embark on the process of learning about one another. From then on, you will be able to establish values and move forward in that capacity.

When giving a speech, storytelling is important to help the audience try to identify with you. You can weave this into the building blocks you use. Convince them to join you in your beliefs. If they feel as though they are a part of your life already, then they will be more willing to accept your provided vision as the speaker. As long as the story is properly set up (meaning it is relevant and concise) you will heighten your credibility whether you produce proof or not.

In negotiation, storytelling is imperative for proof. You must describe situations in which proof had already been administered and stories that give you credibility in providing the proof. "Sure it matters to me, but why should I trust you"- is something that each member of the audience will try to answer in order to heighten their comfort with you. Storytelling is used to create an equal playing field in negotiating so that you can keep the negotiation at a conversational level. By doing this, you can maintain your control over the direction of a negotiation. Allow your audience to offer their stories so that you can better gauge the stories you should use.

Stories and visions are used in order to accomplish the objectives of negotiations, conversations, and speeches. Keep in mind your voice and energy to properly participate in these forms of communication. It is imperative when you are actually trying to have an effect on someone, ending the internal to external process.

Chapter Fifteen

Effect

The effect is the end result of all the communication from one to another that occurs. The "Effect" chapter deals with achieving the most from your communication.

Effect

Note: "And before you leave the market place, see that no one has gone his way with empty hands. For the master spirit of the earth shall not sleep peacefully upon the wind till the needs of the least of you are satisfied." (A Spiritual Treasury)

The effect that you elicit is the end to your transition stage. Your message is no longer in a transitional phase. If your intention is to convey a particular message, you are only successful if that message is accurately conveyed. This can be determined by the effect your message has on your audience. There are many things to keep in mind if you truly intend to have an effect.

Become comfortable with the idea that anything you speak is as tangible as a wooden box. It is as though you are placing an object into the hands of your audience. They can hold your communication and either take value in it or throw it. Your communication is a piece of art as we have previously discussed, and a piece of yourself. So, with respect to the quote, making sure no one has an empty hand is the same as saying that you should share parts of your life with others. You should share your visions and your story and then people will be able to learn from your life and grow. Figuratively, no one deserves to leave empty handed. If you choose not to share, by any means, then the desired idea that you have of yourself shall permanently perish.

LP25: Influence

Everyone craves to know more about who comprises their surroundings. Humans are social creatures and so you can assume upon an initial introduction, that there is at least a minimal amount of curiosity the individual has in you. You can use that curiosity to your advantage now that you understand how to communicate, and thus satiate their appetite appropriately by not offending them, instead engaging them by speaking to their interests.

"If you do not understand your friend under all conditions, you will never understand him." (A Spiritual Treasury)

If you are to have an effect, it is important that you avoid building walls of differences where you intended to build a bridge. This is something many people do unintentionally, and it is because they either create ridiculous expectations about their audience or are too self-deprecating about their own ideas. If you do not know your audience you are sure to stumble over yourself in the course of addressing them. You need to know their visions and stories. If you are to properly converse, speak, or negotiate, you have to work within the boundaries that your audience sets because that is the figurative language in which they speak. The greatest influencers have been those who can subvert a message, make it sound like their own, and place enough spin on the process so that the tactic is beyond recognizable. Knowing the audience allows you the opportunity to play the game. You can only make the rules when you have established an objective alongside an accomplished awareness.

The operational definition for this chapter is below:

<u>Effect</u> is the power to produce results; efficacy; force; validity; influence; the making of a desired impression.

Impressions are completely dependent upon your ability to communicate. If you want to have an effect, you must designate a desirable outcome. Achieving it in the most direct way would accomplish efficient communication. Try to create a list of reasons as to why you would like to communicate better. Of course, everyone says you should, but what are the effects of good communication and why would they help you? Where would good communication skills take you?

Reason 1:
Reason 2:
Reason 3:
Reason 4:
Reason 5:

Place a star by the top three reasons. When you are trying to improve your effectiveness, keep these reasons in mind as a source of motivation.

When you imagine Martin Luther King Jr., or Franklin D. Roosevelt, what comes into your mind? Do you hear their voices and see their faces? When you hear them speak, what happens? Do your ears perk? Do you feel a quiver down your spine? Do you feel inspired? Are you fearful? All of these things are effects. Speakers use words to cause you to *change* in some way, shape, or form. You may change your mood or actions. If you are talking in class, a teacher points you out and asks you not to interrupt the class. So, you look at her because you are embarrassed and you either listen because you are fearful of losing the teacher's respect or you continue because you are fearful of having others lose respect for you. Either way, the teacher elicited an effect. For reference, depending upon the student's response, this would qualify as either a negotiation or a speech, but tends toward a speech. There is a distinct outcome based upon the communication that occurred. The reasons listed above may contain some of the direct effects that you seek to have with your communication.

How should I communicate?

I.   **Watch the body language.**

As previously mentioned, your body language is what stimulates a first impression. You must be cognizant of what you are doing and what it is being conveyed. If you are trying to make a point, use your hands, feet, and eyes to complement that point. Heighten your

LP25: Influence

eye contact by searching to see whether or not the person is actually paying attention. Purse the edges of your eyes to indicate seriousness and concern. Use your eyebrows to parallel the sentiment. If they drop their eyes, take your hands and do one of two things: if speaking within close proximity to someone, use your hands to close the gap between you. If you are speaking to a room of individuals, use your hands to gesture them to move in closer. Turn your feet towards the individual or audience and only slightly lean in towards the direction of your arms. If the person you are speaking with moves backwards, then straighten your posture- you may be either too yielding or intimidating. Relax your shoulders. If they are too tense, you will seem pretentious or weak. Most of all, believe in what you are saying so that your body language will reflect your confidence, and not your uncertainty.

When you are coming to a close, you should press a mental reset button. Reduce your hand gestures to a minimum and turn one foot to the direction you would like to move in next. Use your eyes to reassure your audience by looking at every individual if you have an audience. If you are speaking with one person, look down when delivering your ending statement. Together, these things will spur effects in your audience.

Effect	Feet	Hands	Eyes and Eyebrows	Expression/ Body
Listen closely	Directed towards audience, maybe bent knee	Open to the air, or touching	Pursed and pushed	None/ slight lean
Speak to me	Move around room	Open by the side	Open, normal height	Slight smile/ straightened
I am interested	Direct feet towards audience	Touching or open	Open, one mid-height	Smile/ leaned
Frustration/ consternation	Direct feet towards audience or towards person	Fisted and open arms, for speech or folded hands for an argument	Pursed and one mid-height	Smirk/ motion

Take me seriously	Shoulder width apart towards the audience	Gestured hand, thumb out, movement with speech rhythm	Pursed eyes, and pushed eyebrows	Smirk/ perfectly straight
Avoid Talk to me	Feet in opposing direction of audience	Closed by chest	No eye contact, heightened eyebrows	Unassuming or nervous/ cowered body posture

Within your body language, you can communicate a lot. Because body language is so connected to your beliefs and your energy, it is very difficult to be aware of what you actually do when speaking. It may benefit you to find someone to have a conversation with and have them describe your body language as you tell a story. Try to identify the effect you currently have on your audiences.

Expectations: *"Be Royal in your own Fashion: Act like a King to be treated like one. The way you carry yourself will often determine how you are treated: In the long run, appearing vulgar or common will make people disrespect you. For a king respects himself and inspires the same sentiment in others. By acting regally and confident of your powers, you make yourself seem destined to wear a crown." (48 Laws of Power)*

A.   What you think you are, you will be to others.

Upon meeting someone, expectations on either side play a role. Age, sex, race, and height all play into what people think of you before you say or do anything. These are known as stereotypes. Stereotypes, at times, may be reliable, but it is best to be aware of them so that you can recognize when you are relying on them to make decisions about other people. As a speaker, you should be aware of them so that you can know whether you are working to confirm or disprove them. If you confirm them, the person you are introducing yourself to will work less hard to learn more about you and rely on their previous knowledge to guide their interactions with you. Since expectations have an effect on your listener that are out of your control, it introduces the idea that you must create an image for yourself that speaks louder than any preconceived notions. This does not mean that you act differently from your normal self, but it does mean you must take some energy to develop a new vision to present for yourself. How you present yourself is how your listener will perceive you. If you ignore the interplay of stereotypes however, you will fall into traps that will be nearly impossible to climb out of. Stereotypes are always used as a reserve of assumptions that you can pick and choose from. Anomalies are treated as anomalies, and not as standards. Stereotypes cannot be eradicated from one disproving encounter. They can only be enhanced by them.

The vision you present should complement your purpose. In that way, you will be able to share your visions and stories and they will not contradict your presentation.

Here is the process of the first encounter:

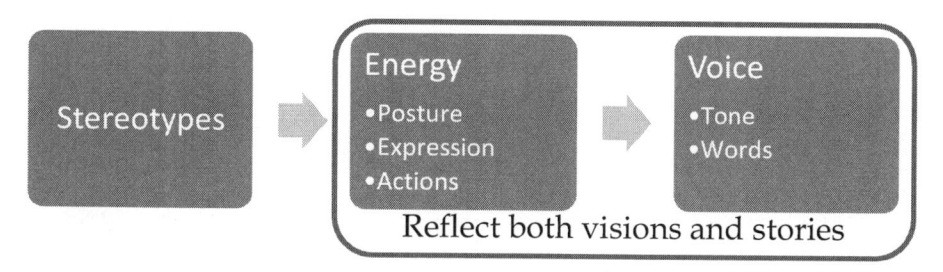

Stereotypes → **Energy**
- Posture
- Expression
- Actions

→ **Voice**
- Tone
- Words

Reflect both visions and stories

The listener then uses each of these steps to draw conclusions on who you are and the kind of relationship they will have with you. If energy and voice are in alignment with your stories and visions, then you can compete with working stereotypes and elicit an effect of the individual being curious as to why you are an anomaly. You must know the stereotypes that the audience harbors so that you can target them in your introduction.

What about the mistakes? Perhaps your vision of yourself is not presented strongly, and this is confirmed by your audience. Recall that first impressions can be reengineered by changing the environment. It is best to remain confident in your mistakes and await the next opportunity to present a stronger version. You should be prepared, however because the more failed impressions you have, the harder it will be to recreate one. Second chances rarely come. Getting it right the first time will save you time and energy.

Presenting a vision involves having a cognitive vision of who you are. As the quote describes, if you want to be treated like a king (have people respond to you in the way that they respond to royalty), then you must think and act like a king. Your thoughts translate into your actions. So, when you have imagined yourself as your purpose, you compel yourself to act in the manner that reflects your imagination. When you do this, you create expectations for people to have for you. Politicians are notorious for this. They act like royalty and righteous leaders. Reality may be far from this, but their actions cause us to place great value in their occupancy of position. We elect people to the presidency who "act" like they are already a president. In beauty pageants, coaches suggest that you perform as if you have already won the crown. How would a beauty queen carry herself? Would she act as though she is vying for the crown, or as though she is the one who brings meaning to it? This is universally true. The saying that implies, "there is no try, but there is to do or not to do", implies the same truth. When you truly believe you are worth a certain kind of treatment, you automatically begin to raise the expectations on you and those around you. The take-away is that you are treated exactly how you believe you should be treated. Act like a king to be treated like a king.

Many people interpret this incorrectly. They feel that in order to act like a king, you must do a lot of convincing to others that you are a worth as much as a king. The contrary is true. Archetypical kings do not have to speak to the idea that they are kinglike. They do not have to parade their wealth. They do not have to belittle others to establish their kingship. They may partake in those activities in order to quiet any dissention. To establish the kingship, however, they carry themselves in a manner that confirms kingship as their proper role in society. They speak like a king. They think and strategize as a king would. They hold themselves up to standards that only a "king" could achieve. Those that speak loudly about their desired position in the world are usually posers and can be spotted a mile away. Be sure that when you practice acting like a king, you are not imitating, but creating a vision based upon your true beliefs.

Intention: *"All individuals who have attained any degree of Self-Mastery do this to a certain degree, more or less unconsciously, but the Master does this consciously, and by the use of his Will, and attains a degree of Poise and Mental Firmness almost impossible of belief on the part of the masses who are swung backward and forward like a pendulum." (Kybalion)*

    B.   <u>Center yourself.</u>

Centering yourself involves a few activities. In the previous chapter, polarity was discussed. Centering yourself means finding the balance in your spectrum. You cannot fluctuate too much in your communication, because the conflicting messages will cause your audience to lose any interest in what you have to say.

Centering yourself also means focusing your energy towards one point. If you want to achieve a certain effect, you must align all aspects of your communication in the direction of your intended effect. If you are seeking to gain attention, then your energy and voice should work together to accomplish that.

Understanding that the world is mental in nature, that all things are perceived and conclusions are drawn on those perceptions, you can do much to alter perception. Being centered allows you to strategize in the mental field. If you are aware of the expectations of your audience, you can do much to manipulate them for your gain. Mastery at this level is only achieved after mastering control over yourself. Metaphysically speaking, you have control over your energy and thus you can permeate energy in ways that are for your intention. So, when you must speak in front of a room, you can center yourself by creating a sense of balance in your mind between your insecurities and your securities through focusing on being confident and clear. You will exude energy that reflects your concentration on balance and cause the room to also be balanced and attentive. You have effectively commanded their energy.

Balancing is a procedure that involves vision, mental reenactment, intentional breathing, and focus. Vision is the mental image you prepare for yourself on what you are going to speak about and your appearance. You must visualize the voice and energy you wish to permeate. By visualizing how you would like to present yourself and the content of your presentation, you will naturally begin to balance your nerves and feel more comfortable with the opportunity.

As for the mental reenactment, you should be able to hear, feel and see yourself going through the motions of your presentation. This will help your mind begin to focus on the occasion and set personal expectations for your performance. You will concurrently feel the expectations of your audience and find ways to work that into your presentation.

Breathing is usually passively done. With intentional breathing, you must become mindful of your breathing rate and begin to slow it down by taking in slower and deeper breaths. This will work to calm you and gain control of your emotions.

Focus is important so that you are able to live within your presentation. Once you are calm, you can forget all of the things you had just worked to mentally create. As you walk to give your presentation, speak from your heart and your centered body will perform almost perfectly on cue to how it was trained. You will release all of the energy that you have just centered because you have no barriers working to hold it back.

Centering yourself will allow you to become an extraordinary speaker.

II.   **Stay in the comfort zones.**

A comfort zone is an area of familiarity. When learning something new, it is best to push yourself outside of your comfort zone. However, if you are trying to elicit an effect, and accidentally venture outside of the comfort zone without guidance, you will lose your audience. This does not mean that you should avoid making your audience think, but it does mean you do your best to make

LP25: Influence

them feel comfortable with thinking. If you make them feel as though there are barriers to their participation, they will not participate. If you create an environment in which participation is expected, then you have created a comfort zone. In small meetings, staying in the comfort zone means you should not intentionally create tension within the group. If you do not reflect the activities your group engages in, then it is the same as having insulted them. You should not change your convictions, however, as there are ways to reflect them, without imitating them. Acting self-righteously in front of a group will only tempt them to test you and then judge you because you have offended their egos.

Acclimation and Reflection: *"Think as you like, but behave like others. If you make a show of going against the times, flaunting your unconventional ideas and unorthodox ways, people will think that you only want the attention and that you look down upon them. They will find a way to punish you for making them feel inferior. It is far safer to blend in and nurture the common touch. Share your originality only with tolerant friends and those who are sure to appreciate your uniqueness." (48 Laws of Power)*

    A.   <u>Communicate with awareness of everyone's insecurities.</u>

Identify your audience's stories and visions. You can then navigate around them. You do not want to blatantly remind your audience of their insecurities, but rather speak in a way that causes them to subconsciously consider them. You should work as a chameleon does in order to gather information. If your audience seems to be upbeat, it would be in your interest to reflect their cheer. You do not have to imitate their every action, but it is best to reflect their energy. In this way, they will feel comfortable around you and share aspects of their life with you. If they are not sharing information, then you are probably not connecting with them to the point where they are comfortable enough to do so. Most people actually use how well you are able to blend in with them as a measurement of how much they can trust you. Business meetings are notorious for such standard-exhibiting behavior. Alcohol consumption or acute wittiness are common themes of an evening business meeting. It is not imperative to do either, but you must reflect the energy that the two activities represent, because you are being judged by your ability to blend in well.

Once you create a comfortable environment, people will begin to share their visions and stories, and through these, you can identify their insecurities. As you continue to avoid conversational landmines, they will open up to you even more. In espionage, this is one way to get your targets to share information with you that can later be used against them. In covert espionage, the comfort zone is usually set by dishonestly sharing aspects of your visions and stories. In that way there is no way to trace your identity.

You only accomplish an insult when you attack something that a person considers to be an insecurity. There are many levels of insecurity that you should be aware of. The same insecurity surfaces differently in different dimensions, and are dealt with differently at those dimensions. Recall that your communication only will have a final effect after being received by your audience and then interpreted according to the four dimensions.

Insecurities in the social dimension have everything to do with interaction and societal worth. In the social dimension, they are purely functional. As a consequence of how society evaluates culture, race, age, or sex, is the manner in which these insecurities exist. So, while the person may not feel hindered due to one of those elements, they are still insecure about them because of societal values. Exclusive groups are hinged in this element and function as both insulting and promising.

Insecurities in the physical dimension are directly related to the sense of personal gratification. Having a competitive nature appears in the physical dimension as the teacher's pet or a person seeking accolades from authority.

In the mental dimension, insecurities exist as the worth of capabilities and limitations. How a person perceives themselves taps into who they believe they are.

In the spiritual dimension, insecurities are centered on a person's beliefs, experiences, and sense of purpose.

The most effective insults impact multiple layers at once. So, while you are communicating with your audience, you should be aware of all of these elements. Insecurities can be used to comfort and discomfort someone. Accidentally committing an insult will cause you to lose a handle on your audience and will render you less effective.

It is best to reflect your audience in content, gather information, and mold your visions and stories around theirs to gain ultimate control over the conversation. When delivering bad news or suggestive insults (a suggestion that could be perceived as an insult such as one on appearance or manner) by which you desire to receive no recoil, there are three mechanisms that exist to afford that result.

The first is through seductive reasoning. You may appeal to the individual's psychology and convince the mark that a specific suggestion is preferential to their current methods. The suggestion must be presented in a disguise as a present or compliment to their judgmental abilities. With this method, the mark must be convinced that they suggestion was self-created. Another method of seduction is through laughter or light-heartedness. Many are deceived by this ruse and will correlate the action to naïveté. They will either build their guard because your laughter pities them in condescension or they will yield all fronts to you because they expect to take advantage of you. The final method of seduction is through false security. You can present false information of great severity to only alleviate it with bad news that is not as significant. Seduction works well when you understand the insecurities of your mark.

The second is the remedy method. We trust our advisors because they have displayed a substantial amount of credibility. If your energy exudes fairness and camaraderie, you can offer credible criticism to someone. To use this effectively, you must be established as an authority on a subject or by position.

The final method is by means of a surrogate. If you cannot afford to accommodate negative attention to your reputation, then you may recognize a scapegoat to translate transgressions. Surrogates are not limited to people. Some individuals use signs or beliefs as a way to relieve the pressure from providing bad news.

Imitation: *"Disarm and infuriate with the mirror effect. The mirror reflects reality, but it is also the perfect tool for deception: When you mirror your enemies, doing exactly as they do, they cannot figure out your strategy. The Mirror Effect mocks and humiliates them, making them overreact. By holding up a mirror to their psyches, you seduce them with the illusion that you share their values; by holding up a mirror to their actions, you teach them a lesson. Few can resist the power of the Mirror Effect." (48 Laws of Power)*

Sentience: *"Know who you are dealing with- do not offend the wrong person. There are many different kinds of people in the world, and you can never assume that everyone will react to your strategies in the same way. Deceive or outmaneuver some people and they will spend the rest of their lives seeking revenge. They are wolves in lambs' clothing. Choose your victims and opponents carefully, then never offend or deceive the wrong person." (48 Laws of Power)*

B. <u>Communicate with care.</u>

Perhaps you desire to prove a point. There is a fine line between persuasion by connection and persuasion by insult. Many people persuade by insult. They belittle the individual with whom they are speaking and their ideas. While this method can be effective, it usually creates fertile ground for future dissension and many times will cause the individual to back into a corner and resort to an unconditional defensive mode. In that mode, no persuasion can be done and arguments end in an agreement to disagree. If you truly want to prove your point, it takes a bit more work than simply stating column A v. column B. Recall that most of our social interactions are predicated in our deeply rooted concepts of self. We do not like to be wrong, and if you prove us wrong on one thing, chances are you are proving other beliefs we have to be incorrect. Presentation of proof requires great care, and when you do not understand your audience, you could be heading for a lethal crash.

Remember:
People want to feel vindicated.
No one enjoys being wrong.
Grudges may be held indefinitely, if not given an outlet.

You must act as a spy if you are to venture into someone's domain. It takes a certain amount of artistry. You must plant seeds that are able to sprout into a new vision, given the right treatment. When giving a speech, sparking a conversation, or enlisting for negotiation, this method is vital. You must begin by stating the current status, or letting the audience define the current status. You can then begin to sow seeds of your vision. You must understand the underpinnings of your vision in order to do this. Try to identify the experiences that caused you to arrive at your beliefs and use that in your storytelling to prevent suspicion from your audience. Then, begin nurturing the planted seeds. By doing this, you are actually crafting a new experience for your audience rather than forcing an interaction from your audience. This process involves your audience actively shaping your presented experience into one of their own, so that they feel it is theirs. In this way, they will feel vindicated because they have conserved their egos.

If someone believes something is their own idea or an answer to one of their prayers, then they are very likely to blindly follow and take the suggestions you offer. You should be careful when you begin to venture into another person's psyche. You may stir up unexpected emotions, and you need to be able to handle anything you may hear from them. This is why centering yourself is very important. When a person decides to trust you with information, you must not be quick to judge them, or they will recoil and find ways to vindicate themselves. You will lose the potential ally you may have had in them. Keep your promises and tread lightly. Even the most harmless seeming individual is filled with a deep canyon of regrets and grudges that will eventually surface as campaigns of vengeance. For some the canyon runs shallower than others, and you should listen to their stories to paint a picture of whom you are speaking.

When listening to stories, you should be an active listener. You can do this by paying attention to all of the words in a story that are associated with stereotypes. Keep a mental track record of all of the stories. Do not assume someone thinks just as you do. You may experience emotions in a similar way, but those emotions are triggered for different reasons. Assume for everything you take for granted as a belief, your audience believes the complete opposite. In this way, you will prevent major first impression miscalculations. Then, work backwards by intertwining potential insecurities into securities and convince them that your ideas are actually theirs because it parallels so closely to their securities. This is what true flattery looks like.

Finally when communicating, there is a technique known as the mirror effect. If you want to surely agitate someone, simply repeat what they do. As you hide your true intentions behind a mirror, you are able to slowly understand people while they grow agitated with you. This is effective when you are dealing with those who may be more powerful than you because as they grow agitated, they lose control and make themselves more susceptible to your influence. When you are mirroring someone, you mirror their mannerisms, language, and process. This is not a recommended method because it spawns the vindictive nature of most people, especially if in the process of the mirror effect, you broadcast one of their insecurities or make them aware of a new one.

III.   Notice their interests/cues.

In all ways of communicating, effective communication relies on speaking in harmony with the interests of your audience. You can gather this information the same way you can gather the insecurities of your audience: through their visions and stories. Use your knowledge to mold your communication so that it retains a certain amount of relevancy. Otherwise, you will be sure to be a lackluster speaker and lose any confidence the audience may have initially invested in you. In order to do this, not only should you be keen on their interests, but you must be genuine in presenting your matching interests. If you are simply speaking about their interests without any passion, then they will assume you are facetious and politely or angrily ask you to leave. This is very important because if you disregard the interests of others, it is as effective as throwing an insult towards them. If you are not genuinely interested, your energy and voice will reflect that their passions are not worth your time. Said aloud, most people would be outwardly offended. Implied, our mental dimension and spiritual dimension responds with abhorrence and we avoid those who are not like us.

Friend: *"Work on the Hearts and Minds of Others. Coercion creates a reaction that will eventually work against you. You must seduce others into wanting to move in your direction. A person you have seduced becomes your loyal pawn. And the way to seduce others is to operate on their individual psychologies and weaknesses. Soften up the resistant by working on their emotions, playing on what they hold dear and what they fear. Ignore the hearts and minds of others and they will grow to hate you. (48 Laws of Power)*

Mentorship: *"Talking in terms of the other person's interests pays off for both parties. Howard Z. Herzig, a leader in the field of employee communications, has always followed this principle. When asked what reward he got from it, Mr. Herzig responded that he not only received a different reward from each person but that in general the reward had been an enlargement of his life each time he spoke to someone." (How to Win Friends and Influence People)*

    A.   <u>Find the common ground and build it. Communicate provocatively.</u>

The visions and stories you communicate must be relevant to the person, and when you decide on the vision you are attempting to impart, include words that encourage your listener to associate pictures with the vision. These images are connected to all kinds of schemas that exist in your listener's mind. By doing this, you can get your audience to immediately accept you and avoid having to vie for their acceptance when you introduce novel or abrasive sentiments. The first quote indicates the importance of interest matching. By doing this, a person can feel as though you have taken your time to try to understand who they are. This is very validating.

Once you are able to figuratively open a person, however, you can explore their fears, hopes, and loves. This level goes a little deeper than interests. The interests are a result of your primary fears, loves, and hopes. If you wish for greatness, then you may fear not achieving it. On the interest level, the hope would reveal itself in a different form, such as an interest in public policy or arts and entertainment. You should recognize the difference between the primary emotion and its manifestation.

As for developing such rapport, you are also able to gain a mentor or mentee out of the encounter. This can be the end-goal of your communication. Mentors can easily become vulnerable gatekeepers of resources you may desire. Keep in mind that both of you are sharing a connection and all parties should benefit from the encounter using the win-win mentality. When introducing such a method with win-lose, lose-win, and lose-lose personalities, you can encounter huge barriers to progress. It takes a bit of craftiness to get everyone to function at the same energy level. Dealing with each of these is a task and it requires you to determine the cause for each of them, and then skillfully create a plan by which you can use their own visions and stories to work toward the benefit of all parties.

LP25: Influence

Part Four Introduction

And the Puzzle-Emergent Properties

Emergent properties are properties that propagate not as a consequence of coexisting individual parts, but are a result of the individual parts working together in an interdependent manner. The results of all communication and its effect are emergent properties. They are not predictable properties, but the person that can master their usage and understand how they interact with other emergent properties will find a great resource when pursuing personal ambitions.

When involved in group work, you have a mixture of personalities, stories, visions, energies, and voices coming to work on the same project. In the process some individuals grow quieter, while others stand to vocally lead the group. Still, others manage to silently, but mentally lead the group because they leave an impression that they are experts in the matter. When creating the final work, some offer suggestions to restart the project. Others believe that minor adjustments should be made. Others are settled and offer no further contribution. Everyone, however, presents the same work to the person in authority so that the project may be taken to the next level, if there is another level. The work is the emergent property. The feelings developed between the team members also qualify as emergent properties.

The best physical way of explaining emergent properties is through life itself. Organisms are made of organic compounds with unique functions that coexist to actually create a system. The system exhibits something we have identified as life. It is not a consequence of just carbon compounds being within close proximity to each other, but it is a quality that emerges from the combination of the working pieces. In biology, it is known as an emergent property.

As a leader, you must know how to channel the emergent properties that exist within a group. This theme is meant to help understand emergent properties and the process by which they can be managed for the ultimate accomplishment of completing the puzzle of which you are a piece. You must understand what it means to serve the larger picture from within your role, and what resources are available to you as a consequence of identifying systems and their emergent properties. At the end of this theme, you will be asked to reflect on your current status of resource obtainment and allocation, and role identification and motivation.

Chapter Sixteen

The Whole Piece of the Puzzle

Identifying how you can work with others is very important to overall success since each person is equipped with his/her own special talents and abilities. By working together and properly managing emergent properties, the product has the potential to be greater, more comprehensive, and unpredictably more beneficial. Emergent properties should be encouraged by you when working in a group, and this segment discusses how to accomplish that.

The Whole Piece of the Puzzle

Note: "We must all hang together, or assuredly, we shall all hang separately." (Benjamin Franklin)

Since we live in an interdependent world, it is critical to adopt a mentality that is conducive for working within a group. You do not venture into the world alone and every action you commit has a consequence that affects you and many others. If you become too concerned with your well-being at the expense of others, expect such a lifestyle to eventually recoil on you. You must observe yourself in accordance with all working pieces if you are to discover the qualities of the emergent properties. What value do you bring to systems? A seemingly strong chain can be easily broken once its stress points are identified and attacked. The same is true for groups. When entering into a group, agreements are made- that each element will perform its part because true value is created when all of the parts are working in synchronicity. Imagine the human anatomy. Would the nervous system work without the brain, and could the brain deliver any value without the nerves that reach our innards and extremities? If the brain were to attempt to function as the nerves do, we would not be human. The emergent properties are created when the systems and the elements of the systems work in a synchronous manner. People are not much different. There is great importance in people working synchronously. Each person is designed uniquely- unique experiences, cultures, influences, talents, and thoughts. Why would we expect ourselves to be just like another person? It is imperative that you define your role within the system and in accordance within other systems, and craft your emergent property value with that definition. You must qualify your value in terms of the impact it will have on systems and elements within your operational systems. Recognize that your group consists of groups and completes other groups. Note the diagram:

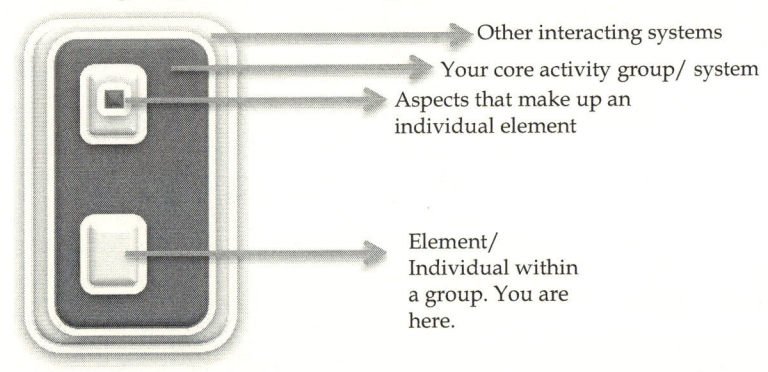

→ Other interacting systems
→ Your core activity group/ system
→ Aspects that make up an individual element

→ Element/ Individual within a group. You are here.

If you try to evade the qualifying process of your value, you will quickly be stamped with an undesirable worth and will miss opportunities that may have been ripe for your undertaking. You will also cause those around you to fall because you cannot carry your weight. Working in a group can be seen in the likeness of a group pulling a boulder up a steep incline. Everyone is harnessed to the boulder so they must pull a certain amount of the weight. If one individual decides to sit because their needs are not being met, they will either have to be dragged up along with the boulder, making the pull more difficult, or they must have to be convinced that they are a necessary part of the team's ability to make it up the hill. If the team validates the individual by speaking in terms of their worth, they are more inclined to actually want to assist in the task. Keep in mind most people do not know their value. If the team argues with the individual, then eventually, the group will no longer be able to support the boulder, and they will all topple down the side of the incline, fatally injuring themselves and others. At the end of the story, the boulder still has to make it to the top of the incline.

When the team is cooperating, they discover emergent properties while carrying the boulder- best practices on maneuvering the boulder upwards, reasons to justify moving a boulder up a hill, and a grander view from the side of the incline. In effect, you must do your part to provide value to a system; so that the system may work, and may interact with other systems. This is how emergent properties are created. Once you have emergent properties, you can then begin the process of learning how to use them for the benefit of your group because you are in an interdependent world.

The operational definition for this chapter is below:

<u>Emergence</u> is the way complex systems and patterns arise out of a multiplicity of relatively simple interactions in philosophy, systems theory, and science.

The definition of emergence implies that in order to have emergent properties, there has to be some interactions that take place prior. Those prior interactions are the previous three themes: understanding systems, understanding how you operate within them, and finally how to move your thoughts from the internal world, your mind, into the external world. Once you have shared your friends and tools with the world, you are able to function within the emergent world. If you can imagine a network of points constantly coming together and breaking apart to form new networks, then that is the vision of the workings of systems. An analog clock cannot display the time without the cogs, cut in different shapes and sizes turning at different times. Elements depend on emergent properties for meaning and emergent properties are devoid of a tangible existence without the elements. Identifying emergent properties takes a set of skills and awareness that you will hopefully develop so that you may be able to move into the next step which involves controlling them. You must begin the process of shifting your mind from "I" to "We".

What will come out of what I have to offer? How may we emerge?

I. When a group comes together, the unexpected happens.

Emergent properties are unpredictable. It is very difficult to understand the reasons behind an emergent property. They are realized after a group has agreed, on a functional basis, to work with each other. Once you understand this, it becomes easy to identify a group's emergent properties. Think of the groups in which you have been involved. What are some of the negative unexpected things that may have happened, and what emergent property is attributable to that unexpected occurrence? Was it a consequence of system-system interaction, or was it a consequence of the internal system elements' interactions?

	Unexpected Occurrence	Emergent Property Origin
Internal System Interactions	Example: We did not meet deadlines	Example: Time management loss due to overlapping and overreaching expectations
System-System Interactions	Example: Did not make desired impact with project	Example: Rules and expectations developed by the group did not match the rules developed by authority.

Internal system interactions are more controllable interactions. They are directly involved in your ability to efficiently communicate. These interactions will allow you to accomplish established tasks and goals. Within this frame, you encounter most of your growth and development. It is best to be open-minded when dealing with internal system interactions so that you may learn more from your group and best work to position yourself as a valuable addition to the group. The rightmost column in the exercise above for the internal system interactions becomes a list of the things you may want to improve, and also develop a vision for you so that you may be able to communicate value to the group.

System-system interactions require the group to be able to communicate efficiently. System-system interactions will, in the long run, define your value to society. These will allow you to accomplish your set purpose or Point B. In these interactions, it is best to keep your mind focused on the future. What is the overall value being contributed via your group? By pushing or pulling the group upwardly, you move yourself into the same direction. The rightmost column in the system-system interactions set are a few guidelines you want to make sure you are abreast of when approaching a new system. These are the nuances of the system. The more you learn about the nuances, the better equipped you will be to define your value within any specified framework.

How do you differentiate between internal interactions and a system-system interaction? The truth is there is no real differentiation because every level can be broken into smaller pieces. The line is drawn relatively in regards to complexity and simplicity. The more elements are involved in the interaction, the more complex the interaction becomes and most likely it will be a system-system interaction. For simple interactions that are usually bound to one step, these are most likely internal system interactions.

Authority: *"Always make those above you feel comfortably superior. In your desire to please or impress them, do not go too far in displaying your talents or you might accomplish the opposite – inspire fear and insecurity. Make your masters appear more brilliant than they are and you will attain the heights of power." (48 Laws of Power)*

A. **I must listen to others.**

Authority is usually very insecure because their power is either granted to them by a higher power or they apply an intense amount of their personal creativity to maintain their position. So, in the case of the quote, if you work to outshine your master or to make him appear foolish, then you will be penalized for it. Firstly, your boss will know not to trust you, and so he will relinquish you of any opportunity that may make you look better. Secondly, he will have his ego offended, and will seek to make sure that you are corrected for your transgressions. Finally, he will feel that the security of his authority is being threatened. These three reasons will limit your chances when trying to seek new opportunities. This is true for all superior-to-subordinate interactions. Reminding someone of their insecurities will assure your impending castigation.

In a group, every one possesses some authority. These three responses will occur if you try to outshine your group-mates, too. It will happen to a lesser degree, but a co-worker can do much to sabotage your chances of earning a promotion, and a classmate can directly thwart your attempt to make a classroom a comfortable environment.

The only way to really know authority, or co-workers for that manner, is to listen to others. Once you know who you are dealing with, you can then work to make authority and your group, seem more valuable. At the same time you must make them dependent upon you for their success. In that way, they have no choice but to give you accolades and promotions. The difference is that they will be happy to do so because you are helping them. This kind of bargain draws a fine line between black-mail and group interdependency. By securing your role on the team, the group will become complacent with your work and enjoy the energy you bring to the task. This is why your role should be fitting to your purpose. You should make yourself indispensable so that you have control over the bargaining chips. Never trade your integrity. If you are in the position where you are requested to abandon your ethics, then you do not truly have control over the negotiation terms, and it is best to try to create a new vision with which to begin. The objective is to fulfill your purpose with a win-win mentality. It is not to hinder the purposes of others with a lose-lose mentality.

If you are in the position of authority, it is important that you offer the group members a platform by which they can express their ideas and opinions. You should remind the group of the context in which they create, administer, and complete goals only after there has been an agreement reached about the overall vision and goal. Once you establish your role as a supervisor, one who "sees beyond", then they will feel as though your knowledge will complement their search for role definition. Listen to them and make good on promises.

Listen to the ideas and perspectives of your group and authority so that you may communicate visions and stories, and deliver your resources and creations to them in exchange for enabling you to climb closer to your overall purpose using win-win methods. At times, such sharing may become contentious. You should welcome discord as long as it furthers the team's movement toward synchronicity. By suffocating contention, such emotions will only sit and fester until someone is so uncomfortable that they lash out in a series of personal attacks or vindictive abandonment of pivotal tasks. The rules of contention should be clearly accepted by all parties so that the win-win method can be aptly applied. The most popular person in the room is someone who allows others to speak after clearly stating the rules of engagement.

Interconnectedness: *"As we continue to grow and mature, we become increasingly aware that all of nature is interdependent..." (7 Habits of Highly Effective People)*

    B.   <u>I must acknowledge all points of views.</u>

In group work, it is extremely important to acknowledge all points of view. This does not mean that you should accept them as true, but you should definitely acknowledge them. There are a few results to this:

Keeps your mind open to other perspectives to better construct your message- you can better understand the context of your vision.

Validates the mental dimension of your group- they do have value and should continue to work to provide it.

This process can be known as a team building process. Trying to force everyone to function with the same energy is very difficult, but exercises that help to make the environment more comfortable to share opinions will do much to create a group with an abundance of constructive emergent properties. It creates new opportunities for first impressions, lays out differences in an explainable way, and helps the group identify where the weaknesses are so that they may be improved upon or wholly avoided. Some team building exercises focus heavily on creating a fun environment for learning. This is very useful, but when the environment or topic changes, the team must adjust and actually learn within the new frame of reference. They start from scratch. In the Olympics, warring nations' citizens and leaders can be seen within close proximity to each other. On the world stage in front of the United Nations, however, reality sinks in and the camaraderie disappears. Inapplicable and simple activities are many times ineffective team building exercises. The individuals still part ways and most likely will not create a bond in purpose.

Some exercises focus heavily on creating bonds through projects. These are a bit stronger because there is a common objective involved in the activity that corresponds directly with the meaning of the group's existence. The group is encouraged to make their opinions vocal. Each participant is then able to determine the appropriate roles for each group member. Individuals in a group can only do this once they have established the value that each person is able to provide.

If you are in a position of authority, the best way to manage a team is to recognize the value that they bring. It is satisfying to the ego when someone feels as though they are offering valuable contributions to a group that is working towards a larger cause.

LP25: Influence

Make sure your supervised team feels as though they are using their talents to find the greatest contribution they can.

Grouping: *"When individual components in an environment come together to create distinct, collective and interactive properties and functions, the results are called emergent properties. These emergent properties do not and cannot manifest themselves unless an organism is looked at in its entirety." (Biology Textbook)*

C.   <u>A group is greater than the sum of its parts.</u>

You must train yourself to appreciate the whole picture. You cannot be limited to only seeing your success, but you must recognize how the success of others validates your position. The world functions with groups. Recall the principle of correspondence- that you can use smaller examples and extrapolate what may apply to more complex systems. If you have a great idea, you probably seek advice or encouragement from people with whom you feel comfortable sharing information. You then try to find people who will assist you in your efforts to make the idea become a reality. The same is true for others who are in positions of authority. They are seeking a group by which they can make something happen and are looking for a few individuals whom they can trust to carry out their agenda. If you act in such a close-minded fashion that you fail to see the successes around you and how you may latch onto one of the coattails through being a part of the group, then you will miss almost all opportunities that come before you.

When joining a group, you should not compromise your integrity. It is so closely tied into your life message, that once you have sacrificed who you are for some cause, then you will be viewed as a traitor to your craft. Eventually, your once admiring group will scorn you, and have no hesitation in letting you drown with a sinking ship. When you join a group, maintain your level of sincerity, and if there are communication issues, refer to your ability to engage in efficient communication. If you cannot elicit a designated win-win effect with the group, then the group's primary objective is not genuinely going to help you arrive at your purpose. Your ability to think using an aerial view is essential to leading a group, especially if the idea is your own. It is important to understand that each person in a room is not as valuable as everyone working together for a common purpose in a room. You must keep that in mind and do your best to encourage everyone to share their value by learning their stories and visions. If each group member enters a group with this mentality, then the group's work output will benefit.

You can accomplish creating this mentality by setting group work in this way:
1. Allow each person to introduce themselves and their background (field)- evaluate passion
2. Allow each person to identify their strongest skill and tell a story that exhibits that skill- evaluate value and method
3. Allow each person to describe the best project they have ever participated in creating- evaluate their standards

By the end of this exercise, you can begin dissecting the current project and set the group's expectations and process. You can use the results from the initial meeting to construct appropriate consequences for the lack of achieving a standard. By having consequences that align with the group's predetermined values and standards, you will create an environment in which scrutiny can be encouraged and clearly administered. The described meetings can be inscribed in the format below:

1. Agreement- Share larger mission and vision
2. Discord- Share opinions and incomplete ideas
3. Individuals- Disperse into smaller working groups to craft plans
4. Repeat

II. **When I expect greatness from myself, others will follow suit.**

Recall that chapter one discussed that followers mimic their leaders. They reflect the values and standards of their leaders. So, you can learn much about a leader by examining his followers. If you are

LP25: Influence

leading by example, then your followers will have something to compare themselves to and have a uniform system to adopt. In the case of group work, this is a significant aspect of the responsibility that comes along with being an authority figure. You must set and live up to self-prescribed and proclaimed standards. If you do not, your followers will be left to their own devices and a new leader will surface from amongst the group replacing your authority. If you maintain a healthy alignment with your standards, then your followers will respect you and be gratified when you commend them in their jobs.

As for working within a group, it is still important that you expect greatness for yourself, but it should be demonstrated, not proclaimed. Group members that speak too much about their standards appear insecure and arrogant. No one places confidence in them and most are waiting for them to slip and fall. So, know your place, and at all times exemplify greatness, but steer clear of triggering insults to the egos of those around you.

The relationship that exists between leaders and their followers can be mirrored in the relationships that exist between parents and their children. Children mostly learn from their parents. They view their standards, and watch how the world treats those standards. If a parent sets expectations that are too high for the child to feasibly meet, or if a parent betrays their own standards, then the child grows resentful and begins to challenge the parent. This holds true for followers. When a group sees authority as an untrustworthy figure that does not genuinely believe in their value, they become resentful and will eventually rebel against that leader. Similarly children should be obedient, exact, and self-motivated to create a role in the family. They are granted independence when they demonstrate responsibility and are in the position to take care of their parents. So, when followers demonstrate responsibility and take care of their leaders, their leaders develop a sense of complacency. Whether to their benefit or demise, the result is the same. You can determine what your idea of a good leader is by what you feel a good parent is. You can make your boss feel deceptively secure about his position by modeling how you feel a good child should act.

Capabilities: *"But (the other's) mind imposed on him the killing of his brother, so he slew him and became one of the losers. Then Allah sent a raven scratching up the ground, to show him how to hide his brother's naked corpse. He said: Woe unto me! Am I not able to be as this raven and so hide my brother's naked corpse? And he became repentant." (Translated from the Qur'an)*

A. <u>My standards become the highest standards for the group.</u>

The height of your standards will be the highest that the group's standards can be. So, if you have the lowest standards out of the group, then the highest grade of work the group will perform, will match only up to your standards. It is the least common denominator effect. This is why when establishing value for each team member, it is important to share individual visions so that a group standard may be created. Recall the image of a group of individuals harnessed to a boulder attempting to maneuver it uphill. If one of the harnesses is weakened or if one person is seated, then the entire group is adversely affected. There is rarely a super human who is able to carry the boulder on his own. If you encounter this problem within your group work, you should take the time, as a group, to reestablish the standards of the group. The standards should be explicit and mutually agreed upon.

As an authority figure for a group, never compare the elements of a group- at least not in front of the group. You can establish standards in front of them, but never compare them. Unequal appreciation is regarded as an insult to ego and security. When you offend both of these aspects to a person, you have created an enemy. As a person in authority, at times it may seem difficult to pretend that everyone has the same value. When you come across such a conflict, the best thing to do is to acknowledge a failure on your part to provide an opportunity broad enough for everyone to demonstrate their value.

As a group member, take personal responsibility for the group. How you work within the group will ultimately determine your societal value. If the group is focused on completing a task, be sure that the group is attempting to accomplish the task in a way that reflects your purpose and the purposes of each individual within the group. If this is not taken seriously, you will gain no real opportunistic value from the project and will limit everyone within the group. There are no shortcuts with real group work, just as there are none with excellence. If emergent properties are to benefit you, take the time to learn about each of the elements within the group: the group members. Emergent properties can also be identified as negative side effects. An emergent property simply requires elements that work together and elicit an effect that neither could accomplish individually. Your group can be engaged in a detrimental combination of activities. If you are not aware of what each one does individually, then you cannot safeguard yourself against the negative emergent properties. So, establish the standards of the group at the beginning by revealing visions and stories, and you can at least safeguard the group from the negative emergent properties that may appear.

You should be in tune with your capabilities. That comes from really knowing your visions. How you truly see yourself is ultimately how you will perform. This quote is in regards to the proper burial of an individual that was murdered. The raven acts as a messenger that provides instructions for what to do as the brother could not determine what to do on his own. The story is one of a man slaying his brother. When you think of a family, you want to imagine a group of individuals who unconditionally love and admire one another. They stick together and work towards a common purpose. The truth is that family members are considered family because you had no real decision in the elimination process of who your family consists of. They are connected to you by genetics, culture, lineage, raising orders, and in many other ways. Family is just as capable of providing harm to you as are others. Families are groups. Family members have the same insecurities and issues with developing visions and telling each other's stories as groups in the work world do. Family members hold secrets that eventually surface and erode the family's once established values. How you act within your family is a direct reflection of the best you will be able to bring to the world.

In the quote, the man was capable of being a loving brother but with the proper incentives to kill, he realized he was capable of the heinous act as well. Those incentives are the same reasons why you find vindictiveness, mind-gaming, and spitefulness within groups. Comparisons were made between the brothers, and so one felt pressured to be just as the other one was. The dejected brother was compelled to prove that he was of the same or greater quality of person, or choose to eliminate his competition. No one wants to be devalued, and as a figure of authority or a group member, you should not make a practice of it. Understand your concept of grouping within your own family. Realize your breaking points and the logical rationales that others use to justify their emotional decisions.

Promises: *"Be wary of friends-they will betray you more quickly, for they are easily aroused to envy. They also become spoiled and tyrannical. But hire a former enemy and he will be more loyal than a friend, because he has more to prove. In fact, you have more to fear from friends than from enemies. If you have no enemies, find a way to make them." (48 Laws of Power)*

B. <u>How I respect the deadlines will determine the amount of confidence I have in the group's value.</u>

A friend promises what he cannot deliver, and an enemy promises vengeance. When you respect and confide in your team, you do everything you can to prove yourself to them. When you feel as though your group has little to offer you, the response is to lower your own standards and expectations- these are friends who have gotten too comfortable. Enemies function for their benefit, and so they never fall into the trap of such joint complacency. They are constantly evaluating their competition and seeking ways in which they may overshadow or purge them. So, if you find that you are having issues with time-management tasks, then most likely, you have lost confidence in your team along the way. They provide no motivation for you to want to excel. This is why you see people completely disregard simple tasks or perform poorly in easy classes. They simply have not identified the value in them and thus subconsciously render it "beneath" them.

Time management-heavy tasks include reading, project coordination, writing, calling, and many others. Complete the following exercise.

Task You are Pushing	Skill Required	Authority	Missing Confidence in...

Once you have completed the chart, you should contact the designated authority and discuss the points in which you lack confidence. Confidence is self- construed, but the group is still involved in the process. In the initial vision building steps, they determined your value. So, the group members must be included in this reflective process. By starting from the root, you will be able to see these tasks easily completed. Preventing procrastination takes effort and it is necessary that you have confidence in the group you are reporting to or in the decision that must be made for the procrastination to disappear. You must identify what prevents you from wanting to complete the task. The answer is not laziness. It is usually some fear or unresolved issue at the heart of it. It grows into your lack of confidence in the group's value, and you begin to question your activities, standards, and visions. Identify these core issues early, discuss them, and then see a world of opportunity open up in front of you.

Sameness: *"Let us do evil, that good may come? Whose damnation is just? What then? Are we better than they? No, in no wise: for we have proved both Jews and Gen'tiles, that they are all under sin;" (King James Bible)*

C. <u>My views about life reflect the views people in my life have.</u>

Realize that you are a consequence of the many things that occur around you. Then, realize that the same is true of other people. You have no real ownership to your life because you did not give yourself life. You do have ownership over how it is carried out. When it says your views reflect the views that others have, it does not mean that you are identical to the people who have influenced you, or that you have identical beliefs, but it suggests you do reflect those beliefs. If you were never exposed to certain people or certain things, your outlook on life would be different than it currently is. If you were born to a Catholic family, it will influence you differently than if you were born to a Muslim family. If you were exposed to homelessness, then you will reflect the lessons learned from that encounter. You should take pride in all of your experiences, because others have not had them and will gain value in their lives by having you share them. It is your responsibility to do so. No one will share your story quite like you. Even biographers try to interview the person they are writing about. If they did not consult them or their writing, then they would surely misrepresent them and their experiences. One thing to keep in mind is that you are still separate from your experiences. A good leader understands this. A person may take in many influential factors, but will make decisions that are unique to whom they believe they are. This is why you can have two individuals go through extremely similar lifestyles, and conclude their lives at different positions.

Your stories and visions are a part of those creations that you carry as tools from Chapter 5. You share them, as described in Chapter 11. You use them effectively as described in this chapter. You use them when establishing standards for a group and then finally to prepare for the emergent properties because of the group's heightened awareness of itself. The quote implies that all individuals have their own opinions regarding ethics and process. To weigh one as greater than the other is a fatal group mistake. You can use efficient communication from Chapter 15 to administer a new vision, but you must understand everyone's point of view before embarking on a reprogramming excursion. Everyone has used their environment as a way to test their hypotheses on life, and consequently was either encouraged or discouraged by the results. Their mentors have offered them advice, and they too have filters set up through their four dimensions. They carry dreams and aspirations with them. You must believe that who you are truly does reflect those you have met and the same is true for others. If you immediately embark on a crusade and castigate people for not being as you are, then you have committed a major crime to the world. You have destroyed stories and visions. You can prepare for emergent properties by working with what is available within your group. Usually, it is more than enough. The proper incentives must be presented- unique to each individual. The penalties should align with group-determined values and standards. In this way, group process is enforceable.

III. **<u>A stronger group gets noticed.</u>**

To attract opportunities, it is important that you stand out. You must be conspicuous in your efforts so that opportunities may come to you. You must appear to be useful. Remember, if no one is impacted by your efforts, then the efforts are for naught. The stronger your group is in effort, the more that it will stand out. It will attract opportunities that correspond to the efforts. This is why it is important to be sure that the work the group commits to is related to the purposes of the individuals that comprise the group. So, by creating a standard for the group, you are creating group value. As you develop bonds through stories and visions, you grow stronger. Teams that work well together dominate over those that do not. Regardless of talent, if a team cannot set aside differences, mitigate uncertainties, and manage the project, then the products will be unfavorably affected. When a team accomplishes these things, it can remain convicted because its activities are guided intrinsically. Upon success, each participant is able to accelerate their purpose.

Groups that are strong are groups that people have placed value into. We place value into entities that we feel provide some benefit to us. When a group is able to make their ideas seem real and effective, people adopt them into their systems. The group must position itself by making its ideas as real and effective as possible. They must convince others that their ideas are truly the ones that should be considered. When presenting true ideas, there is a lot of competition. You must make your ideas more true to their cause than others if you are to gain the attention of an audience- be it your boss, or the world in which your entity functions. Your group must be willing to internally refine itself and externally define itself.

Just as reflection is needed in your own growth, the group must also reflect on itself and offer feedback through efficient communication. A group may reflect on itself by preparing a task list, and determining milestones. It may also do so by using the standards as a way to craft a rubric and gauge the team's potential. Each member can then grade the other members on their ability to work together and meet the group's standards. The team can then use those grades as a way to evaluate the current status and chart a pathway forward. It is great to use each of the scores to derive an averaged value for each person and the group's average value based on each individual. An example of some categories for establishing standards may be:

A) Deadlines
B) Time Management
C) Asking for Help
D) Motivation
E) Leadership
F) Attendance
G) Role Expansion
H) Communication

For each category, the group should carefully decide what each one means, the ranking system, and what each rank means. You can also prescribe solutions for each rank. Rubrics can become increasingly complex, but the objective should be the same. They should require your team to reflect on their current status, and track their progress. Going through this exercise will only strengthen your team and if done regularly, your team can be encouraged by observing how the rankings change over time, and as a group, you can tailor the group's assets and emergent properties. You can also use evaluative measures to apply some objectivity to the penalty and incentive consequences for negative and positive behaviors.

Unity: *"Would that I could be the peacemaker in your soul, that I might turn the discord and the rivalry of your elements into oneness and melody. But how shall I, unless you yourselves be also the peacemakers, nay, the lovers of all your elements" (A Spiritual Treasury)*

A.   Power is within a large, united group.

Strength can be noticed in a few ways. One of which is through authority and numbers. At least a 3:1 number ratio is necessary for a direct attack in numbers from one group to another. If you are trying to win against another through brute force, and not through stealth, then gather two of your friends, and confront your antagonist. In argument, have three counterpoints to every one point your opposition may present. He or she will either flee or surrender to your tactics. Triangulation works because it creates a closed polygon around a point of focus. In political triangulation, an adversary has nowhere to turn to rebuild their arguments. In business, if you seek the three most powerful individuals in an organization and allow each of them to have buy-in on your terms, then you are guaranteed access to the business. Movements are powerful because we are naturally intimidated by large numbers or people focused around a singular cause. If so many people believe one way, it must be true- truth established by numbers. In groups, it is important to make sure that you have numbers on your side.

Even if your group is small, its support should be broad and resounding. Your group can literally bully its way into new opportunities. When pushing an idea, the more camouflaged it is within known and accepted frameworks, the more support it will seem to have. Build support by winning small campaigns to increase your support network or by explaining your ideas with the justification provided or endorsed by other, more renowned figures. Naturally, we respond to broad support of an idea as a reason to accept the idea as true, and we value the entities that are able to describe and discern truth. Your group must be a truth providing entity. It must take its ideas from conception and place it within the contexts of what is understandable to the system. In doing this, you demonstrate value in your group and in the idea the group presented.

If you do have large numbers of people within your group, then they should work to propagate your message. In order to motivate them to do this, you must explain how their value is inextricably tied into the cause. You can do this by finding the common story within your group and using it as an example of your envisioned advocate. Once this is communicated, they will do most of the work for you. They will find avenues to make their purpose more recognized. You just have to provide the resources for them to use. Once repeated enough times as true, an idea becomes accepted as truth. Whether you decide to reference people, money, or resources, do not underestimate the effect of creating a façade of large numbers. There is power in numbers, and positioning your group for systemic success involves a careful evaluation of your numbers.

Success: *"The Nazarene was not weak! He was strong and is strong! But people refuse to heed the true meaning of strength" (A Spiritual Treasury)*

B.   Strength means triumph.

Another way for a group to be recognized for opportunities is to establish truth through success. While something may be small in size or stature, it can be positioned to be adopted by a system because of its history of success. Your group must provide value in its methods by sharing its stories. The archive of stories that your team has aggregated over the years can be used as stories for the group if your group has not yet created ideas or successes. A business plan's selling point to its investors is its management team. If the management team's stories seem successful and applicable enough, an investor feels confident in the team's ability to execute. Give your group value by digging into the stories of each team member, and by also collecting stories from the group's successes. There is much power for you to wield by having the biographies of the people who are on your team, and the previous success ascertained through the team's active methods.

When you demonstrate success, you have given credence to your ideas. In effect, you establish that the ideas you create are ones that should be admired and highly valued. Companies use their customer satisfaction data with previous products to sell new ones. Politicians speak on the positive highlights of their track record to convince voters that their assumption of greater power will yield positive results too. When communicating your triumphs, be cautious. It must be done properly to not create unnecessary enemies. When speaking about triumphs, offer credit and benefit to multiple parties. Those that hear your message will not feel strife against you, but will strive to one day also be mentioned on the list with others who have benefited or contributed to your group's triumphs.

Your team can be viewed as strong by adopting proven methods and demonstrating success. It can also be proved as strong by garnering a sufficient number of people to support you or at least create the image of wide-spread support. From each of these levels, your team will experience a myriad of emergent properties. If you spend the time to craft the vision of the team properly, taking into consideration everyone's purpose, and then by positioning your team to produce accepted results, everyone will be steps closer to their end goals.

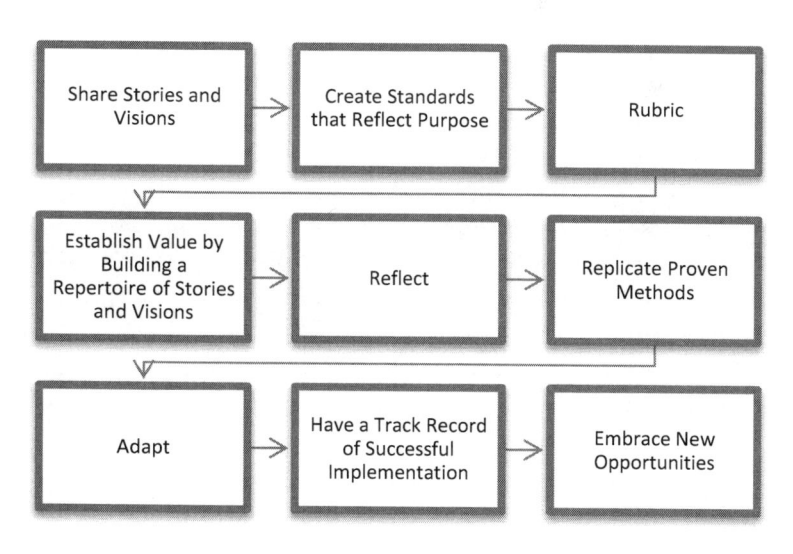

```
Share Stories and Visions → Create Standards that Reflect Purpose → Rubric
                                                                      ↓
Establish Value by Building a Repertoire of Stories and Visions → Reflect → Replicate Proven Methods
    ↓
Adapt → Have a Track Record of Successful Implementation → Embrace New Opportunities
```

Stress: *"Trouble can often be traced to a single strong individual – the stirrer, the arrogant underling, the poisoned of goodwill. If you allow such people room to operate, others will succumb to their influence. Do not wait for the troubles they cause to multiply, do not try to negotiate with them – they are irredeemable. Neutralize their influence by isolating or banishing them. Strike at the source of the trouble and the sheep will scatter."* (48 Laws of Power)

C.   The group is weak without me.

You are a representative of your group. Your group must not have weak links. You cannot be a weak link. Materials break at their weakest point. You must be flexible and connected in order to prevent such rupture. Competing groups will identify your weakest member and pour value into them so that they may change allegiance. Weakness is not limited to a measure of capability, as capabilities are expressed through sufficient incentivizing. Weakness is captured in vision determination. If an individual is distressed or unfulfilled by their designated roles, then they will become a weak component and will cause havoc within your group. If a member of a group is seen as weak, then the entire group suffers in its public relations. This is true for ethnicities, a country's ambassadors and citizens, company representatives, religious advocates, and many other types of grouping entities. Take the job seriously. How you behave reflects on everyone else, because innately, we understand that we are all influenced by our environments. So, when a child is acting rudely, most people assume the parenting was poor. This is true across the board. When you graduate from your college, other people believe they are interacting directly with your college when they interact with you. You cannot do much to bolster the reputation of an entity, but you can do much to denigrate it. Bolstering your group's reputation can be done through the previously mentioned methods of large numbers and recognized success. Never demonstrate group weakness unless you are seeking to be disdained by the larger community. In general, a group that displays its weakness can easily be taken advantage. In dealing with emergent properties, it is not good to display group weakness, unless the group is deemed to be too perfect and not secretive. A secretive group must always hide its weaknesses. There is no real value within a group that outwardly displays its weaknesses, although there is a form of marketing that can be extremely useful when trying to draw attention to your group. Such marketing activities may succeed in highlighting both your group and the competition.

All reflective work on weaknesses should be done internally, within the group, so that the environment is always conducive for sharing. If it is done outwardly, the emergent properties will most likely be negative- though on occasion some groups do get lucky. What are you currently doing to not be the weakest link within your group? How do you know when you are exhibiting weakness? When you do not take the time to engage in the process of making the team strong, then you are concurrently making it weak. Some groups just eliminate their weakest members, and it is an appropriate way of resolving the issue. Such actions may however leave hard feelings and spur up unanticipated competition. It is best to provide and repeat clear group standards throughout evaluative processes. This is not an activity limited to figures of authority. With such an evaluative environment, weaknesses usually weed themselves away. To limit the influence of negative emergent properties, you should either renegotiate the standards of the group or reflect on the perceived value of each member. If a member still demonstrates weaknesses, then the group's new idea, with which to make a strong idea, must be to remove or intentionally exclude the weak person.

You must now transition from thinking in terms of "I" to "We". Your group is your vehicle by which society will be able to establish your societal value. Leverage opportunities by preparing for emergent properties and the world will begin to open itself to your influence.

Chapter Seventeen

Necessary to Serve

The mindset you should have when establishing and executing a task is that the task is ultimately meant to serve some greater purpose. Every individual should employ this mindset in their team. Having the mindset of "serving" allows for certain creative elements to flourish and of course, for the identification of a specific role priming an optimal environment for emergent properties.

Necessary to Serve

Note: "Every man is the descendant of every king and every slave that ever lived." (Benjamin Franklin)

The idea that Benjamin Franklin was attempting to capture in the quote is the interconnectivity that we all have and the amount of uncertainty and chance associated with our origin. Someone in your lineage was the kind of individual you, at times, separate yourself from. There was also someone within your lineage that was the kind of person you are currently aspiring to be. There is no inherent greatness associated with your bloodline, but you must consider how your lineage affects who you have become. With the amount of chance interspersed in your call to existence, you must understand that there is value present in each person that is in existence. When you realize that your life could have very well been created in the context of wealth, and just as equally likely created in the context of poverty, then you can begin to value and appreciate the birth status of others.

Adopting a mentality to serve requires that you not only recognize your value, but the value in the opportunity to serve the purposes of others. You must appreciate your interconnectivity with others and the responsibility associated with your birth- conditions and influences. Your purpose does not exist in a vacuum, and the

LP25: Influence

experiences you have as you develop are meant to gear you to specifically pursue your purpose. The existence of others gives meaning to your existence. Pursuing your purpose without any real consideration to the amount of planning that has gone into your life is beyond careless. Each action you commit has a reaction that will affect the world around you in ways that are immeasurable. With such great power, you must take responsibility for your actions and engage in activities that are purpose-enabling for others. When you maintain an agenda as such, then you will find your purpose much easier to access. Other people who exist as gatekeepers and magistrates for resources will only open them to you if the resources are rendered usable to the benefit of all parties involved- not just you.

Servant leadership is a buzzword in many professional and academic circles and its overuse can sometimes dilute its impact. So when people refer to servant leadership, what exactly are they referring to? Can it be described in universal terms and can a process be attributed so that you may gauge whether or not you are enlisting yourself in servant leadership? What is servant leadership? What do you serve to others? Whom are you serving? These are all very important questions that will allow you to take your leadership –ability to make decisions- to the next level. Remember, the end of the transition phase lies in context of groups and systems, so bear in mind that the frame of reference for servant leadership is within the larger context of the connected world.

The operational definition for this chapter is below:

When one <u>serves,</u> it means to render assistance; be of use; help; to contribute to or to promote. The word finds its origin in the word "slave".

To be of use implies that you have utility. It implies that you can supply for a need, whether explicitly or implicitly. The use of the word "slave" breeds negative connotations. No one wants to see themselves as a slave to anything, but the origin of the "serve" is from "slave". So, it would be important to understand the context that slaves occupy. They were active hands to accomplish a predetermined objective. Slaves were not compensated by anything tangible, but were given the opportunity to live. A slave was usually a prisoner from a foreign country or neighboring nation in times of war. Slaves were used to build the foundations of many of the commoditized systems that exist today. They were assigned values based upon their skill or design and the application of their skills to the markets of the captor nation. So, even if a person were worth much in one nation, if the new nation that captured the person could not find a practical use for the slave, they were rendered worthless. Some would have to prove their worth so that the new nation could reinstate their value. The lifestyle of a slave was to be obedient to his value and his purchase designation. If the slave faltered from it, then the value would drop, and the slave would either be exhibited as an example or killed.

"Serve" came later and has more positive connotations associated with it. Serving indicates a bit more autonomy. Assistance is an option. The luxury of deciding to help rather than being forced to help is how people view the word "serving". With that, the meaning of servant leadership is leadership with the choice of assisting. There is no imperative to help, but it is expected. We describe leadership as an act of having the ability to make decisions. You can qualify your leadership based on the decisions you make: your decisions to act or not to act. When we create that dichotomy between slave and serve, the chasm is in option. When there are options to do bad or good, we expect a reward when we choose to do good things. As a consequence, servant leadership is a popular and meaningful term, and tends to spark many positive emotions and associations when referenced.

What, why, and who am I serving?

I. **I have a role, purpose, and design.**

In Part 2, the focus was about defining your purpose and appreciating every role you occupy. Much of what influenced your designated purpose was your design. How you act, think, and feel are all a part of how you see your purpose. Again, your purpose does not exist in a vacuum. So, when you think of your role, purpose, and design as a piece of the larger picture, you are creating a more accurate view of your playing field, as referenced in Chapter 5.

Just as a reminder: What was your determined role? What was your Purpose? What Forces and Focuses do you have? It is important to keep them in mind as you move forward in understanding servant leadership. Within the context of a group, you are liable for serving all three of these aspects to who you are.

Humility: *"Always make those above you feel comfortably superior. In your desire to please or impress them, do not go too far in displaying your talents or you might accomplish the opposite – inspire fear and insecurity. Make your masters appear more brilliant than they are and you will attain the heights of power." (48 Laws of Power)*

A. <u>I must serve my role.</u>

You have an obligation to your designated role. While it may be temporary, it is your responsibility to identify your role and then dominate it with everything that you have to offer. When you are serving your role, everyone who comes into contact with you will comment on your efforts. You will find yourself learning and growing daily in the process. You will only be able to grow when you humble yourself to listen to the advice and good will of others. Keep in mind that you are not only serving yourself, but the importance of your role. Serving your role consists of a few phases: identification, objective accomplishment, maintenance, and expansion. This process applies to both the context of the individual and an individual within a group of equal status elements.

Identification involves speaking with your group and sharing your stories and visions with the group in order to characterize what you will be able to contribute to the group. You must be actively involved in the process to create group standards and overall group vision. This process also includes helping others determine their roles within the group. The role is not described by tasks, rather it is described by personalities. Which expertise will you bring to the table, and what conflicts may arise from your personality in the context of the group? Most groups jump into setting objectives, and fail to really stimulate their group members when doing this. Identification is a very important step in group determination. When these factors are consciously voiced, precautions may be taken in order to prevent major hurdles down the line. Identification also involves rule determination. You must be well versed in the nuances (ethics) of the system in which you participate. So do not blindly offend people because of your ignorance of the system's customs.

Objective accomplishment requires a few steps. The group must understand a given task at hand, formulate objectives in order to accomplish it, and then execute. In understanding a given task, the group must work together to dissect a problem and then sort it according to each person's personality. This is when you can assign specific job roles to each group member. The team should then be tasked to "own" their specified tasks. If they encounter problems, the Identification stage should have expanded everyone's comfort zone enough so that all feel free to ask questions to clarify the group's expectations. The group should formulate plans to assist each role in its method of accomplishing their agreed upon objectives. This will keep the group functioning on a systematic level. Many great ideas get lost in the fact that each person functions in respect to their silo. By concurrently devising an action plan, the team can avoid such task myopia. The execution should take into consideration all of the information discovered during identification.

In maintenance, you must take time to reflect and ask for feedback on your role. You must be strong enough to accept the criticisms others will provide, and you must be flexible enough to adopt or adapt the advice they offer. In maintenance, you will also have to do the same for the other members in your group. When you are serving your role, you are committing to your excellence, and the excellence of others.

Finally, when serving your role, you must commit yourself to growing your role in meaningful ways. This does not imply that you should take over someone else's job, but you can focus on making your job more efficient and impactful. Do not attempt to grow your role to a point where you cannot manage it, but grow it at a pace that helps you become more fulfilled in it, and in a way that helps the group appear to be stronger, in accordance with the methods outlined in the previous chapter.

Motivation: *"And death on earth, to son of earth; is final but to him who is; ethereal, it is but the start; of triumph certain to be his; if one embraces dawn in dreams; he is immortal! Should he sleep; his long night through, he surely fades; into a sea of slumber deep; for he who closely hugs the ground; when wide awake will crawl 'til end; and death like sea, who braves it light; will cross it. Weighted will descend." (A Spiritual Treasury)*

    B.   <u>I must serve my purpose.</u>

Serving your purpose means you have firstly, designated a purpose, and secondly, focused your activities towards achieving that purpose. Recall that a purpose is broader than a role is. You should position your role so that once your group interacts with other systems, your purpose will begin to shine. When you intertwine your purpose with your role, you will notice an extra amount of motivation appended to your activities. You must keep in mind your life message and your focuses and forces. These will keep you immortal, and if you are serving your purpose within the context of a group, you are positioning yourself and your group for new opportunities. Aligning your role to your purpose takes some creative energy. You must be able to place your role into the larger context of systems and also into the context of your life. How will this role be viewed with respect to your entire life? If it were to occupy a chapter, what would be obtained from that chapter?

Since your purpose is determined within the context of multiple systems, when you serve your purpose, you are simultaneously considering those systems and the value that you may bring to them. You should find ways in which your role may serve as a stepping stone or incubator for the achievement of your purpose. In order to properly entwine the two, you must be well aware of what your role consists of and not pervert it to the point that you are no longer serving your role. You must be humbled to your initial agreement. On the other hand, if you are too concerned about your role and maintaining your role, then your ceiling will be your role.

Just as it is important for you to entwine your role into your purpose, it is important for you to exhibit servant leadership and assist your group mates to entwine theirs. It may mean reflecting on their stories and visions, and helping to draw a path for their success through objective accomplishments. When you are serving your purpose, you actively do this when working in your group. Make sure your mind is expansive enough so that when a time and opportunity are ripe, you can recognize them and either move your team towards the new opportunity, or accept moving to a new group where your value is more deeply explored.

Current Organization	Designated Role	Tasks	Created Purpose-Aligning Tasks

Uniqueness: *"My soul spoke to me and said, "The lantern which you carry is not yours, and the song that you sing was not composed within your heart, for even if you bear the light, you are not the light, and even if you are a lute fastened with strings, you are not the lute player." (A Spiritual Treasury)*

C.   I must serve my design.

You must be true to your capabilities. You were designed uniquely, and you should not try to overreach your abilities. Ask for help and work up to your expectations. It will encourage others to do the same. You should master the tasks that excite you and develop competency in supporting tasks. This means when in a group, you should clearly communicate your value through your stories and visions. Through these stories and visions, your group should be able to clearly identify your passions and know which tasks excite you. You were designed in a certain way and you must not pretend to possess skills that you do not have. Speak about your abilities that you are confident in and to their effective importance. While sorting objectives, do not give a task to an individual who exhibits no excitement for that task.

What is your design? Your design is the breakdown of your four dimensions. The next time someone asks you what your strengths are, you can answer them by going through each of the tiers and describing the relevance of each activity that encompasses that tier.

An example is below.

Dimension	Activity
Social	Impactful group work and communication
Physical	Writing papers
Mental	Determining trends and crafting solutions to problems
Spiritual	Noticing how these trends may affect the future of the group, we can prepare for the next wave of innovation. We are uniquely placed to position ourselves to be at its forefront.

This kind of description flows and helps to paint a picture for the audience or the other group members. It is unique to you and it describes the value you can bring both in full objectives and in supporting tasks. Practice becoming comfortable with your design, and then throw the ownership to a greater cause. It will alleviate any jealousies you encounter, and will afford you the authority that will be necessary to see a task to completion.

II. <u>As we serve, we understand a larger source of intellect.</u>

As we work to serve our roles, purpose, and design, we are slowly building a larger intellect. The larger intellect can be described as the collection of all resources available. It is the emergent property of such a collection. As we continue to serve, we grow this pool. Our creations, resources, and friends are added into this intellect. This source can be later accessed for the collections and used to further our services. As we help our groups, they also add to the growing collection of resources. When this grows, we expand our horizons and maximize our potential both as an individual and as the human race. The greater intellect plays an active role in our lives since we are constantly interacting with it. Every new concept you discover is added and archived for later. In Chapter 9, where roles were discussed, it was noted that your life functions on an infinite plane, which you can slowly discover more about. Serving your role, purpose, and design is the only way by which you will be able to discover more. You want this archive to be as extensive as possible so that you may ultimately achieve your purpose without lack.

Systems: *"But the masters, rising to the plane above, dominate their moods, characters, qualities, and powers, as well as the environment surrounding them, and become movers instead of pawns." (The Kybalion)*

A.   <u>The greater intellect allows us to maintain our current status.</u>

When you add your experiences and knowledge into the greater intellect, it directly begins to influence you. As you learn systems and the elements of systems, they begin to evaluate you. They begin to move you to where you can best serve your role. So, the comfort that you feel is purely a result of the greater intellect that you have established within your frame of reference. You are allowed to maintain your job, attend your school, and function in society to the extent that the greater intellect affords you. Without these systems at interplay, society crumbles, and value in the social domain is absent. With the inclusion of these systems, life becomes valuable and meaningful. As you are gathering experiences to include in the greater intellect, you should concurrently learn the nuances of that intellect so that you may be able to work in anticipation of how its systems will evaluate and place you. By taking such an initiative, you will gain more control over your plan simply because you can better prepare for the opportunities that you will be placed in. If you continue to live unaware of how factors influence your life, then you will lose any inkling of control because you will not be able to prepare yourself. Recall that preparation involves understanding and exhibiting maturity.

Understanding: *"The lips of wisdom are closed, except to the ears of understanding." (The Kybalion)*

B. <u>The greater intellect allows us to manage on the same plane.</u>

Ultimately, you will only be able to have intentional influence over the systems that you are able to add. You cannot intentionally influence what you do not know. When the quote mentions the lips of wisdom only speak to those that can understand it, it means that you are limited by what you cannot perceive or conceive. The aggregation of experiences that you will perceivably have will only consist of what you are able to understand. Your plane is expansive in directions that you can conceive. You will not be able to understand beyond these points.

While this may seem to be a limiting thought, recall that the greater intellect is completely accessible by you. You are able to interact with it, add to it, and share it. When working with a group, you must share your collections with theirs and the resulting growth will be in multiples. The more you learn about the greater intellect, the more influence you will be able to wield. Learn the nuances of what you do know, and you may discover some of the unknown unknowns.

Transmutation: *"This principle, by establishing the mental nature of the universe, easily explains all of the varied mental and psychic phenomena that occupy such a large portion of the public attention, and which without such explanation, are non-understandable and defy scientific treatment."* (The Kybalion)

C. <u>The greater intellect will complete your final image.</u>

As you are vying to reach your final destination, the collection of systems that are a part of the greater intellect will ultimately determine your final image in the eyes of society. Your image is comprised of your visions and your stories. It is your "life message". We all serve the greater intellect in different capacities and it this body of all experiences that influences your life in the respective manner. All things that are a part of this greater intellect are spiritual, mental, physical, and social in nature. It is comprised of all energies so you can access it to alter the energy of others. Beyond adding and sharing it, you can use it. So why must you serve? Only a servant will have access to the source.

III. I consider who receives my service.

So you have learned what you serve: your role, purpose, and design.

You have also learned why you serve: access to the source and control of the resources.

Finally, you must consider who you serve.

In serving, there must be a recipient of all that you do. It is important that when you are serving you keep in mind all of the recipients of your servant leadership. Usually this aspect is the sole focus of servant leadership, but as a good leader you recognize all of the implications to leadership and what it now means when you say you are serving. Something to keep in mind about serving is that even though someone is receiving your service, it may not necessarily be beneficial to them. Services are neutral. Even though they reflect your purpose, role, and design, there may be unintended effects for some. A new invention of yours may replace someone's job. Assisting the neediest of our society may only further their decline into helplessness because their position in society is reaffirmed by your actions. Be conscious of your services and know that with all of your services there are negative and positive consequences. For each positive service you feel you are administering, determine how it could adversely affect the recipients of your service. Once you break down the positives and negatives to a service, use your values to highlight your course of action. Once you connect those pieces, you can begin to become an effective, efficient, and intentional servant leader.

Service	Affected Group	Positive Effects	Negative Effects	Value Match
Role				
Purpose				
Design				

Ego: "*The soul is a newly developed element in Nature- and like other elements it has its own inherent properties. Consciousness, desire for more of itself, hunger for that which is beyond itself; these and others, are the properties of the soul, the highest form of matter."* (A Spiritual treasury)

    A.   <u>I receive my service.</u>

The first person to receive your services is yourself. Contributing to a cause through your own efforts is self-validating. It is a way of reminding yourself that you are fortunate because of your ability to decide to serve. You heighten your confidence in your abilities because alongside serving comes admiration-be it silent or vocal. You are providing value through your existence and this is why it feels good to serve others. You can appreciate the assistance you are providing because it becomes up close and personal. You also receive growth in the greater intellect and your understanding of it. Serving is a direct way for you to consciously acknowledge your capabilities and the conditions of others. Especially within a group context, you are able to see how interdependency works to create a product. It is a thrilling experience for your ego, and positions you to be closer to accomplishing your purpose as you are profoundly serving your role, purpose, and design.

Courting: "*The perfect courtier thrives in a world where everything revolves around power and political dexterity. He has mastered the art of indirection; he flatters, yields to superiors, and asserts power over others in the most oblique and graceful manner. Learn and apply the laws of courtiership and there will be no limit to how far you can rise in the court."* (48 Laws of Power)

    B.   <u>People receive my service.</u>

People receive your purpose, role, and design. It has a courting effect. People grow to rely on you and admire you because of your services. You should take the accolades and chalk it up to an uncontrollable urge to pursue what you were designed to pursue. When you use the term servant leadership, this where most people jump to immediately: How do I effectively engage in community service- the community needs me?

When engaged in traditional community service, you must definitely pay attention to the nuances. People like to know that you have considered their well-being in your engagement with them. They do not like to work harder than what seems necessary and they want to know that you are genuine about your efforts. This means your motivations must be pure when engaging effective community service. You must sincerely reflect on the activities you are about to engage in. Otherwise, your recipients will silently paint you as opportunistic and superficial. If your community service is only halfway thought-out, it will be evident when you leave. Recipients will feel insulted because you simply showed up to remind them that they need help. Your efforts will fade away as each day passes because there was no real help provided. Your friends, however, will admire you for being a model citizen and helping the needy. Do not use people as your pawn for establishing societal value. Instead, use people in their entirety. Learn what their skills and abilities are. Learn their stories and visions, and then determine the best way to help their situation. Some of our neediest are mentally trapped. They have been convinced that their designated role in society is to be needy. So, they optimize that role, and other efforts must be taken to help them find new roles. This is not to denigrate the value of community service, as it must be done, but next time consider where your energy is going and whether or not it is efficient usage of your valuable and powerful energy.

Outside of the traditional meaning of community service is a less traditional way of community service. Whenever you perform an act to the community whether you receive pay or not, you are serving your community. In the general context, you should be aware of the people who are affected by your actions, thoughts, and feelings. When you consider the consequences, you are actively serving your community. What are the positive and negative and outcomes to all of your decisions? People will attribute your value based upon the amount of community service you do. [This is why some people have high monetary value.] They offer a service that people have accepted as being something of great value. Many tend to complain about the salaries that professional athletes and entertainers have, but they neglect the fact that they contribute to the value that they have attributed to these individuals. Whenever you purchase a ticket to view a show or game, you are entering into an agreement. The service is worth the prescribed monetary value. They cannot be paid more than what is present within the system that they are a part of. Some systems are more lucrative than others, and that is a result of the hard work the participants have placed in establishing their system's value. No profession was ever paid a dime until they were able to demonstrate a value and convinced someone to agree with them. Systems participate in markets and transact their determined societal value. As a member of a system, you must take it upon yourself to provide something of societal value so that there may be transactions of value between your system and other systems.

Past and the Future: *"Every cause has its effect; every effect has its cause; everything happens according to Law; chance is but a name for law not recognized; there are many planes of causation, but nothing escapes the law." (The Kybalion)*

    C.   <u>History receives my service.</u>

Finally, the history of humanity receives your service. Every triumph you have and every person that joins you becomes inscribed into the visions and stories of others. Your actions will cause others to behave and think in a certain way. The entire chapter on effect describes ways in which you can have a direct effect on other people. Anytime you affect someone, it is written in our historical archives. It becomes a story that gets passed on to others. Not only will future generations gain from your servant leadership, your ancestors are validated by it. If you can imagine the past, present, and future in concurrent existence, then it is much easier to understand the relevance of such a statement. Their lives are immortal because they have shared their stories and visions with those around them. When their stories and visions meet yours, there is a certain validation process that society undergoes. This is why it is significant when we have our "firsts". There would be no significance in their triumph if we had no recollection of history. A 'first' would be just as significant an accomplishment as a 'last' because we would not have anything to compare. History allows us to verify value and progress.

Evaluate your value and progress by observing your actions with respect to the future and to the past. What will the future inhabitants of this planet have to say about your life? How did you affect the system you were a part of? What groups prospered during your time and which groups fell into extinction? Add perspective to your purpose and evaluate whether or not the world is better now than it was before. What are the reasons for such a transition, and how does your system affect it? Finally, how can you affect your system? Each level is an emergent property of the next. Contextualizing history is an imperative for servant leadership. When Martin Luther King Jr. embarked on his purpose, was he considering only the immediate future or did he inspire others with a vision for a future that only history could capture? When your mind is broad enough to ponder on history, then it will be ready when an opportunity is ripe enough to present itself for the taking.

Realize that your actions affect systems. These systems are manufactured as emergent properties of our history. So when you interact with a system or influence its value, you are directly influencing history. So the people who will come after you will come to know a system after you have modified it. If you wield no influence, then they will know it as it was before you ever came to existence. While the idea of systems in the metaphysical light is entertaining and definitely exploratory, the point is simple. Servant leadership yields results because of its focus. In servant leadership, you serve your purpose, role, and design to yourself, people, and history in order to grow the greater intellect so that purposes may be obtained.

Chapter Eighteen

Dalton's Theory

There is no empty space. This literally means no person is meant to singularly occupy space. Every person has a specific contribution to make and it should be valued when this contribution is discovered. This segment is an analogy prescribed by the scientific theory of Dalton.

Dalton's Theory

Note: "It explains that THE ALL (which is the Substantial Reality underlying all the outward manifestations and appearances which we know under the terms of "The Material Universe"; the "Phenomena of Life"; "Matter"; "Energy"; and, in short, all that is apparent to our material senses) is SPIRIT, which in itself is UNKNOWABLE and UNDEFINABLE, but which may be considered and thought of as AN UNIVERSAL, INFINITE, LIVING MIND." (The Kybalion)

The Kybalion focuses on the metaphysical interpretation of life, and with that comes an abundance of analogies. In light of how concepts that are true can permeate all through life, this chapter is meant to demonstrate how a theory, accepted as true on one level, can be applied to our social structures. Analogies are futile if you are not able to apply them to something outside of the comparison itself. In communication by voice, when you create analogies which exist on another emergent property level, you construct visions. The visions should give you a heightened sense of awareness and understanding so that you may make better decisions and better represent an idea that you desire the audience to receive. You must relate what is easily understood by your audience as an axiom to a more complex concept or manifesto by way of a true analogy.

Society is intricate and its ebbs and flows should be understood if you are to become an effective and efficient decision maker. All things that you envision may at some point join the substantial reality. Recall that visions originate in the mind and then manifest in the world. If society is constantly creating a substantial reality, would it not be wise to consider the underpinnings of society and increase your awareness of your socialization? You can use other analogies to accomplish the same goal.

In many cases, mathematical modeling is very similar to an analogy. You try to predict future information by making a model out of prior information. When you have a large set of data points, computers are used to analyze the data and construct a best fit equation that matches all of the points that are within a range of variance. If you try to fit a straight line to a data set with only one point of data, the options are countless. If you want to fit a polynomial to data that only consists of two points, you will find that to be quite difficult too. However, when you fit a line to two data points, you can then extrapolate to predict what other points may fall onto that line, and thus predict future data. Projections and data analyses are derived by a more complicated version of data fitting, but the concept is primarily the same. Can you use a sample set of data, model it, and extrapolate to configure future data? Imagine that with an analogy, you are attempting to find rhyme and reason within your set of data points so that you can predict what may occur in the future and prepare for it.

The operational definition for this chapter is below:

A <u>theory</u> is the analysis of a set of facts in their relation to one another. It is an elaborate hypothesis assumed for the sake of argument or investigation.

Theories are used for and created by investigations. As you add to your greater intellect, you begin to manufacture theories as to how you should conduct your life and demonstrate your societal value. We take great pride in our ability to do both of these. This is why mentors can be courted by promising that their lives are validated through your successes. They can be convinced that you are an apprentice of theirs, and that their value is attributable to yours. Each person is a bundle of theories interacting with systems. This book is a representation of multiple theories sewn together so that many are able to evaluate its credence and meaning.

In this chapter, we will focus on developing a corollary using Dalton's theory. Dalton's theory is with complete regard to the composition of matter. The opening quote relates the metaphysical properties of matter and reality, and Dalton's theory deals with the physical properties of matter. Since people all take up a considerable amount of space, and create an emergent property called society, we will use Dalton's theory on matter to metaphorically provide a list of guidelines to the working elements within society.

How does Dalton's Theory Apply?

I. **Dalton's Theory: All matter is made up of extremely small particles called atoms.**

Concept: Society is made up of pieces called individuals.

All of matter is comprised of individual building blocks. In our case, society is a system made up of smaller segments known as individuals. When you insult a system, you are concurrently insulting the individuals that make up the system. When you affect a system, then you are affecting the individuals within the system. Just because the system is an emergent property of the pieces does not mean you are not affecting the individual pieces. So, when you think of the systems such as those that deal with politics, business, law, technology, entertainment, and religion, you are really referring to the individuals that comprise the system. This is why these social systems vary from culture to culture. The systems reflect the core ideals of the culture that they are a part of. Each person represents a part of the whole system. They function interdependently to create their systems. By themselves, they may not exhibit the defining qualities of the system, but en masse they create the system as an emergent property.

Reflect on the systems you participate in. Who are the individuals that drive the system? Who are the ones that simply receive it? When considering materials, there are some atoms that influence the structure of the material more than others. Keep in mind that the atoms that make up matter do not have to be identical. Different atoms exist and function conjointly to create more complex matter. Society can be seen in the same light. People of different elements- energy states- are able to influence society differently. Complete the exercise below:

Systems you participate in:	Drivers of the system:	Your current contribution:

Systems can include the country in which you reside, your culture, religion, profession, family, or interest group. Individuals occupy space. Individuals, as do atoms, have properties and all coexist to the manifestation of what we can understand to be society.

II. **Dalton's theory: All atoms of a given element are generally identical in size, mass, and other properties. Atoms of different elements differ in size, mass, and other properties.**

Concept: All individuals of a given energy state are generally identical in activity, effect, and other characteristics.

In chemistry, atomic states vary by vibration or energy. Interacting atoms at differing energy levels can result in materials that exist in solid, liquid, gaseous, or plasma state. When people occupy similar energy levels, either through emotions, countenance, or actions, then they are similar to one another. A person consumed in anger, whether tall or small, rich or poor, will display identical characteristics. They will elicit almost identical effects. In the analogy, your energy is your element. People can be grouped and classified as "predictable" by these elements. What are the different energies present within your groups? When you can identify the different energies, then you will able to group your teams more intentionally to yield the results you may want. Such differing energies affect how they connect to one another.

Treating individuals as representatives of their element is one way of being able to properly identify their role within your system. Just as atoms can be altered and tend towards the lowest energy level possible, people can be altered in energy and usually tend towards their comfort zone.

How do you identify different energies? Companies use interviews and tests to identify high potential candidates. The description "high potential candidate" indicates a certain amount of growth potential. How willing you are to exit your comfort zone is a great indicator for your growth potential. In chemistry, this is your electronegativity, radioactivity, or ionization energy- an atom's susceptibility to alteration. You can also determine someone's energy level through speaking with them and learning where their insecurities are.

Which element are you in? If you wish to alter your energy state, you can do so by reflecting on those who you aspire to model yourself after. In your attempt to model them, you will actually adopt their world views and begin to behave as they do. If you only reflect their personalities, then you will only superficially assume their energy level. It only becomes genuine when you have identified with their experiences and use their motivations as your own.

You can identify your potential by completing the following exercise. For the first line, indicate how you feel about your current workmanship. For the second line, list how you could improve that feeling and add value to it. Continue to do this until you cannot think of a new level.

| Energy Level 1 |
| Energy Level 2 |
| Energy Level 3 |
| Energy Level 4 |
| Energy Level 5 |

When someone asks you about your weaknesses, respond by indicating what you will do to raise your personal expectations as based on the above exercise. If everyone in the group completes this activity, then you will all be able to ascertain what specific steps should be taken to improve the group's value and better channel your group's emergent properties.

III. Dalton's Theory: Atoms cannot be created, or destroyed.

Concept: Individuals cannot be created nor destroyed.

Because people leave lasting effects on systems, their stories and visions are never truly erased. They may not physically continue to exist, but people continue to live through their lineages, and life messages. This portion of the analogy does not consistently work within the physical dimension. Technically, one could argue that atoms had to have been created at some point- whether as a result of energies merging or through some other method. However the story may go, individuals, for the sake of understanding society, cannot be created nor destroyed. They can only be rearranged.

In the context of group work, it is important that you do not strive to eliminate a person. Their ideas will never truly go away. For every idea you attempt to stop, another identical idea will appear in the form of another individual. Value the presence of the individuals you are exposed to. They bring special value to systems, and if you take the time to understand their potential, then you will be equipped to help steer the emergent properties in a way that benefits you and your group. The idea of permanence is true for system interactions, too. All of history can be concurrently

LP25: Influence

witnessed around pockets of the world. This is why the increase in accessibility to technology is so intriguing. It plays into the analysis of any system you partake in.

In the case of a business, imagine a company identified as a competitor. Your business can choose to affect their business, or attempt to eradicate it through acquisition and subsequent phase-out. The result of the former is the inability to reduce the potential of an identical company's surfacing as its replacement. If you are to acquire a new company, be sure to incorporate its practice and employment philosophies if you are to truly "outcompete" it. It is a numbers game, as described by the section delineating between a strong team and a weak one.

In government or foreign policy, the situations are even more nuanced. After an enemy of the state has been identified as a threat to national interests or security, these individuals are usually found to be supported by networks and archaic, persistent, and contagious ideologies. With such support, the eradication of the shepherd simply means the sheep will eventually seek and locate a new shepherd in his place whether by consequence of other systems or by personal volition or vindication. Whatever the compelling mechanism may be, they will be easily swayed because it was not the person they adopted, but the ideology that the leader had embodied. They will seek his shadow. Win-win mentality would incorporate the elevation of these followers who have rendered themselves to be flock. To expose them to more robust and confluent influencing systems (culture, logic, duty, and emotion), the support network can then be open to accepting a new ideology.

IV.   **<u>Atoms of different elements can combine in simple, whole-number ratios to form compounds.</u>**

<u>We say</u>: <u>Individuals of different states can unite en masse in order to form complex systems.</u>

How are most organizations structured? Usually, they are structured around the concept of a pyramid. There are people at the top who manage the organization, and there are those that build the support for the system. An organization that has too many managers usually topples over. So, for every manager, there should be so many support-developing workers. This type of structure goes well beyond our organizations and actually reflects the structure of many of our systems. Structures will be explored later. We give such complexity the name "bureaucracy". People of differing determined societal values- usually a result of energy- come together to create structures. These structures have associated emergent properties because they reflect the culture of the individuals that partake in them.

The special thing about groups uniting is reflected in the analogy. When atoms of differing or identical elements join to create a substance, it is then granted greater meaning, and the presence of emergent properties is evident. The substance has a role to play. Elements provide some value, but it is in their combinations that you can create an infinite reality of resources. Consider the elements you put together. If you place someone who operates purely from motivations derived out of fear with someone whose motivations reflect hope, what is the result of the combination?

When making investment decisions, you should be able to clearly identify the levels of organization involved in your investable entity. If there is any confusion in role determination or objective identification, the entity is likely to fail. The team should be well aware of its vision and stories in order to better define roles and set purpose aligning objectives. The compound, not the elements, in the end, matters.

V. **In chemical reactions, atoms are combined, separated, or rearranged.**

Concept: In pursuing unity, individuals will be exposed to forces that combine, separate and rearrange them.

When atoms combine, they consume and release energy. In the case of groups, they accomplish the same thing. Finding the most useful

LP25: Influence

arrangement of individuals involves separating them, combining them at different energy levels, and rearranging their energy levels. All processes will yield different emergent properties.

When people are placed together, they experience tension. Unity is not a consequence of identical people wanting to do identical things. Unity is a process that involves effort and leadership. It involves creating a vision that is adhered to by all parties. Making this vision workable requires tailor-fitting the personal weaknesses and strengths of the party. They are individual elements working in different manners to accomplish an agreed upon objective. Individuals can be combined, separated, and rearranged to find the best way to achieve unity. Why would a group want to achieve unity? Unity makes a group appear stronger (larger and validated). If you are to propagate positive emergent properties and utilize them effectively, position your team accordingly.

While trying to actually achieve unity, a group will experience pressure that works against that objective. If you wanted to leave a lasting effect on a system, simply do one of the three: Exert pressure on the system by introducing a new element, separating the system in a divide and conquer fashion, or rearrange the system so that it is no longer recognizable.

Introducing a new element can be caustic because at some point, most groups become comfortable in their established arrangement. This is why most chemical reactions do not occur spontaneously. If the reaction were spontaneous, then it would have already occurred in the system before you arrived. You must provide energy to begin the chemical reaction. When you are introducing a new element, you are adding a new energy amount and structure that will force the system to buckle into adaptation. The system has to identify the value of the new element and rearrange itself if it wants to continue to function in the way it had before or naturally succumb to a change. Examples include strategic hires, products, espionage, new technology, and change in location.

If the system is separated, this can cause a chemical reaction. Recall that systems have interdependent natures. When part of the system is courted away- could be done through your service provisions- then the remainder of the system must quickly recapture its full function with only a portion of itself. This is very hard to do. That is why a company in a transition phase is at its weakest point. They are most likely to buckle in order to survive. During a transition, be sure to cover your bases. Be able to answer "why" and have a plan with built in evaluative measures and moments.

If you are pressured to act quickly, set in motion concurrent short term and long term plans. Expediency is never a great argument for justice, but there are momentous and unpredictable occasions by which you must employ your gut feeling and witticisms. Do not gamble with your opportunities- calculate the inherent risks. If you have the option to welcome additional information without further worsening a serious predicament, then wait. Parse your words. If you do not have such a luxury, then make a bold decision, and have your subordinates evaluate it privately for crisis management and causation. Have another group drafting the expected repercussions. Once the moment has subsided, be in the process of developing the long-term plan that includes and begins with the expected results of your gut-decision. You can safeguard yourself from the situations that leave you cornered by constantly expanding your knowledge of systems and community of actively sought mentors and mentees.

System rearrangement is much more difficult to accomplish. You must be in an influential position or have access to one within the system in order to accomplish this, but it is the most effective. In a rearrangement, all positions feel new and the system will have a definite change. The other methods result in more incremental changes, whereas system rearrangement affects the psychologies of those that partake in the system. Examples of this involve training programs, acquisitions, mergers, or a rebranding process.

You may argue the merits of the methods of this analogy in system alteration, because in all cases "energy" is technically being introduced for the "change" to occur. This chapter is not meant to present a debatable case, but to discuss the more topical interactions that are occurring when toiling with systems. In essence, rearrangement involves "adding a new element" and so does divide and conquer, but the discussion relies on the prominent action and not the technically argued action.

Sun Tzu describes these conquering or change-inducing methods in more concrete detail. You can also create a straw-man or booby trap by which all blame can be projected into a process or inexistent entity. The booby trap involves truly identifying with your audience and knowing their next moves so that you may cater to their individual psychologies. Recall, you can identify the energies within a system by building rapport with the individuals that comprise that system. Once you can identify their energy, you can extrapolate and make predictions regarding those individuals' behaviors. You can match their energies because you practice the mirror effect and then you can best figure what combinations of those individuals will move a chemical reaction from unspontaneous to spontaneous in order to yield results and materials that carry value and work for your servant leadership. No person was meant to simply occupy space. Each person is equipped with qualities and combination proclivities. Each person must respect their design as explained through the analogy provided by Dalton's Theory.

Chapter Nineteen

Aggregate Resources

This chapter is based on the Theory of Abundance. It is a mindset that the world is infinite and that much of it is a matter of trade. The possessions of an individual continue beyond his or her familiar environment but incorporate the entire world as the market. It is a difficult concept to grasp and put to practice, but many successful people simply believed it and so their limitations were much fewer than those who did not.

Aggregate Resources

Note: "Work on the hearts and minds of others. Coercion creates a reaction that will eventually work against you. You must seduce others into wanting to move in your direction." (48 Laws of Power)

As you continue to pursue purposeful leadership, you will accumulate many resources. There are several ways to do so. There are three main recognized methods: by force, by flattery, and by chance. When deciding on how to best handle your resources, it is important to have a perspective on what the resources actually are and how they are transacted. As mentioned in Chapter 5, resources are one of the tools that you need for your journey. Resources can make your journey more efficient, or they can present burdens if they are defective or weighty. When procuring resources, it is best to convince the gatekeepers of resources that sharing their resources will benefit them. The quote references "speaking" to the hearts and minds of others. This simply translates into communicating hope. Everyone possesses desires. By promising people the fulfillment of their desires, they will grant you access into their vaults.

Realize that resources are emergent properties. As described in previous chapters, resources originate as creations of others. They are firstly created in the mind and then manifest into a substantial reality. It takes some craft to know how to properly manage

LP25: Influence

resources. Many books have been written that use the skill of intricacy to explain where a king should place his infantry or how an investor should diversify his portfolio. Some are explicitly written for human capital managers so that they can shape their companies for maximum profitability by reducing the operational costs. Time is also a resource because we have applied constraints and measurements to it. As a consequence, books will venture into lengthy dissertations regarding the proper way to apply time management skills. The objective of this chapter is to prepare you to become adaptable so that whichever resources you obtain will be useful rather than burdensome.

The operational definition for the chapter is below:

An <u>aggregate</u> is the collection of units or particles into a body, mass, or amount

This chapter is entitled "Aggregate Resources" to reflect the exact mentality that you must possess when attempting to achieve your purpose. "Aggregate Resources" is based on "Abundance Mentality" in which the world consists of ample amounts of all things for everyone. This kind of mentality supports win-win mentality, and will leave you in a state of full responsibility for your possessions and circumstances. You can no longer blame systemic issues as your excuse for diminished performance. Believing that there is enough available for everyone is motivation in and of itself.

Psychology check: What are your apprehensions associated with this mentality? List five of them, and in the following column, attempt to evaluate a manner by which you can circumvent the limitation. Then, you may proceed.

| Reason 1 |
| Reason 2 |
| Reason 3 |
| Reason 4 |
| Reason 5 |

So how do you recognize where resources are? In previous chapters, resources have been described in many ways. You must define what resources are necessary to accomplishing your purpose, fulfilling your role, and supplementing your design. Aggregate resources are another form of groups. Just like all other groupings, resources abide by the same rules. They can be subverted through divide and conquer, combination, and rearrangement. There is strength in numbers and success, and possession of defective resources will only lead to your demise. Every resource must be evaluated and considered for its function. If resources are inappropriately used, then the emergent properties from their usage will be negative.

You can evaluate them by the energy they bring. Money is a great example of a resource with a lot of energy. Since resources possess energy, their energy can be diminished, increased, or maintained. It takes energy to change energy. They ebb and flow and express polarities-the traits of energy possessing entities. They can be understood via analogies. The resources you directly interact with supply you with a certain amount of energy. Finally, resources cannot be completely destroyed or created. They can only be transacted from one form to another or from one location to another. They can be restructured to provide more value or increase in impact, but they cannot ultimately be fundamentally created nor destroyed. No idea is absolutely new. Ideas are recycled and viewed from different perspectives, and these perspectives are infinite.

What are community resources and how do you leverage them?

I. **There is nothing you do not have access to.**

Firstly you must come to realize that all resources are accessible, it just takes craftsmanship to design the right keys. By believing the opposite of abundance, you are functioning under the scarcity mentality. Scarcity mentality results in the participation of a zero-sum game. Basically, if you are gaining, then someone else must be losing. Zero-sum does not take into account emergent properties. It also can prohibit the pursuance of a win-win mentality. It supports a win-lose mentality, in which if you win, then the other person must lose. While this is a mentality that can be very beneficial, it limits your creativity. It becomes harder to expand your role for efficiency because your problem solving focus is not geared in that direction. It opens the opportunity for people to identify and target your role as a prominent leader. If the person doing the analysis is the "loser", they will seek to influence and cause harm to you. A win-lose mentality will accomplish objectives, but the chances of it being a creative or novel approach will be slim if present at all. A win-win mentality, however, compels the user to be creative because everyone must positively gain after the encounter.

A win-lose mentality is very useful when vying for success in the business world. There are competitors, a limited market, and increasing compliance demands. It is natural to revert into a win-lose mode when building a monetary or financial empire. The alternative mentality, however, demonstrates that there is an unlimited market as long as the value is properly administered. It contends that the competition is not really competition, but a potential partner in developing an extremely powerful oligarchy. As a matter of fact, some of the most powerful businesses utilize each other in order to ensure their success. While in some respects, they may be competitors, they are coordinating to a certain degree to maintain their relevance. The trick is to woo all participants into wanting to be a part of your resources so that they may have access to you and you may have access to them. You must demonstrate value to be a part of such a group. Many times we feel angst towards large businesses, but realize, they are only large because they have demonstrated remarkable value and worked to develop strong ties with gatekeepers. Imagine if the most innovative companies ceased to innovate. If they did so, the result would be a lose-lose situation for consumers and corporations. Therefore, both parties work to support each other. Corporations provide items of value and consumers provide a pump with monetary energy flowing through it. Both parties must work to communicate with one another.

When seeking resources, you may only directly manage a few dollars, but within your community there is an abundance of resources and many people who are anxious to share their resources. You must determine which resources you need and then find ways to obtain those resources. If it is money, there are probably billions within your city. If you need people, there are plenty of people who are available, seeking jobs or volunteer opportunities. The list goes on for all resources. If you need time, there are ways to maximize your efficiency by delegating your obligations to others who may be more proficient or through creating a new task management process. Realize that all resources are available and accessible to you. You are tasked with understanding how to retrieve them. It begins by understanding the way in which resource transactions occur.

Transaction: *"Everything flows, out and in; everything has tides; all things rise and fall; the pendulum-swing manifests in everything; the measure of the swing to the right is the measure of the swing to the left; rhythm compensates." (The Kybalion)*

A. <u>All things in the world exist as physical expressions of energy. Ownership is temporary.</u>

The fact that ideas manifest into a substantial reality, a physical entity, has been amply referenced. In a mentality of abundance, it is imperative that you understand the meaning of this statement. Thoughts and actions reside in the energy state and when they become creations, they become the resources of others. Resources flow from one location to another. They occupy the hands of individuals at different energy levels, and are used in the way that the individual deems as a best fit. Resources circulate just as energy does. No one owns resources indefinitely. They are meant to change hands in order to continue to propagate value. In this way, the entire world can be seen as a marketplace. Time, money, land, creations, and many other things are constantly being traded back and forth to provide a specific value. With regards to being a purposeful leader, resources are obtained to meet the objectives of a purpose. What are some of the resources that you need in order to progress your idea further and add to the growing pool of abundant resources?

One of the hardest aspects to obtaining access to resources is in identifying the gatekeeper. Many people desire to claim more than they may possess, and so they will compel you to chase a mark that is actually nonexistent. You can best identify a person's position and resources by having them share their visions and stories. They will reveal their accessibilities. Note their body language when sharing. Then, ask questions that pertain to the system that their resources are a part of. They will reveal the story of their participation. If they are able to answer, then they most likely are the gatekeepers. If they can only partially provide some information, then it implies their position as a gatekeeper has minimal impact, and there are other, more influential parties involved. The process is:

1) Vision
2) Story
3) System Application

Services	Needed Resource	Location of Resource	Gatekeeper
Role			
Purpose			
Design			

When trying to understand a gatekeeper, you must communicate *to* them a few things:

1) Value
2) Abundance
3) System Knowledge

Gatekeepers are participants of systems. You must demonstrate to them that you acknowledge the nuances of their respective systems and then court their confidence by demonstrating value and growth. It is not enough to communicate that you will provide a maintenance service; most gatekeepers are assured that they are able to accomplish that objective on their own. With a mentality of abundance, you must demonstrate that you can make more out of less.

Value has two aspects to it. There is intrinsic value and there is societal value. Intrinsic value is immutable, whereas societal value changes as quickly as the second hand on a clock. When communicating value you can demonstrate intrinsic value in the purpose of the idea. Purpose is accessibility-centered while mission is activity-centered. When demonstrating societal value, you must use stories that validate the purpose. Does society appreciate the idea for its purpose? If not, what do they appreciate? The answers to those questions are what the gatekeeper attempts to determine. For example: Supplying computers to all children of developing countries has the intrinsic value of increasing those students' accessibility to the world. The societal value involves the cost-benefit analyses. Societal value may also be expressed in terms of interacting systems. While purchasing computers for students may not recover its costs directly from students or the educational system, it may result in the expansion of the economy of that country, which affects the world's economy.

With regard to abundance, the gatekeepers want to believe that they are doing the most with their resources. Whether or not people are positively affected is an added benefit, but the most important aspect is to be able to communicate the other sources by which your idea will attract a larger pool of resources. An abundance of resources is attractive for a few reasons. The primary reason is that an abundance of resources affords options. People like options, just as serving connotes more positive emotions than slaving. It also indicates a certain amount of a comfortable increase in efficiency. When you are able to grow the value of your resources, then you become more comfortable with the process that is allowing such an effect. The same is true for gatekeepers.

Finally, having system knowledge means speaking the language, knowing the system's protocols, and sharing insight in productive processes tailored for the system. When you are able to do this, you have provided proof that the other two are possible. Each gatekeeper has their own way of viewing systems and value, so it would benefit you to make mentors out of identified gatekeepers.

The transaction appears like this:

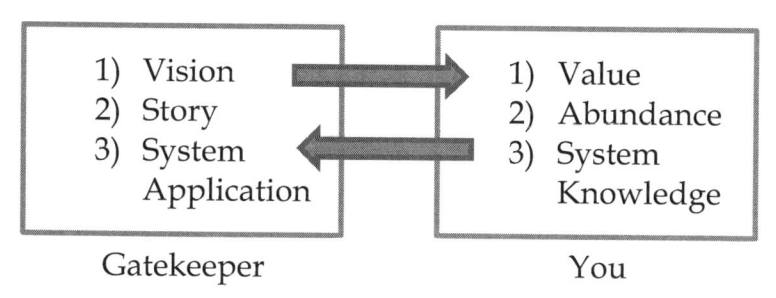

Gatekeeper	You
1) Vision → ←	1) Value
2) Story	2) Abundance
3) System Application	3) System Knowledge

You must compel the potential gatekeeper into revealing their true authority.

Energy: *"But the Masters, rising to the plane above, dominate their moods, characters qualities, and powers, as well as the environment surrounding them, and become Movers instead of pawns. They help to play the game of life, instead of being played and moved about by other wills and environment." (The Kybalion)*

    B.   <u>All emotions in the world exist as circulated causes and effects.</u>

You will have to deal with emotions when handling gatekeepers and accessing resources. If you are to maneuver as a mover, then you must accept responsibility for changing the energies of your gatekeepers. They must feel comfortable around you. You can accomplish this through your energy and your voice. The previous section describes the subjects of your communication, but you must present the entire package. You can easily route the best path to influence your gatekeeper by recognizing the cause and effect nature of resources. Because all resources are translocated, the gatekeeper had to have obtained their resources from someone or somewhere. Their energy was also recycled. So, you have the ability to transmute both the gatekeeper and his allowances. How he feels about his resources are only a consequence of his life experiences. You can create an illusion for your gatekeeper wherein his deepest and most selfish desires are attainable, but only through you and your visions. The illusion you craft must be related to the resource of desire. The gatekeeper will only allow you to access what he feels you may comfortably utilize. If you create an illusion that references a resource that you do not desire, do not expect the gatekeeper to read your mind. By creating the illusion that it is only attainable through your efforts, the gatekeeper will be compelled to lower his guard and trust you and your expertise. The energy he will exchange with you will no longer be strained, but boundless to the full extent of what he has to offer. Keep in mind that energy states are not fixed. They may be altered, and you have the capability to directly influence the energies that exist around you.

What are the aspirations of the current gatekeepers and how could you craft their illusions?

Gatekeeper	Desires/Wishes	Aspects of the Illusion	Administering the Illusion

Ordainment: *"And he said to himself: Shall the day of parting be the day of gathering? And shall it be said that my eve was in truth my dawn?" (A Spiritual Treasury)*

C. <u>All people in the world exist as cyclical fulfillments of purposes.</u>

The propagation of resources is a self-fulfilling prophecy. Gatekeepers who obtain resources are most likely replicates from the gatekeepers that held the resources from before. This is because as you pursue a purpose, you focus your efforts to engage with certain systems. You seek resources within those systems, and then the next generation appears and approaches you for the same resources in order to fulfill their purpose. They are seeking your resources because they are in line with their purpose. You should view everyone who is drawn to you to seek your resources with respect. Chances are that the encounter is not by accident, and they are very similar to you.

Knowing this, there is much you can learn from those that have served history within your system. You can learn the traits and values of gatekeepers before and anticipate the traits and values of the gatekeepers to come.

It is also important to understand that gatekeepers are not occupying purposes, they are occupying roles. Roles are constantly being turned over. As new people move throughout a system, roles are assumed by new individuals. When you are trying to access the resources that a gatekeeper manages, then you are accessing that role and developing a key that is unique to the gatekeeper. Roles have new replacements all the time, and while the gatekeepers are similar, they are not quite identical. You still have some work to do in order to develop rapport with the gatekeeper and woo him into entrusting his resources to you. Just as you meet a new vendor whenever you visit a department store, so will you meet new gatekeepers when you identify the resources you wish to pursue.

Current Gatekeeper	Previous Gatekeeper	Similarities	Differences

II. **There are ways to collect and allocate everyone's resources.**

Obtaining resources requires a specific set of skills. You must know how to seek them first and then you must know how you can effectively aggregate them. You can place them into systems, people, or objects as a way to store them. The instructions you leave with them will ultimately determine how they mature while being stored. If you place money into a savings account, you will see that it serves to maintain societal value because the growth is usually tied to match inflation rates. If you place your money into an aggressive investment portfolio, then you will see that it serves to amplify the societal value. Neither may actually happen, but the intention behind what you do with your resources will determine the kind of gatekeeper you are.

Once you have resources, you must leverage them to actually perform the necessary duties to grow closer to your purpose. An example of an investment portfolio that yields annual returns of +10% shows that your money can grow. However, simply having money sitting in a vault does not put it to energy-propagating use, but it may bring value for future use. At the point of sufficiency, you can begin to administer resources in ways that will position you and your system to increase its value. Your resources must be used at some point. Effective allocation is a skill that takes time, mission, and power to develop.

If you have communicated value to a gatekeeper, then you must exhibit that value. You must expand your system knowledge and maintain a mentality of abundance so that you may apply all of your creativity to your resources. As you demonstrate an ability to manage resources, others will be drawn to you either to request your resources or to manage their resources. Distinction comes along with apparent efficient resource management, and with distinction comes more resources. If you do not know how to manage your resources, then eventually future opportunists with no will to generate abundance will take advantage of you. You must be an effective gatekeeper for your resources. This does not mean you create obscure and impenetrable barriers for its access, but it does mean that you create learning opportunities for those who truly want to engage and benefit from your resources.

LP25: Influence

Take an inventory check of your resources before progressing:

Resource	Description
Money	
Time	
Land	
Creations	
Ideas	
Stories	
Any Other	

Prediction: *"Control the options: get others to play with the cards you deal. The best deceptions are the ones that seem to give the other person a choice: your victims feel they are in control, but are actually your puppets. Give people options that come out in your favor, whichever one they choose. Force them to make choices between the lesser of two evils, both of which serve your purpose. Put them on the horns of a dilemma: They are gored wherever they turn." (48 Laws of Power)*

A. <u>Spread an idea in the form of "joining the collective".</u>

Use your methods of predicting people to assume the influences of their decisions- culture, duty, logic, and emotion. Then, give them options that are imbalanced to favor your win-win purpose. When you are collecting resources, it is very important that you approach the gatekeepers with a structured framework on what to offer. Trades should appear to be even and binding. You can accomplish all of this by creating an option that "benefits all". If they join you on your crusade, then they will be positively affected or known for standing for a cause. When using the joining the collective mentality, each person must be persuaded through the lens of their main influences- culture, duty, logic, or emotion.

By using this method, you allow yourself more flexibility than simply coercing or stealing for resources. "Joining the collective" forces you to consider the well-being of the gatekeeper. If done correctly, it also grants you unlimited access to the resources without the fear of subversion because the gatekeeper now has a vested interest in your success. Using the concept of "joining the collective" involves identifying and understanding your mark, approaching your mark, and proving potential to you mark.

When allocating resources, joining the collective can be just as useful. This mentality helps everyone who has access to your resources feel a sense of responsibility for handling them properly. They feel indebted to you because you have granted them access. Imagine how you would feel if one of your mentors gave you access to his resources after negotiating with you- you would feel liable for their usage. Negotiation is very important when allocating resources. Some gatekeepers freely serve their resources without this step, and the recipient feels as though the resources are not that important- otherwise, they would have been harder to gain access to. We regard items that are difficult to obtain as more valuable than those that are easy to obtain. So, you should make it difficult, and educational to obtain your resources.

So the break-down is as follows:

Collecting:

Identify and Understand — Approach — Proof

Allocating:

Identify and Understand — Approach — Negotiation — Proof

Differentiation: *"Get others to do the work for you, but always take the credit; Use wisdom, knowledge, and legwork of other people to further your own cause. Not only will such assistance save you valuable time and energy, it will give you a godlike aura of efficiency and speed. In the end, your helpers will be forgotten and you will be remembered. Never do what others can do for you." (48 laws of Power)*

B. <u>Use hierarchical distribution.</u>

Specifically when allocating resources, you must set assignments for them. Everyone cannot use all of your resources in the same way. It is important that each resource be distributed through a channel so that it may be useful and not burdensome. By trying to multitask and manage all of your resources, it is certain you will unintentionally misuse some of them, and others will linger and go to waste. The mentors and mentees that you have can take temporary ownership of some of your resources and manage them. Your efficiency will increase, and you will not be limited to giving all of your resources to one system or individual. Use distribution channels that are already accepted by society or create organizational structures to administer your ideas/ resources. You can maximize your effect by doing so.

Refer to your inventory of resources and try to identify new gatekeepers for each resource. Then, associate objectives with those resources so that when you delegate those resources, they come with clear directives. This is how gatekeeper roles are established. They must manage a particular set of resources. Without clarity in their role, your gatekeeper will frivolously exercise use of the resources and avoid being held accountable for their misuse.

Inventory Item	Objective	Potential Gatekeeper or Role Design

You can use this when establishing a business, managing your talents, or upon taking up a new job. If you do not use hierarchical distribution, you will find that fulfilling you role will become too difficult. As a matter of fact, that is one way that you can tell when you should consider delegating a resource to someone else. If you are behind schedule or missing deadlines, then chances are you have bitten off more than you can chew and should either relinquish a resource or share part of the responsibility of a resource.

For some, they simply do not have more resources, because they have convinced themselves that they could not handle them. So they engage in activities that shrink resources instead of grow them. Once you have constructed a plan for how you can allocate resources, you will then be able to successfully seek them. Otherwise, you will lack confidence in your management process and unconsciously avoid obtaining the resources. Resolve these fears by expanding your knowledge of systems and developing a plan for resources that includes avid system knowledge. You will find resources begin to flock into your possession because you recognize them and have increased your own utility.

Desired Resource	Gatekeeper	Fear Associated with Gatekeeper	System

Reflection: *"Think as you like, but behave like others. If you make a show of going against the times, flaunting your unconventional ideas and unorthodox ways, people will think that you only want attention and that you look down upon them. They will find a way to punish you for making them feel inferior. It is far safer to blend in and nurture the common touch. Share your originality only with tolerant friends and those who are sure to appreciate your uniqueness."* (48 Laws of Power)

    C.   <u>Express group energy and you will not make an incorrect move.</u>

Finally, when managing your resources, there is the possibility that you may lose them. You can lose them because you have no valid plan for them, or someone with a win-lose or lose-lose mentality pilfers them from your influence. The best thing to do when approaching gatekeepers and potential gatekeepers is to reflect their energy. It is the surest way to build rapport with them and identify their insecurities. When you are aware of their foundational mentality and weaknesses, you can then develop options for later employment. Within the context of a group, you can blend in by speaking their language, expressing silent contempt for what displeases them and vocal adoration for what they love. People are attracted to and trusting of others who are similar to them.

When reflecting energy, never mock your group. It will make your efforts seem disingenuous and will probably enflame them. Also be careful of what you repeat. If you repeat something that may later be used against you, expect that it will be the case. So, even though your co-workers may engage in insulting a boss, do not actively participate. Such remarks can later be used against you. Instead, reflect the same energy. That, in fact, you are displeased with your boss without ever actually stating it. If you disagree with the group, do not appear judgmental in your voice or in your energy.

If you adopt this when handling and collecting resources, you will not make an error that will cost you the opportunity afforded by them. If all else fails, copy the methods of the person who has successfully applied it. Your efforts will not go unnoticed and people will still keep their confidence in you.

So, we function in a substantial reality in which ideas are manifested as resources. Resources are creations of others and they should be collected for your use to serve your purpose, role, and design. They are the emergent property of the energies that make up society. You can supplement your efforts with resources to improve yourself, your team, and your system. In order to collect them you must build rapport with gatekeepers, the holders of resources, by demonstrating value, system knowledge, and the "Abundance Mentality". You can use the "joining the collective" method to accomplish all three. Finally, once you have resources, you must allocate them. You can effectively do so by constructing hierarchical systems, managing channels of resources, and by reflecting the sentiments of those that comprise the hierarchical structure.

Chapter Twenty

The Whole Picture Part 2

This chapter focuses on your reflection of everything discussed in previous chapters and prepares for the next theme. Try to get a good look at how you are working within all of your groups and how those groups play their roles in society.

The Whole Picture Part 2

Note: Complete the exercises in groups if applicable.

Theme 1: Dreams of the Goal

Chapter 1: Roles of Leadership

What do you expect to accomplish as a leader?

Which of your activities do you deem to be effective?

What defines your leadership and what is your "final destination"?

Chapter 2: Moments of Leadership

> *What moments in your life have shaped your leadership?*
>
> Most exciting time:
>
> Subsequent conclusions:
>
> Worst Experience:
>
> Subsequent Conclusions:

What are your main influence factors?

Duty   Culture   Emotion   Logic

What current obstacles do you face?

Description (motivation of obstacle)	System	Objective if obstacle were absent

Chapter 3: Dimensions of Life

What is your focus? What do you want to change in all dimensions?

Dimension	Productions	Motivates production?	Results
Social- What is the value of the fruit, testimonies			
Physical- The description			
Mental- The Design, how well does it work			

Chapter 4: Win-win Mentality

Under which circumstances do you find yourself reverting to a win-lose or lose-lose mentality? Why?

What restricts your practice of win-win?

Time   Resources   Circumstance Nuance

Can you work around these?

Chapter 5: The Future

What are your tools, and who are your friends?

Resources
Creations

Mentors
Mentees

How does your purpose look from the ground? How does it look from the air?

Ground	Air

Theme 2: How Do I Play a Role?

Chapter 6: Who Am I?

What are you limited by?

What is unique about you?

What skills/talents do you possess?

LP25: Influence

What is your new set of circumstantial blessings?

Which prejudices restrict you?

Who influences your perceptions?

Perception of...	Bad Influence	Good Influence	Operating Prejudice
Role			
Design			
Purpose			

What do you believe about your limitations?

How do you feel about your current circumstances?

What events have shaped you?

What is your purpose?

Chapter 7: Concentrate Your Forces

Which intersection did you identify?

How are you preparing for the proposed dangers? (3 ways)

A)
B)
C)

How are you preparing for the proposed achievements? (3 ways)

A)
B)
C)

Chapter 8: My Life Message

What content do you feel is in your life message?

```
┌─────────────────────────────────────────┐
│                                         │
│                                         │
│                                         │
└─────────────────────────────────────────┘
```

Who has negative opinions about you? What are those opinions? Why?

Individual	*Negative Opinion*	*Reason*

Are any of these things you would like to change?

Can you work within those frameworks?

Individual	*Influence Factor*	*Hologram*

Chapter 9: The Plan

What is your Point A, and what is your Point B? How do they compare?

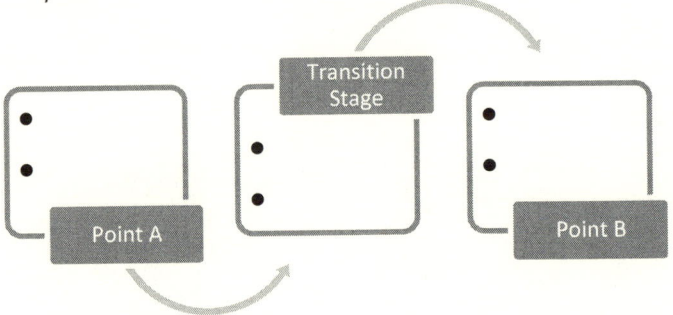

How are you preparing yourself for the transition?

Chapter 10: Responsibility

What are your responsibilities? What influences your responses?

What are some of your values?

What are your ethics- priority morals, in addition to the "standards of leadership"?

To eradicate a bad habit, you can subconsciously condition yourself by completing a "+/-" chart with your presumed positive and negative traits. By repeating the exercise daily, you will find that your mind will begin to try to refute what you enlist as a negative. It will attempt to counteract it and develop goals.

Positive (+)	Negative (-)

Theme 3: The Transition Stage

Chapter 11: Internal to External

> *What are you trying to communicate and why?*

Chapter 12: Voice

> *What would you like to improve when it comes to your voice? What do others think of your voice?*

Chapter 13: Energy

> *How do other people feel around you? What "vibes" do they get? How do you want people to feel in your presence?*

Chapter 14: Communication

> *Try to tell a story to someone. What process did you use to convey your story? How effective was it?*

Chapter 15: Effect

Tell another story to someone and decide on a specific reaction you would like. After telling your story, did it compel a reaction from the person? Was it the desired reaction?

Theme 4: And the Whole Puzzle- Emergent Properties

Chapter 16:

What do groups accomplish?

Current Groups:	
Name: Description- purpose of group: Designated role: Weaknesses and strengths: Reason for participation:	Name: Description- purpose of group: Designated role: Weaknesses and strengths: Reason for participation:
Purpose you serve through participation in both:	

Chapter 17: Necessary to Serve

How do others feel about your participation? What do they feel your motives are? Are they correct?

How do you serve your role, purpose, and design?

Role

Purpose

Design

Chapter 18: Dalton's Theory

What are your groups analogous to?

How can the analogy be used to help you better understand and position them?

Which groups require new energy in your surroundings?

Which methods (separate, rearrange, addition) should you use to supply the new energy?

Group	Method

Chapter 19: Aggregate Resources

What resources are within your vicinity that are necessary for me to serve yourself, others, and history?

What are your responsibilities?

Which resources are difficult to manage? What systems are they within? What channels do you use?

Resource	System	Channel

LP25: Influence

How can you relieve some of your pressure?

Once you feel comfortable with your answers, it is time to move into the next theme, Community Activism which is about actually accomplishing the goals you set and achieving your final destination.

Part Five Introduction

Community Activism

Community activism is about being effective in your environment. This theme is primarily self-directed. It is mainly comprised of activities which require the context of your current initiatives. There are some pointers to consider for each of the chapters, but they are simply meant to provide guidelines for you to develop your own plan and purpose. Your concept of community activism should be broad enough to encompass both voluntary services and paid services. You have the freedom to engage in a multitude of different activities, but you must be able to recognize your inherent and potential societal value, and utilize and develop it accordingly.

Now that you can appropriately handle emergent properties that come alongside working within groups and systems, you can tailor them to actually accomplish something. "Community Activism" is the final stage of the entire series which included thinking in terms of the big picture, analyzing your role, translating your thoughts to the outside world, and gauging emergent properties.

At this point, you have yet to accomplish anything. You have created theories and identified gaps, but now you must act. Your environment is awaiting your action because it is interdependently structured. It is relying on you to bring your purpose into the substantial reality. So, you must visualize your end product and apply it throughout the next five chapters.

Those who think and do not act are just as useless as those who act and do not think. Imagine if our greatest innovators, workers, philosophers, researchers, rights advocates, and others, harbored all of their creations. What world would you live in? How could you possibly achieve your purpose without the others who have vivaciously fulfilled their roles? They did not let their limitations hinder their progress, and neither should you. You possess a certain amount of greatness that others are curious to experience. Let that internal light shine brightly by being well prepared to complete the beginning of your journey to truly effective and efficient leadership

LP25: Influence

with a purpose.

For the next few chapters identify a project of interest. The project may be a group project or event, a new company, an innovative idea, a volunteer project, a traditional community service project, or a research project. You can complete the exercises vis-à-vis your project and by the end you should have a plan for the resources you need and be well on your way to making the project a reality. Use the skills from previous chapters to supplement your efforts in this section.

Chapter Twenty-One

Differentiation, Purpose, and Talents

As mentioned before, each person in a group has a specific role and much of group work is involved in discovering those roles. This segment states that there must be a separation of roles in order to prevent confusion and promote responsibility. Use your designated project as the context for this chapter.

Differentiation, Purpose, and Talents

The operational definition for this chapter is below:

Differentiation involves becoming distinct or specialized; acquire a different character.

When assigning your resources, differentiation should be an integral prerequisite. Crafting a hierarchy can help to sort where some resources should go and how certain roles should be defined. Differentiation is a process that humans have been employing for a long time. When we were primarily an outdoor society, there were hunters and gatherers. Each individual assigned to a group was responsible for their role and most were assigned to roles for which they had a design affinity for. When creating a structure for your project, you must keep in mind that if the roles are not fit to the talent of the individual being assigned to it, then you will probably experience rapid turnover in that position because neither party's expectations will be met. There must be enough job specialization that the person assigned a role can experience autonomy and not have to be concerned about their competitors. By doing this you can keep those that work with you content and focused on managing their resources.

LP25: Influence

What structure best accommodates your project?

The Pyramid. The pyramid is the most common form of hierarchy within social systems. It is easy to understand and manage. Those at the base support the system, while those nearer the top manage and direct the support system. There is clear stratification in a pyramid as support members usually identify well with other support members, and management identifies with management. Note that, for more specialized jobs, this trend may not be as evident. In programming or engineering divisions, managers will communicate frequently with their support staff.

The base is usually concerned with short term objectives and adaptations while management is concerned with long term trends and strategic decision making. There is a transitional group in the middle in which there can be ample amount of job crossover and uncertainty. Metaphysically, pyramids are used because they are strong. They do not bend or conform, and are steady and massive structures with a secure center of mass. Organizations that exist in this framework are easy for other systems to recognize. Since it is a recognizable structure, most either make contact using a top down approach or they try to erode the pyramid by eating at the base. So, for ease of interaction and implementation of a strong identity for an organization, the pyramid is the structure of choice for your project. The pyramid is a weighted-decision model.

The Sphere. The sphere is used to a much lesser degree. The sphere is superior to the pyramid in that it has the ability to retain its shape while still being flexible. In this structure, no one person has any real power over the next and it truly exemplifies the idea of organizational interdependency. A sphere can only be attacked because it is an infrequently used system. So, most are confused when exposed to an organization with such a non-existent hierarchy. Boards utilize a spherical structure. All of the members are equal in value, but occupy distinct roles. Boards are usually appended as external entities of the pyramid structure of business. Stratification is not evident in spheres. Implementing new processes and making internal changes is very difficult in the sphere. For consistency and avid group think, the sphere is a likely candidate.

The sphere is a consensus- decision model.

The Cube. The cube can represent two kinds of organizational structures.

On the one hand it can be a simple cube with only a few faces. This is exemplified in some sole proprietaries. It is steady as a pyramid is, but there is no differentiation between roles. Everyone works towards the same goal regardless of job overlap. Implementing new internal processes is not very difficult in these systems. Organizations do not usually plan to be simple cubes, but will inadvertently become them. If you are seeking to grow in scope or revenue, and you find that your current project is "cube-like", then it should undergo some changes. You should invite an external person into the organization to inspire new ideas. Hopefully he or she can whittle some designated roles for individuals in the group. The simple cube is a singular-decision model.

On the other hand, the cube can also represent a very complicated organizational structure, such as the Rubik's cube. This involves a complex series of checks and balances that work their way through a system. There are many faces that are very specialized and at times overlapping. The government may appear to be a pyramid, but it can also be seen as a complex cube. There are groups that serve as checks and balances for each other within one line of command. When introducing all elements of the government and the election process, you eventually find a system that is very stifling and predominantly focused on incremental changes. Shedding dead weight or finding new talent becomes an overbearing task because no one has ultimate say, but everyone has a say and is accountable for one another. The complex cube is very difficult to erode and is able to keep a constant hold on resources. It is inefficient when implementing rapid and comprehensive changes, and must be exposed to a lot of pressure in order to do so. Organizations do not usually begin as complex cubes, but evolve into them depending on the interactions with other systems. The cube is a weighted and consensus-decision model.

LP25: Influence

What is the structure for your project/ organization?

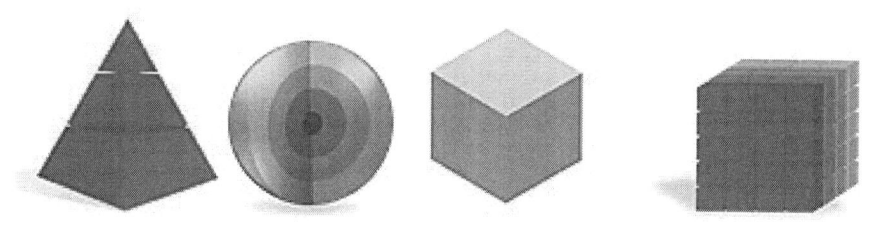

Purpose of Project:

Structure:

Reason for Structure:

Designated Roles	Tasks	Skills	Resources	Gatekeepers

Differentiation is very important when attempting to achieve community activism. You must have a structure that complements your organization's or project's objectives. You can extend the list of roles as you continue, but try to identify at least three specific roles above.

Achieving community activism…

I. The collective can only exist when the individuals commit to the greater vision.

The people that occupy your designated structure can jointly be termed the collective. In order to have them participate in the structure, they must be committed to a greater vision. The vision is the way you describe the purpose of the project. What is the vision?

If the project were to achieve everything it was created to achieve, what would it look like?

What would the community look like?

How would you be affected?

How would others be affected?

How would history be affected?

Once you have clearly defined a vision, you must make sure that the other involved individuals are committed to it. You can do this by having them envision their role within the larger picture: the vision of the project. When everyone is not on synchronous pages, it sows internal seeds of discord. Eventually, some will feel compelled to rebel against the vision because of their lack of commitment to it. To prevent premature implementation of a structure, share the broader vision with each person. Also, encourage them. You must develop a culture that stresses interdependence. Let them build and design their desired roles. Have a candid conversation about the needed resources and skills. This will allow everyone to justify, for themselves, their appropriate role within the organization. You will have more responsible members of the organization. Purpose does not change, but roles do. People are equally capable of identifying roles within the group that best benefit them and the group. If you allow them to set the terms of their roles, then you have just created a loyal member in your organization.

> A. <u>The commitment involves a sense of self-acknowledgment.</u>

Engage your team by allowing them to craft their own roles based on their talents and individually determined long-term goals.

Recruitment. Identify the kind of person you want to fill in the roles and then target them. You can target your audience by making your project take the form of an entity that your target audience would 1) recognize and 2) identify with.

> 1. Recognize: What are some similar organizations or projects? How are they structured? What are their objectives? What have they accomplished in the past? What is your differentiator? What is your target audience's most used mediums of communication?
> 2. Identify: What stories and visions are common amongst your target audience? What does you target audience hope to gain, in general? How will your project or organization meet that demand? Where do you find your target audience?

Use the space below to answer these questions for your project.

Recognize	Identify

Formal Interviews. Your objective in a formal interview is to construct questions and scenarios which will help you determine if the prospective team member is a good fit for your project. You have the opportunity to share the vision and story of your project, and gauge their reactions based on energy and voice. For your benefit, identify individuals who predominantly use the win-win mentality. This is so that you may manage emergent properties as a gatekeeper. You can discover this through asking questions that insert an ethical dilemma. Also, gauge how motivated the potential member is by the questions that are asked. Are they interested in their role in the company/project? Are they interested in the vision of the company/project? Create some formal interview questions.

Questions to ask to learn win-win:	Questions to tie into vision of project/ organization:
Questions to identify voice:	Questions to identify energy:

If you are placed within a group, and have no influence over the assortment, then it is still necessary to craft a group vision and determine how each person fits into the objectives of the project.

Informal Interviews. Once a candidate for a role is chosen for that role, you should meet in a comfortable environment and have a candid discussion about the skills necessary for a job, and how that person plans to achieve developing those skills and the capacity to which they would like to contribute to the group. You can help them by asking questions about their tools and friends.

Leading questions about role:	Leading questions about project/ organization vision:

Questions about friends:	Questions about tools:

B. <u>The commitment involves self-responsibility.</u>

Ensure that every team member acknowledges the importance of other team members by creating a culture of interdependency.

System Flow. Everyone who partakes in the project should know the systems that they are interacting with. Providing flow charts for team members indicating process is important. These are created by you, but developed organically as members begin to find a rhythm with their tasks. By keeping the system flow updated and meaningful, you can prevent many administrative processes from slipping under the radar or becoming redundant. Technology can assist in this pursuit. Using your predetermined roles, try to create a representation of a likely way your system may flow.

Rubric. The organization/ project should be subject to some form of consistent evaluation. The rubric should consist of categories that all members have identified as important. Rubrics are where incentivizing can be applied: perhaps there is a monetary gift when objectives are met, or keeping a job instead of being fired. Other incentives include items/ events that satisfy other group member desires. These incentives can be determined by learning about each person in the informal interview.

What are some measurements that your project or organization needs to take to observe progress?

What do your members care about/ want as a reward?

Transparency. An organization that internally circulates information about its members is an organization that will have members who are concerned about how responsible they are. If a meeting is called after every incident, you can be sure that incidents will infrequently occur. Public humiliation is more subtle in the current world, but it is practically the same as when transgressors were placed in a public square to be criticized and admonished. Politicians and prime executive officers suffer via mass media. Transparency affords the same thing. Perhaps for smaller groups, a metaphorical "hot seat" may accomplish self-responsibility on the part of group members. No one enjoys having their ego bruised.

    C.   <u>The commitment requires leadership.</u>

Provide opportunities within the project's purpose that will compel your members to make decisions. Be sure that the vision of the project is so clearly defined that they are able to exercise some autonomy.

Idea Contribution/ Meetings. Meetings should be held in environments where everyone feels comfortable offering contributions. You can add props and incentives to the meeting to get everyone thinking. In order to encourage the active participation of every member, you can assign everyone to give a presentation during a following meeting.

II. **Community activism is achieved through an effective, efficient, and purposeful collective.**

While you may think you are the only individual who is affecting change, keep in mind that there are many supporting elements to being able to accomplish that change. You must acknowledge the involvement of all participants. If you start a company, you have utilized the resources of the government, other companies to provide you with your supplies, and individuals to help you efficiently position it. Community activism is only accomplished through the efforts of the collective, so you must recognize and expand your interdependent role within the collective so that it may grow stronger.

A. **Each individual must be aware of his/her strengths.**

Enroll yourself and your members in professional and leadership development workshops so that they may be encouraged to continue to challenge themselves. Also, draw conclusions from the rubrics so that everyone can align their activities with the direction of the organization/ project. Attach objectives and plans to your assessments. In addition to the rubrics, find individuals with experience to speak to the new members of the project/ organization. This will encourage them to strive harder because an investment has been made in them. Finally, creating a mentorship program will allow your members to adapt to the project/ organization culture more rapidly.

Books	Mentors	Mentee Programs	Workshops

B. <u>Each individual must define for himself or herself the vision that he or she finds for his or her legacy.</u>

Be sure that every member has a vision for their role. They will work to pursue this vision as long as they are given the space to do so. Differentiation works best when each person feels autonomous, but has specific, clear, manageable, and meaningful objectives, and a framework where support may be requested. It allows people to gauge themselves and feel comfortable with accountability because they have established mutually recognized standards. If you are in a position to delegate tasks, be sure to give tasks that are meaningful and important for the success of the organization or project.

What are the key milestones for your project/ organization to be successful? Let your team decide which milestones appeal to them and have them create plans to accomplish those milestones.

C. <u>Express group energy and you will not make an incorrect move.</u>

Enforce a project/ organization culture by explicitly describing the desired work environment. Everyone can participate in adding to this description.

Safety	Ethical Standards	Relationships	Work Standards	Diversity

Chapter Twenty-Two

Cogito Ergo Sum

"I think, therefore I am," is part of an old axiom. The adage continues to be that we are because you are and you are because we are. This chapter discusses the significance of an individual being an active thinker. When someone is able to think, by default, they become important. They can be influenced or influence others, and that concept is fundamental to the function of any group or individual activity.

Cogito Ergo Sum

The operational definition for this chapter is below:

<u>Thinking</u> requires having a conscious mind, and to some extent, the acts of reasoning, remembering experiences, or making rational decisions.

Many people view themselves as outsiders of systems, or non-interactors. The truth is that everyone influences systems simply because they exist. Since you exist, you think and you respond to your environment. You are always actively engaging with your community. So, you should be aware of how you are engaging and be sure that you are active in the manner that you deem represents who you are.

As a thinker you are unique in your ways. You are unique because of your experiences, beliefs, desires, and capabilities. You choose to be a pawn or a master. To believe otherwise, is to elect a position as a pawn. If you choose not to think for yourself, then others will indulge in thinking for you. You will truly be a product of your environment.

You must take time to separate yourself from your experiences. You must believe that your experiences are to you as are taking classes are to being a student. You are supposed to learn from them and use them as tools to help you pursue your purpose. If, instead, you become your experiences, they may work to erode your sense of self-worth and purpose. This is where you will find yourself in social depression- not clinical depression. You will portray yourself as a victim, and identify every excuse to avoid ever becoming anything. You worked to counteract these hindering beliefs about yourself in the previous chapters. Now, you must put them to use since you are a thinking creature.

Thoughts manifest into the substantial reality. All of the resources with which you interact are a consequence of someone else's creations. Resources are a consequence of cause and effect and the manifestation of thought. Simply phrased, with your thoughts, you can create a substantial reality.

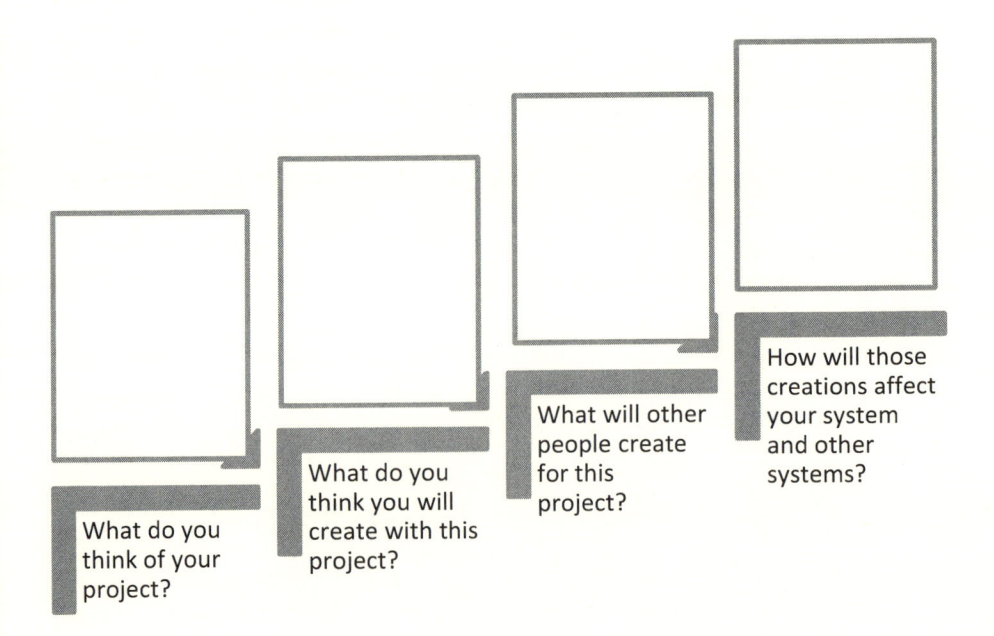

What do you think of your project?

What do you think you will create with this project?

What will other people create for this project?

How will those creations affect your system and other systems?

LP25: Influence

Achieving community activism...

I. **That I exist means many things.**

A. <u>I have an effect on others.</u>

You and your members must all adopt this mentality. By fostering an interdependent environment, you can provide value and meaning for each person. When defining forces, Newton's third law states that all forces have an equal and opposite force when interacting with a new system. The force may elicit a different effect, as dependent upon the composition of the new system, but the energy has been transferred. Depending on mass, in a collision, some objects will stick together; some will bounce apart at velocities that are equal in magnitude and opposite in direction. Some objects will remain stationary, while the other bounces. When you act upon a system, the system will respond according to its design. However, both parties must *account* for the existence of the interaction. The response may be different by each party, but they both partake in the transaction. Accountability, providing a response to a stimulus, is inherent and should be factored into your decisions. You have an *effect*.

B. <u>I have a purpose.</u>

Since you were uniquely shaped and molded, you can assume that you were designated to a purpose. Otherwise, there is no reason to have diversity. We have people of different size, shape, color, make, culture, energy, and the list continues. If we had no special purpose, then we would all be clones of one another. Purpose can be intrinsically derived. Some people were born with genetic defects that concurrently safeguarded against other diseases. It can be argued that part of their purpose was to exhibit the new gene so that it could be researched and used to protect other individuals. Mistakes inherently have the purpose of being studied. If the *Comet* commercial jet mistake was never made, we probably would not have the planes we have today. If Edison or Tesla had not made their mistakes, we would still be clamoring for ways to transform energy.

It is a shame how many people are lost to their purpose because of their inability to think for themselves. Develop an adaptable environment by easily being able to implement changes that team members suggest.

    C.   <u>I have an obligation to utilize my abilities.</u>

When you are given an idea, only you can actually make it manifest in the way that you envision. Others have their own purposes to pursue. So, if you do not pursue your own, you can expect the idea to fade away. Perhaps someone who is seeking to define a role may simply take your idea from you. If you have a thought, then you must own it, and make it come to fruition. If you choose not to, then there will be a time when you will regret it. If you skip on pursuing your personal legend, your purpose, then it will haunt you and you will run out of people to blame for your predicament. Bitterness and depression will ensue.

If you treat your thoughts with respect and spend time developing them, they will reward you handsomely. Make sure that everyone, in your group, is using their talents and resources to the fullest but you should be strategic about their usage. You can encourage this kind of team work when you provide incentives for your team to plan and be creative while on the job.

    II.   **<u>Community activism through yourself must involve:</u>**

    A.   <u>Deliberate expansion of my role.</u>

You should continuously expand your role when engaged in community service. Recall the exercise which identified supporting industries and services to your crafts.

How can you expand the role you currently have based on trends within your system and the interaction of your system and others?

LP25: Influence

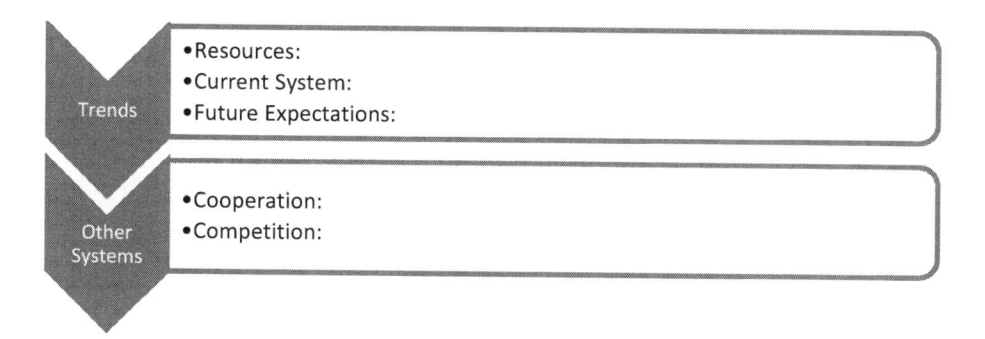

- **Trends**
  - Resources:
  - Current System:
  - Future Expectations:

- **Other Systems**
  - Cooperation:
  - Competition:

For resources. List your entire inventory with regards to your system.

For current systems. Describe the current value of your system. What is the culture of the system? How do managers view your role? Does your system interact with other systems? Which ones?

For future expectations. What might your current role consist of in 5 years? How will global and local culture changes affect the culture of your system? What will be the associated value with your current system? Are there any obvious inefficiencies within your system and role? This category specifically should describe, based on trends, what will most likely occur with your role as a visionary, manager, an employee, a student, or as an individual. No role exists in a vacuum. While you are living in the present, you are concurrently experiencing the slow evolution of the future. Simply put, life continues to move forward. Be the master of trends and model them using one of the most complex tools you have- your brain. Devise conclusions and operate in conjunction with them to develop a series of actions for yourself and your team.

The next section, "other systems", involves your understanding of your system in the context of apparent chaos- the interaction of multiple orders. In particular, the exercise focuses on both competition and cooperation.

For cooperation. If you are to maintain relevance in your system, you must plan how you can coordinate with other systems. Which resources can be shared, and with whom? Which resources are invested, and what gains will come from such correspondence? You can use the Chapter 7 diagram outlining the supporting industries to better determine what other systems you should consider. Foster emergent properties.

For competition. You must be aware of redundancy. Just as individuals are unique, projects should be too. There are many ways to deal with competition- industry coordination, subversion, erosion, and innovation.

> *Industry Coordination involves the joint coordination of seemingly competitive entities' to either corner or define a market.*
>
> *Subversion involves the adoption of a competitor's value(s) or product(s) in order to diminish their differentiation in the market.*
>
> *Erosion involves the castigation or defamation of a competitor through identifying low quality, ethical, production, or personnel standards.*
>
> *Innovation serves to widen the differentiation gap by either introducing a completely new method or idea within the same market for the same service, or an enhancement in convenience, cost, or reliability of an industry standard.*

These methods can be employed in conjunction with one another. Refer to the standards of leadership and your team's defined ethics to guide appropriate actions that will not serve to erode the values of your project while you are attempting to eradicate your competition. Also, be sure to understand the structure and the vision of the competition so that you may select the best methods of correspondence. How does your project fair up with the competition?

B. <u>Involvement of no fear during the creative process.</u>

Your thoughts should not be rooted in fear. Fear is a very limiting emotion. It can be strategically applied, but when trying to be creative, avoid thinking in fear by focusing on a vision. There will be many times in which you will need to solve a distinct problem.

LP25: Influence

Creativity will be an imperative, but fear will serve to obstruct it. The following diagram represents the physical process and the thought process involved in obtaining a creative solution to a problem.

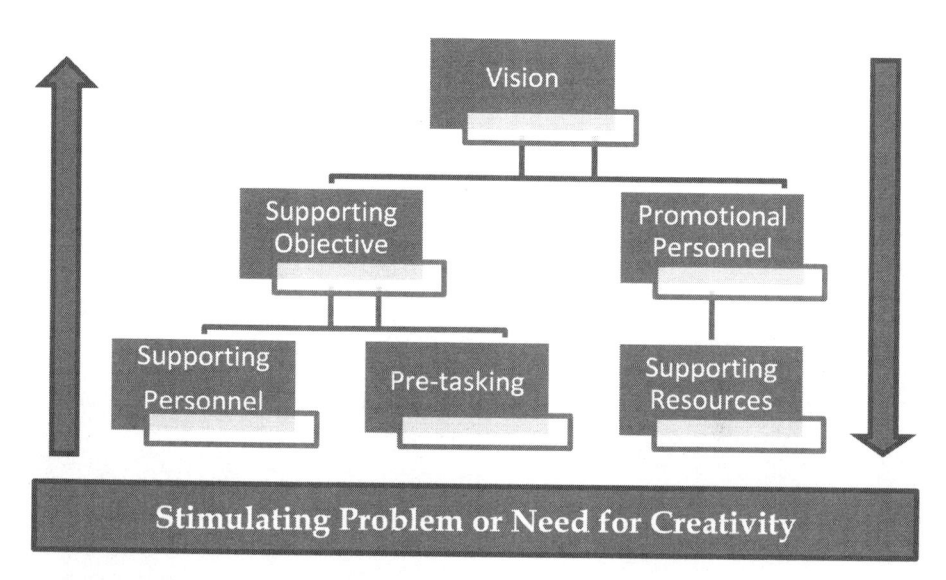

```
                          Vision
                            |
            ┌───────────────┴───────────────┐
      Supporting                       Promotional
      Objective                         Personnel
            |                               |
    ┌───────┴────────┐                      |
Supporting       Pre-tasking           Supporting
Personnel                               Resources

         Stimulating Problem or Need for Creativity
```

This schematic represents the flow in which you should use your resources and the flow in which you should think. The arrow on the left from bottom to top is represents flow of process and personnel involvement- the use of resources. The arrow on the right is represents a thought process. It demonstrates how you can ensure you align your focus and your activities. From bottom to top and left to right, the explanations are below:

Supporting personnel are meant to represent other group members and experts who are affiliated with the new idea you are trying to craft. They either provide you opportunities to explore or directly share in the discovery process alongside you.

Pre-tasking is an imperative and involves preparing your list of resources and supporting personnel. It involves developing an action plan for what you plan to gain or obtain from each.

"Supporting resources" include books, accurate and trustworthy documents on the subject matter, and materials gained from opportunities provided by supporting personnel.

"Supporting objectives" involves constructing the overall goal of what the new idea is meant to accomplish. It also involves actually creating the idea.

Promotional personnel on this level function as promotional avenues. They provide passive support but may purchase, test, try, or administer your creation. You can consult these individuals for feedback.

Finally, vision is the grand goal that the new idea you have created helps to accomplish.

What are some key differentiators you have developed?

Point	Value to System (high to low)	Determinant (metrics and why)

What gives your idea uniqueness?

Point	Qualitative	Quantitative

C. <u>Acceptance of my individual faults and strengths.</u>

Where you lack, a team member may thrive. Jealousy is an insecurity that when allowed to take root, prohibits both the person who is jealous and the object of the jealousy. Own your strengths and let them motivate you alongside your resources and your passions. If there is no alignment in your forces and your focuses, then you will encounter emergent properties that are negative and unmanageable. Also, by clearly stating your strengths and expected contributions, you allow other members to define their roles as complements to yours. This dynamic is healthy and encouraging. Leaving an "empty" role simultaneously blows the dog whistle for someone to incur the responsibility.

Encourage this environment and realize how your method of conveying thoughts to a group will truly compel your existence and consequently, your effect. As you exist and think, so do your fellow members. In a group, each member relies on the existence of the others. Embrace this idea and you will be rewarded for it. Use the tips in the previous chapter to build your team and use this chapter to define your team and their purposes, as a consequence of their existence.

Chapter Twenty-Three

I and Me

This chapter references a previous mention that an individual is a divided entity. There exists the component that creates with the mind and feels, and the component that creates within a substantial world, with substantial meaning. It is the full circle of creating something composed of matter.

I and Me

The operational definitions for this chapter are below:

A Principle is an accepted or professed rule of action or conduct, a fundamental, primary, or general law or truth from which others are derived, a fundamental doctrine or tenet; a distinctive ruling opinion, and a personal or specific basis of conduct or management.

Gender archaically means to engender, which means to give birth to.

When establishing a project or organizational culture, you must adopt associated standards. Standards come out of prioritized values, and values are determined by your morals. These are the principles by which your project/ organization functions by. All of these principles are a consequence of a philosophical explanation of "gender".

The word "gender" is now usually used in terms of sexual classification since the French influence upon its meaning. The Middle English version used it to represent the engenderment of something. In the older philosophies, the "engender" definition is used. "I" and "Me" represent the conflated notions of both sexual classification and the process of engenderment. In the cited philosophies, the words were used to represent categorically different aspects of the human mind. These metaphorical aspects of the human mind were capable of all of creation. In religious context, the two components describe divinity and the image of likeness of divinity. The use of the word gender changed into classification, and now we have our conflated notion of the word. "I" and "Me" are now designated as the masculine and feminine derivatives of the human mind, respectively. This is reflected in many of the archaic symbols that represent a multitude of religions and schools of thought. As humans, we like to categorize processes and organisms. So when principles are formulated, they are "engendered". They go through a two part process in order to achieve manifestation. The two steps in the process are represented by the "I" and the "Me". The "I", is the evaluation of creation itself while the "Me" is the thought of creation. All ideas were created twice- once by mind, and subsequently by matter. Things are rendered useful only after they have been imagined useful. Both are needed for a complete idea to come into fruition. So, this chapter discusses the philosophical meaning of the masculine and feminine principle and the manner by which all other principles are able to exist. The importance is derived out of recognizing whether or not your project possesses the ingredients for a substantial reality.

What principles guide you in the project? Why is the project significant to you? From where did these guiding principles manifest? What do these principles create? Refer to the diagram below to gain insight into these questions. It shows that the system exists in a describable state prior to your involvement, and your vision describes the world following your influence. The process of manifestation is directly tied to your ability to acknowledge the system as it was before and the associated mechanisms of implementation. Have you done enough to become a subject-matter expert? If not, revisit Chapter 6 to gain control over limitations, Chapter 7 to identify your system, Chapter 9 to plan your preparation, and the previous chapter to develop creative ideas.

Before your idea: → | Your beliefs about the world:

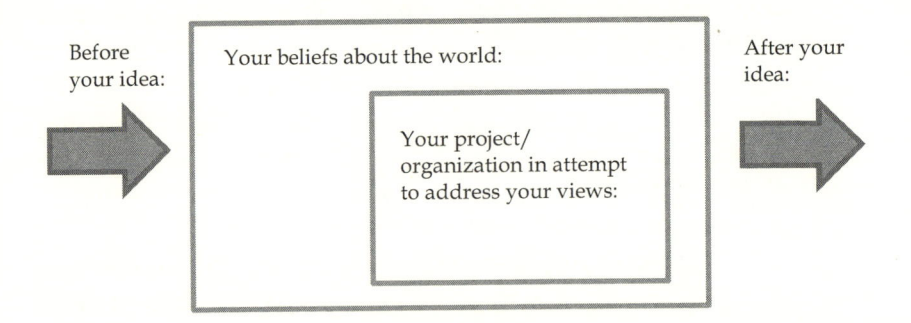

[Your project/ organization in attempt to address your views:] | → After your idea:

What conclusions and assumptions are you making about society by implementing your project/ organization? These are the bases of your principles. Your organization should reflect these conclusions and assumptions and the vision is what will happen to the systems after your idea has been implemented. For effective vision communication, recall that others may not share your world view post-influence. You must describe the vision using terms that are known and certified. Your argument/ group must be strong. Refer to Chapter 16.

You can clearly see how your idea is truly an emergent property of your ideas about society, or the system you are attempting to impact. Since it is an emergent property, channel it by drawing the big picture, recognize and credit your services, reflect on analogistic (with the quality of an analogy) features, aggregate and channel resources, and survey progress.

You can fill in the chart below for your project in defining the big picture:

World View	Assumption	Solution	Post Solution

LP25: Influence

Once you have incubated your thoughts, you must then move them to the external world in the form of a creation. Use this chart to extrapolate how the "Me" can be turned into the "I".

In the "Me" column, place your thoughts and ideas. Thoughts are boundless in your "Me". Take the time to visualize these aspects.

For the "I" column, think of the systems that are at play, and try to conceive the "Me" idea in its tangible form. All of these should pertain to your project/ organization.

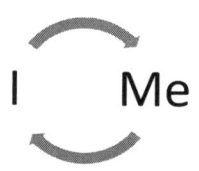

Me	I

I ⟲ Me

As you can see, the "Me" and the "I" are tied together and rely on energy to make up the difference. Recall, all things are mental in nature. After you have determined the two operating components for creation, you must note a balance is inherent in its use. The "I" column consists of the most probable services you deem as valuable to offer. How do you value them? What systems attribute value to these offers?

"I" Column	Service/Product Translation	System

What works of art or analogies have been associated with the systems?

Systems	Analogy	Tenets

Finally, which friends and tools do you need for the "I" column to manifest?

"I" Column	S/P Translation	Mentor	Mentee	Resources	Creations

Achieving community activism...

I. **Gender exist on all planes and manifests differently within them as the masculine and feminine principle.**

   A. <u>The "I" and the "Me" are expressions of gender.</u>

Avoid being too polarized in the way of "thinking of creation". Once an idea becomes mature, it is time to work on making it a reality. What stages of development can you create for your organization before you make it a reality? A generic set of the "Me" stages may appear like this:

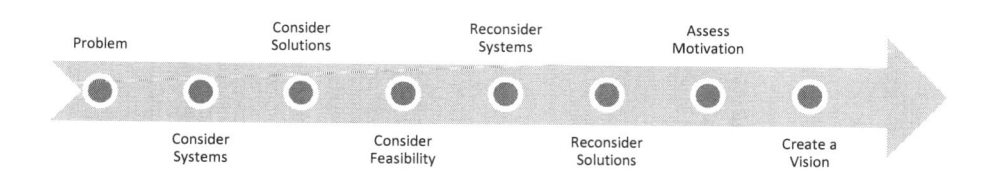

Problem → Consider Systems → Consider Solutions → Consider Feasibility → Reconsider Systems → Reconsider Solutions → Assess Motivation → Create a Vision

All of these occur within the mind. This is before an idea is ever shared with anyone. At the point of creating a vision, you have developed a creative thought in which you must exercise the act of communicating it to another person. It is in this phase that you begin to engage with your "I". A generic set of stages to manifestation may appear as such:

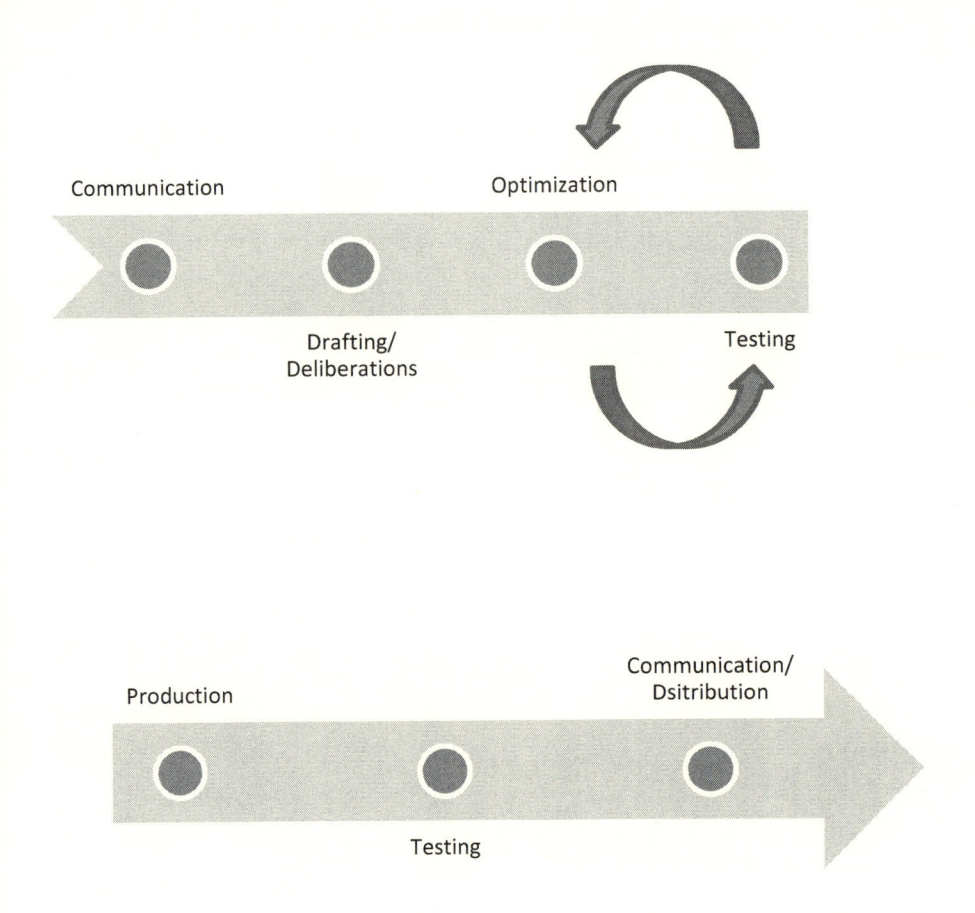

Communication — Drafting/Deliberations — Optimization — Testing

Production — Testing — Communication/Dsitribution

B. <u>The universe is a broader manifestation of the unity within the universe.</u>

The statement seems a bit recursive, but it is another example of the correspondence principle, "as above, so below, as below, so above." If the universe exhibits "gender" unity, then the elements of the universe exhibit the same "gender" unity. The masculine and feminine principle is the foundation of every other principle, and stand to represent how connected all things are- a direct connection between what you believe and think, and what you physically experience and create. As nature tends towards unity and process,

LP25: Influence

so do people. Within your project/ organization, you should be aware of the masculine and feminine principle. Which aspects are in which part, and how do you get ideas to move into becoming a substantial reality? You will have an opportunity to develop this in Chapter 25- Methodology.

II. **The Masculine and Feminine principle is the cornerstone to the operation of everything that comes to be.**

    A. <u>Community activism needs both components.</u>

You must first envision an idea, and then you will be able to create it. Even things that are discovered by "accident" had to have its use imagined before taking into effect. Envision all of the inner workings of your idea so that when you actually begin engaging with your creation, you are prepared.

What are you currently doing to make the project/ organization a reality?

Internal: How are you preparing yourself in system knowledge, uniqueness, and maturity? Are there applicable win-win discussions impending post-influence? What are the limitations?

Transition: How are you preparing your message? Which stories and visions apply?

> External: How do systems respond to your idea? How are you judging/ gauging those responses? What are the expressed strengths- by number and credence? How do systems interact with your idea- structure?

    B.   <u>There must be a cyclical approach to gender just as is there is in life.</u>

Your ideas should flow from internal to external at all times so that you may constantly evaluate them and determine how they can best be positioned for manifestation. You can use your external experiences to influence how you conceive your ideas.

Refer to some of the key differentiators you created with your new idea. What are some of the aspects that you could spend a bit more time reflecting on? You should set aside some "Me"-time and really focus on your ideas and attempt to configure new ideas. The following diagram will allow for two things: decrease your over-commitment to one point of view, and two, help you arrive at a new idea. Use the following process with every idea you would like to refine or adjust.

LP25: Influence

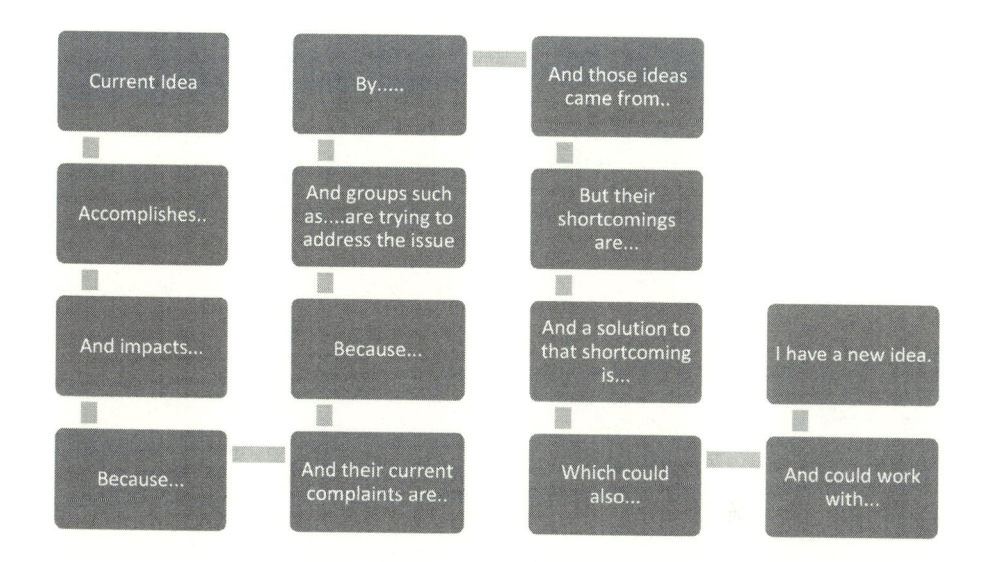

```
[Current Idea] → [By.....] → [And those ideas came from..]
      ↓              ↓                    ↓
[Accomplishes..] [And groups such   [But their
                  as....are trying to  shortcomings
                  address the issue]    are...]
      ↓              ↓                    ↓
[And impacts...] [Because...]       [And a solution to    [I have a new idea.]
                                      that shortcoming
                                      is...]
      ↓              ↓                    ↓                      ↓
[Because...]    [And their current  [Which could         [And could work
                 complaints are..]    also...]             with...]
```

C. **The group must constantly evaluate its application of the feminine and masculine principles.**

Your project should do an equal amount of "thinking" and "doing" in order to be efficient and effective. Failure to adapt and consider alternatives will leave your project/ organization in an unpopular, immutable, and vulnerable state. What are you currently doing in your organization/ project? How much reflective thinking is occurring to evaluate old and new ideas? Conservatism can be a great thing, but stubbornness is a hindrance. It breeds pride, and will eventually lead to the demise of your project/ organization. If you are too preoccupied with process, then when new ideas sprout, they will be uprooted either voluntarily or by force and reappear later as a competitor. Pay equal attention to those that think and those that do in your organization. Which roles in your project/ organization are mainly associated with thinking, and which are associated with doing?

Thinker	Doer
Role: Task:	Role: Task:
Role: Task:	Role: Task:
Role: Task:	Role: Task:
Role: Task:	Role: Task:

This philosophy is very complex and manifests within all of the four dimensions. The most important aspect with regards to project development is to keep in mind that when creating, there are two distinct and equal processes that work in conjunction with one another. They require that you think and then do. Most thinking requires no consciously recognized impulse. An example is an emotion. Usually, no thought is seemingly required to elicit an actual emotion, but the brain is still responding to some stimulus. For this reason, emotions are controllable and can be manipulated. Reengage your thinking so that it is deliberate. Think of and master your unconscious processes, and it will be great practice when organizing and managing a group. The elements that are easily taken for granted can cause the most turmoil if there is a defect. A manager must lead with a vision and become a rescuer when the team is in trouble. You should exhibit a balance between the "I" and the "Me", and so should your team. As it also holds true to the principle that all things are thought of first and then they manifest into the world, you should apply the principle to every dimension of your project. You will see that your project will have the ability to ebb and flow with changes in the system. If you are not balanced, your project will act like a pendulum which compensates for a disturbance by swinging wildly in the direction opposite to which it began.

You should make sure that there are evaluative and reflective processes in place to gauge creative processes. Your organization/ project should have an internal support system for both of these tasks. Assigning directives without both processes of creation will ultimately lead to defective parts of your project/ organization. Offer freedom by having a work flow that encourages and rewards the application of both thinking of creation and creating.

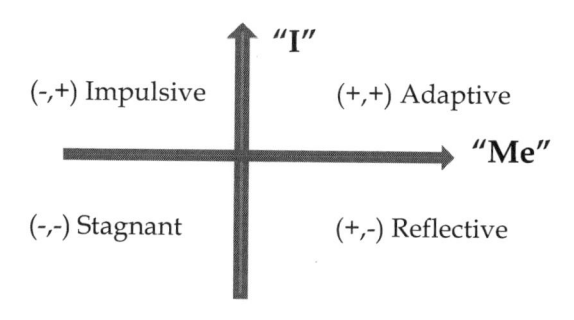

```
                    "I"
                     ↑
   (-,+) Impulsive   |   (+,+) Adaptive
                     |
                     |─────────→ "Me"
                     |
   (-,-) Stagnant    |   (+,-) Reflective
```

Chapter Twenty-Four

What

The compelling statement here is "What are you going to do?" You are nearing the end of the entire curriculum and it is now important to consider what you are going to accomplish. You can put all of the things you have discussed into practice. Determining the "what" is easier than you may believe.

What

The operational definition for this chapter is below:

An **objective** is something that one's efforts or actions are intended to attain or accomplish; purpose; goal; target

When dealing with efficiency and effectiveness, objectives are the center of attention. Leadership must have a purpose and with purpose appends goals. There must be a goal with your project/ organization. In addition to setting objectives, you have to prepare your range of success. Under which conditions will you continue to push forward, and at what point will you have to reconstruct and make comprehensive changes to your organization/ project?

Your Target

On Target

Reevaluation Range

What are some measurements that you are going to use for each one? A few suggestions for your project/ organization are listed below. It is important to analyze these measurements in context: why or why not? Some categories apply to organizations as a whole, and some also apply to projects, groups, or departments within the organization.

Total Revenue
Total revenue is the amount of money your project/ organization realizes on a daily, monthly, quarterly, or annual basis.

Profit
Profit is the total amount your project/ organization realizes with the total costs subtracted out. Many companies generate a lot of revenue, but overhead costs are so high, that they are not profitable.

Number of Products
You may want to designate a number of products or services for a given period of time. Limitations may include available labor, feasibility, time, and costs.

Production and Distribution Time
This is the measurement of the time it takes for a product to go from raw material to a product of quality or the time it takes for a service or product to be requested and delivered. This is another important measurement that can be used to identify if there is inefficiency in a production process. This measurement can affect volume and customer satisfaction.

Employees
These are the individuals who are a part of your project/ organization. Your designation on a number of employees can be used to maximize profitability. "More people" generally translates into more products or services, but cost per employee must be taken into consideration, and there is a point, in every organization or project where more people means a decline in productivity. There is a bell curve for every project/ organization, but they are internally derived and depend on the nature of the project or organization. Job differentiation can be used to temporarily oppose the bell curve and make it flatter on the top. The graphs below are generic and exaggerated to show the trend.

While not exact, case studies from previously established projects or organizations similar to yours can be used to anticipate your growth curve and identify where problems may originate. Your curve may be different, but you will be more prepared to establish a size that is suitable for your structure and type.

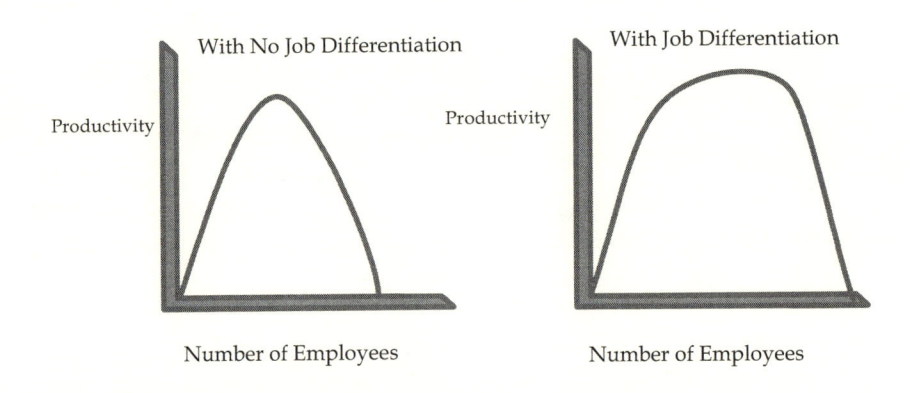

[Chart: Productivity vs. Number of Employees — With No Job Differentiation (narrow peaked curve)]

[Chart: Productivity vs. Number of Employees — With Job Differentiation (broader plateau curve)]

Environment also affects productivity outside of the number of employees. Are there enough benefits/ incentives associated with productivity? The work schedule and work-life balance play major roles in productivity.

Turnover

Turnover is the process in which an employee is replaced by a new employee due to insufficient performance on part of the company or the individual. In an organization, turnover can be extremely detrimental. If the reason for turnover is discontentment, then it means the individual was not content with the performance of the organization or project. It could also be due to the environment, compensation, or potential for growth.

If the reason is a missed quota or target for a particular worker, then the reasons could be that expectations are unfeasible or the individual was not effectively brought into the vision of the organization or project.

For either case, if turnover is too high, then the project/ organization should consider what is driving it and attempt to accommodate changes.

Diversity

This category can be very important and its parameters are dependent upon you. Gender, nationality, education, and other qualities can be used to determine diversity within your group. Diversity can be very important for groups attempting to grow. Increasing the talent and knowledge pool can break impending barriers incurred with expansion. The negative effects include an impact on group culture and potentially increased internal competitiveness.

Number of Programs and Investments

Number of programs is self-explanatory as a category. In some organizations/projects, this may be used to determine its effectiveness. Programs can be events, service projects, or specialized and strategic initiatives. They all require a blend of investments in relationships, labor, and money.

Products/Services Revenue per Target Audience Member

This may be very important if your target market is very small. Your service or product may be available in multiples per person. You must determine this target through analyzing your market and their corresponding needs. This is usually done in averages.

It can be increased in multiple ways:

Promotional Products

Additional products are offered at discounted rates. It increases the total revenue per customer by providing incentives for the customer to increase their total payment by increasing their purchasing power.

Product Grouping

You can offer sets of products for prices that are discounted from purchasing the products individually.

Example: You can purchase 1 of x, 2 of y's and 3 of z's, or order package two with 2 of x, 2 of y's, and 2 of z's.

Arrangement of Different Applicable Products

How potential consumers choose products can be completely determined by impulse, depending on the nature of the product.

How products are displayed can ultimately influence which product is purchased. Those that are presented first can have higher prices than those shown last, and so on.

Presentation of Multiple Applicable Products or Services
For any given potential customer, there can be a presentation of products that would all benefit them. This method is similar to the previous method, but engages with the customer in an all at once fashion, and not at a product by product basis.

Maintenance Fees
If applicable, maintenance fees can help to supplement costs associated with maintaining contact with your clients and covering any potential liabilities. It is a great source for residual funds from a sale.

Extended Payment Period with Interest
Many times, for large purchases, interest can be added to payments that are extended over a period of time. Most consumers do not mind this arrangement because their cost during a shortened period is much less than the total purchase price of a product or service at one time.

If creating a service project, you can determine how much each person should receive from your organization's service.

Target Audience per Product/ Service
You want to know what the interest level is for specific products so that you can modify what you make available. If only the demand for the complete set of products is reviewed, it will be difficult to determine which products are in demand, and which only deplete resources. Once you view the profit provided by each product, then you can make decisions to cut any excess.

In traditionally recognized service, how many people are being served per item or person? Much of this segment deals with scope with regards to traditional community service projects. Institutions or groups providing resources would be curious to know how many people benefit from every dollar donated.

Number of Members in Target Audience

The extent to which you can market a product or service, should match, or be much greater than the number of people that you are targeting. You will rarely ever reach 100% of your entire market. If this is not the case, then it may not be viable to continue to pursue distributing your service or product in the manner you have chosen. What is your target for such an audience size? How many people do you have access to? Generally, you can use the 10% rule. Out of the many that you can contact, 10% will actually purchase or participate in your product or service- 1 out of every 10 people.

So, generally speaking, if you are targeting 100 people, you should make 1000 people aware of your particular venture. This rule is highly variable as aforementioned, but can get you started in developing a marketing mix for your idea. While these numbers may seem daunting, do not forget the principles of aggregate resources. The resources and people are within your reach, you must know how to access them. You should meet what you can accommodate.

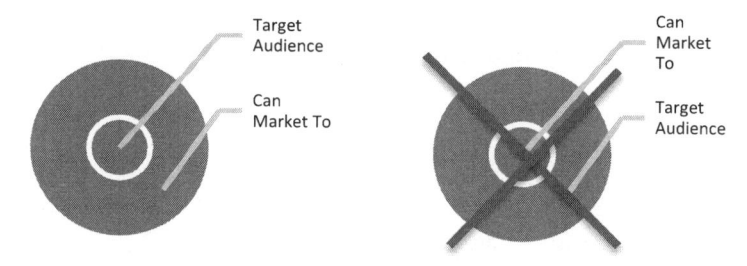

Cost Per Person

Whether you are doing a service or providing a product, you should keep track of how much it costs per person who is either employed or serviced by your project or organization. For an employee, activities that may cost include salary, benefits, training, and some government compliance aspects. You should monitor whether or not these costs are growing or decreasing, and why. If costs are increasing because of training, then perhaps there is a system inefficiency that is causing the cost per person in training to increase. If you designate a target or range for this category, then you will be in a better position to negotiate with your employees and reconfigure the organization or project.

Total Expenditure

These are your expenses. Depending on the accountant, it can include all liabilities or the liabilities after debt recovery. This can be seen with some large technological purchases that organizations have. These purchases tend to pay for themselves over time, but can reflect otherwise according to the accountant. As an organization or project, you should definitely be aware of your total expenditures to see if you are truly incurring a profit or suffering a loss.

Debt

Debt is an amount that is owed because some extension of credit was extended to you. Debt usually brings along other associated costs and expectations on behalf of the lender and yourself. Loans and credit both qualify as incurred debt. Resources that have been supplied by an investor will have associated expectations. Regardless of the liability share, it is best to accompany the amount invested by other parties with an amount invested by you. In cases that you are liable for risks associated with your organization, keep the ratio of amount you invest to the amount another group invests as high as possible.

Manufacturing Costs

This is a subset of costs associated with your service or product. Manufacturing costs include all costs required for your product to go from raw materials to end-user quality without the costs of labor. This amount can be reduced by creating a more efficient or unique system for product production or service. Set targets for your organization to reduce inefficiency and be able to provide more for less cost.

With regards to a service project, you will be able to broaden your scope at a much lower cost of resources.

Compliance Costs

This is another subset of costs associated with your product before it reaches a consumer. These are usually imposed regulations by the government or a professional group. If there are "standard practices" in your field, then the costs associated with accommodating those regulations are considered compliance costs.

Taxes and Tax Savings

Be sure to monitor how much is being paid in taxes and where you can find potential tax savings.

Cost per Product/Service

This value is the total cost of getting a product to a customer or client. This considers all expenditures and the number of units you are producing. Watching how this value changes can indicate whether you are becoming more sustainable or not, but it is best to see the breakdown as an itemization. In that way, you will be able to identify inefficiencies and begin fixing them.

Some texts will suggest that cost per product or service only includes some expenditures. While, it may be done this way, it creates a rosier picture for your organization. The downfall with including all expenditures is that it creates a picture that may not reflect success in your business. The price per product may go up, but it may be due to an increase in other costs that are incurred with growth, rather than inefficiency.

Price per Product/Service

Price is what the customers pay. Cost is what you pay. Your price should fall somewhere above your cost. If you set revenue or profitability goals, you can use those to determine the price of your product. You must take into consideration your market and what your market perceives as affordable. You can use price to determine your market (e.g. more expensive items may appeal to those with more expensive taste). Price consistency is another concern. You should be able to anticipate price fluctuations by keeping track of demand, supply, and inflation.

Supply-Chain Costs and Prices

If you are in the middle of a supply chain, say the provider of wood in a vertical market, then you receive your resources at a given price, and you distribute the refined resources at a given price. Costs are factored into each step so that each step increases the value of what is being exchanged. If there were no increase, then you would create a trend of decreasing profitability in an entire supply chain. With this in mind, realize you can only "lower" your prices, if you can affect the supply chain that precedes your position. If you can successfully cut the profit margins of those that precede you or close an efficiency gap, then they can offer you a lower price because they incur a lower cost, or have limited their revenue. Then, you will be able to lower your prices for your customers. If you cannot produce a product that fits within the target range of determined or acceptable prices, then you can either change your product to fit that target, or opt to decline pursuing the creation of the product.

You can use the supply chains to determine the sustainability prospect of your particular service or product.

Insurance on Liabilities

There are ways to limit your liabilities, and hiring a great lawyer may be a step in the right direction. Insurance costs can be mitigated by taking preventative measures to limit great liabilities. Having someone who manages quality assurance and a strict quality assurance system is a great way to avoid major recalls or issues with your product or service. Quality assurance can oversee compliance with government regulations, product performance and safety, and distribution methods. If you open a store that sells directly to consumers having the option to "return" items, then it can become expensive for the store. To safeguard your profits, you can effectively offer "store credit". This retains all of your earnings on a given piece of inventory. If you are providing a single service or product, "store credit" is much less effective, and will only add pressure on your buyers when they are evaluating the risk involved in a potential purchase.

Product/Service Satisfaction

Another target that should be used for your organization or project should be your users' satisfaction with your products or services. You can use testimonials, rankings, and references as qualitative or comparative measurements of your success. It may also be imperative to measure consistency. Do you consistently meet expectations?

Employee Satisfaction

Employee satisfaction is a measurement that has been taken more seriously in recent days. This is an indicator of how "happy" your employees are. Having a high employee or membership satisfaction ranking will help to draw in new talent for your project or organization. A happy organization is usually a more productive organization- as long as clear goals are set. If there are no clear and multi-faceted objectives set within the organization, happiness can be false indicator. You should have employees that are happy with their role, embody the vision of the organization, and have ample opportunities to apply their talents in developing their role.

Region or Scale Coverage

Your coverage is another measurement. Outside of scope in numbers, being cross-state, national, or international may be a part of your target goals.

Technology

Efficiency and effectiveness should be a key consideration for your organization: communication, management, etc. To stay up to date, you can designate an objective or amount for technological investments that can be pursued. You can track the most recent uptake of new technology and whether or not it has provided a sufficient return on investment.

Intellectual Property

Patents can prove to be strategic and lucrative assets beyond the intrinsic value the patented entity may possess. You may associate goals with your patents and patent portfolios as a form of recourse in the case of a depleting cash infusion or as a method of pushing influence on other practicing entities. Intellectual property may be obtained through investing in technology and management, as most specific and definable processes and entities can be protected.

Strategic Partners

To effectively expand your scope and increase your efficiency, aligning your project organization with strategic partners is an imperative. Partners in the project world function like mentors and mentees in the individual world. They can provide resources, advice, and a platform for your growth. Being strategic implies a win-win mentality. Both entities must gain something from the partnership and can concurrently address industry and competitive issues. "Strategic" implies both short term and long term goals. Partners can be utilized to accomplish both.

Mergers and Acquisitions

Mergers and acquisitions are a more extreme version of having strategic partners. One of the entities will lose its identity or be molded anew. When an equity firm acquires a company, it does not do so to swallow it, but it does attempt to rebrand it. So, restructuring and process infusion usually occur. People lose jobs and products and services are discontinued. Usually, however, these acquisitions provide an expected overall benefit for both entities. Your goal with merging and acquiring should be to identify the win-win solution.

> *In acquisitions...*
> *Vertical integration is a type of industry acquisition in which the manufacturers, refineries, suppliers, and product producers are owned by the same entity. In this way, they manage control over*

the supply chain and influence pricing structures more so than if they were not.

Horizontal integration involves industry acquisition of entities similar to yours. You can have control over distribution type, number, and scope with this kind of acquisition.

You can meet the demands of your organization by strategically merging or acquiring vertically, or horizontally. Set targets and qualifiers for those mergers and acquisitions, and work to achieve them.

Productivity
Project productivity can be difficult to measure, but by conjoining all of the aforementioned categories, you can use those targets as a way to measure your productivity. Pick the categories that are relevant, and weight them according to goal priority or impact. Then, you can measure your project or organization's overall productivity.

Full Budgeting
Budgets are great target tools for projects and organizations. They require the exercise of anticipating the needs to accomplish specific goals for different aspects of the same project. The combination of a Gantt chart and a budget can be very powerful.

The most important aspect of a budget is perhaps that you are able to identify your "gap". Your gap is the deficit between what you have, and what you need to meet your goals. If budgeting is not exercised, you are effectively guessing your needs. When you know your gap, then you can extrapolate it over a period of years. You can determine if you will meet your projections. If it seems like you will not, you can then identify that gap and find ways of filling it. Recall, the world has an abundance of resources.

The aforementioned section can be used to determine your objectives and should be done within the context of your group. For each of these, robust analytical work may be performed to produce projections. By evaluating which measurements best pertain to you, you will gain insight into some of your best-suited business practices. Also, projections and forecasts can be created from any of these, preparing your group for sustainability.

Achieving community activism...

I. <u>Know your objective.</u>

Clearly, it is important to know what you are trying to accomplish with your project or organization. After this is determined, then you must evaluate the feasibility of that objective. Once you have determined that you have the volition to pursue it you can begin to make it manifest by adding parameters to measure your progress, and sharing your vision with others. Allow them to partake in the vision creation process. Continue to redefine and refine the objectives.

A. <u>Recognize an issue.</u>

Establish a grip on a problem and your current method of solving it.

Problem Identification Categories

Vocal or latent complaints:

Proposed reasons for such complaint:

Previous attempts to address complaint:

B. <u>Be familiar with your strengths.</u>

The process of determining your "what" will require experience, process, and the presence of opportunities. On the other end, you have planning, execution and evaluation which will be discussed in the next chapter.

```
  Experience   Process                Planning   Execution
       Opportunity          ⇒              Evaluation
```

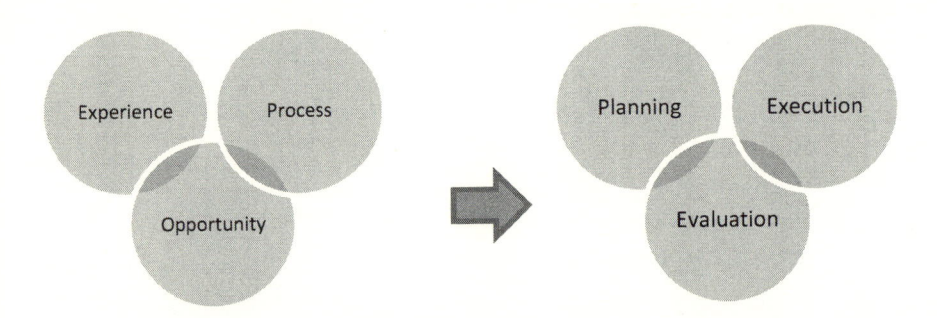

Experience. Using your strengths and weaknesses, identify what you will most likely need to produce your product/ service. This can help you determine which roles are needed to complement your role. Try to determine which other roles of expertise are needed:

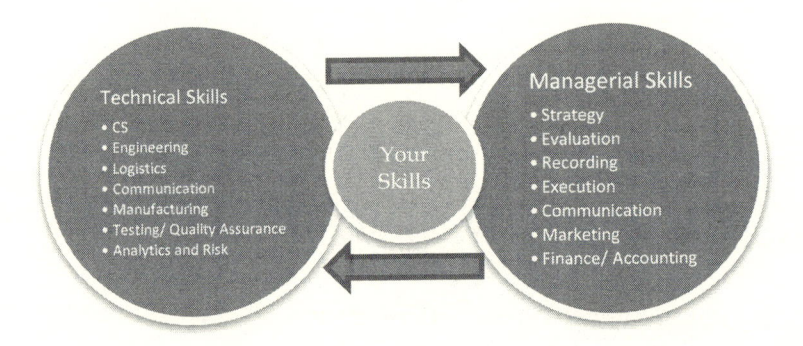

```
Technical Skills                          Managerial Skills
 • CS                                      • Strategy
 • Engineering            Your             • Evaluation
 • Logistics              Skills           • Recording
 • Communication                           • Execution
 • Manufacturing                           • Communication
 • Testing/ Quality Assurance              • Marketing
 • Analytics and Risk                      • Finance/ Accounting
```

Process. When designing your processes, you must have at least two processes:

Workflow

- Internal Information Flow
- Documentation
- Production Process

Transaction

- Sales Processes
- External Transactions

Workflow can appear as such:

Product Development:

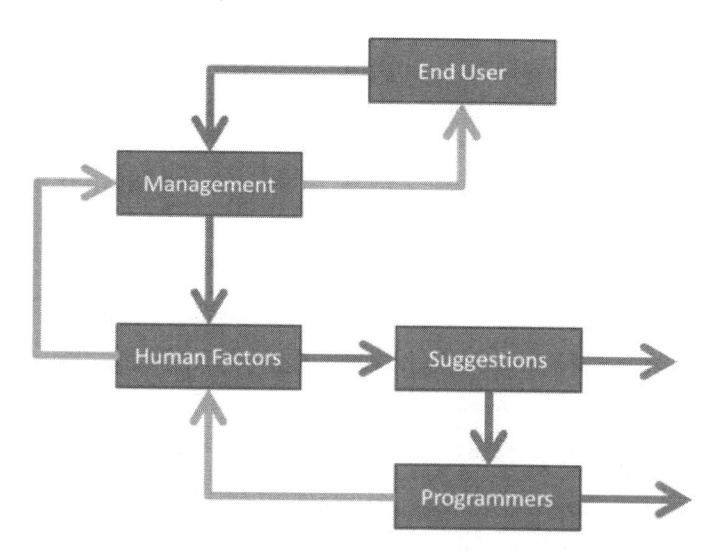

```
          ┌──────────┐
     ┌───▶│ End User │
     │    └──────────┘
     │          ▲
┌─────────────┐ │
│ Management  │─┘
└─────────────┘
     │ │
     │ ▼
     │ ┌──────────────┐     ┌─────────────┐
     └▶│Human Factors │────▶│ Suggestions │──▶
       └──────────────┘     └─────────────┘
              ▲                   │
              │                   ▼
              │            ┌─────────────┐
              └────────────│ Programmers │──▶
                           └─────────────┘
```

Opportunity. Lastly, for opportunity, this includes identifying areas of abundance, knowing your gap, and identifying occasions of serendipity.

Potential Product/ Service	Resource Needed	System of Abundance	Create a Potential Opportunity

C. <u>Tell someone else.</u>

Finally, you have enough to seek out your potential group members. Share your vision and your story with them, and make sure they are involved in the creation of the complete idea and its solution.

Make a list of those who would be interested in working with you to develop your project or organization. For each person, include the name, contact information, potential contribution or role, and then an anticipated reason for the interest in a particular position. When you finally contact the person, speak to interests and craft the vision in those terms.

Name
Contact
Potential Role
Reason for Interest

Once you have established your team, use the Problem Identification categories to re-evaluate the systems and solutions that are currently available. Include everyone on the team in these discussions. After this analysis is complete, revisit your proposed solution and refine it so that it can accomplish any new elements added to the overall vision. Use incentives and your knowledge on emergent properties to have everyone use their creativity in discovering new possibilities with the solution. Reviewing an idea requires a few important aspects:

Modeling: In modeling, allow the person who created the idea to describe the idea in its totality. He or she should be encouraged to use pictures, analogies, research, reports, case studies, charts, graphs, stories, or models.

Evaluation: Each person should then have the opportunity to offer advice to the solution provider. Using a SWOT analysis is one method for maintaining consistency in the kind of evaluation the group performs. SWOT is an acronym for Strengths, Weaknesses, Opportunities, and Threats. Through performing such an analysis, each person considers trends, systems, intrinsic value, societal value, and feasibility. All of these are great categories. If a similar product or service exists to the one that is being presented, that can

LP25: Influence

be described as a threat. The evaluation can either take place in an informal setting or on a formal stage in which reports are prepared for the presenter.

Feedback: The content prepared in evaluation by each of the group members is then given to the presenter. The presenter should have a few options. They can try to address each of the concerns raised in evaluation, or they can allow the group to offer a potential fix for the concern.

Each member should have the opportunity to model their solution at least once. Once all ideas have been discussed, the group can then consolidate best features, modes, and processes for further development. Having such a reviewing system will allow management to maintain its flexibility. Offer credit where credit is due and do not shy away from confronting issues (use methods mentioned in the previous chapters). Management should involve flexibility, in terms of adaptability, and clarity.

Be sure to document the group's progress. It is great for reference and serves as a reminder that change must occur at times. Document the programs, growth, decline, targets, evaluations, and changes. Documentation is very important if you are a company seeking to go public. It can also lower your costs associated with compliance or risk. Someone or a group of people should be dedicated to documenting the activities of the group.

After determining what to pursue, the group can set targets for their expected performance from their product or service within their project or organization. Those expectations are the beginning of brand development. How you set up your standards, vision, and mission should all be aligned with the energy emitted by your group and any associated symbols. Your brand is given birth by the pervasiveness of the consumer-received messages.

To get started, you can use the list of targets from the beginning of the chapter before moving into the next chapter. What measurement methods will you utilize?

Category	Reason	Unit	Time	Goal

Chapter Twenty-Five

Methodology

Now that you have determined what you want to do, come up with a plan for execution. Remember the qualities of "The Plan" and "Concentrate your Forces" in order to really get started.

Methodology

The operational definition for this chapter is below:

Methodology includes the study of underlying principles and rules of organization of a philosophical system or inquiry procedure, and the study of the principles underlying the organization of the various sciences and the conduct of scientific inquiry.

When positioning your project or organization, you must develop your methodology. What is the internal system that it operates by and what are the methods of the system within which it operates? After you and your group have determined both elements, you can then begin to plan how you can accomplish objectives to make such methods become a reality. Methodology, in this chapter, will include planning, execution, and the evaluation of such execution.

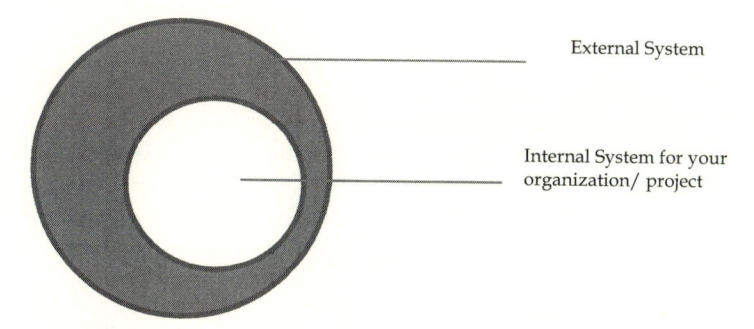

External System

Internal System for your organization/ project

You can create a methodology by establishing rules and standards. The group should be involved in this process. The rules should be strict enough that they ensure the stability of your structure, but loose enough that they are adaptable to changing circumstances. Rules can include the rules of inquiry, engagement, and adaptation.

Rules of inquiry are those rules that directly involve the development of your product or service. This set of rules predominantly focuses on the process by which new ideas are accepted into consideration and the process by which ideas can be filtered out.

Rules of engagement have to deal with people-people interactions. You want an environment that nurtures creativity and is comfortable to those that are within and outside of your project or organization.

Rules of adaptation are those associated with making changes to those already constructed. Whether your rules are changed through amendments or some other method, it should be clear and procedural. It should be unbiased so that no one can easily subvert your project or organization down the road.

Some rules are already provided by external systems, and the system by which you operate. You must consider the legal system and etiquette and best practices of your system. You must search for these rules and reach out to potential mentors for answers to some of the questions you may have. Then, you can proceed to develop your own so that your system can work in conjunction with the other systems, or strategically position it to work towards the changing of the system you are within.

If you outwardly are attempting to overthrow a system without developing any internal inroads, you will find your tactics will be greeted by well-prepared foes. Taking a divide and conquer approach is the best choice. Work within the system to plant seeds of dissent, and then outwardly confront. This will incur the kind of sedition you seek.

What are the system rules that are at play?

Rules of Inquiry

Your System:

System Rules:

Legal Rules:

Customer/ User Rules:

Supporting System Rules:

Rules of Engagement

Your System:

System Rules:

Legal Rules:

Customer/ User Rules:

Supporting System Rules:

Rules of Adaptation

Your System:

System Rules:

Legal Rules:

Customer/ User Rules:

Supporting System Rules:

When completed, you can then begin to plan.

Achieving community activism...

I. **Pursue your objectives.**

You have set objectives, and now execution is the agenda. Planning is a part of both setting objectives and executing them. There should be operational plans set in order to accomplish the intended objectives. Your project and organization should reflect a brand both in its substance and in its method. Developing your method of accomplishing objectives requires sincere reflective thought. You must stay tuned to your resources, the needs of your team, and the greater vision.

A. **Think point A to point B.**

How will customers feel and what will your project or organization appear to be at its Point B?

Quality	Current	Year 1	Year 3	Year 5
Size or Scope Brand				
Strengths				
Weaknesses				

B. **Plan.**

Now that you understand that plans are preparation, use the vision of your project or organization to help you craft your plan. Include weaknesses, forces, and focuses in your plan so that you can properly be positioned for its greatest success.

LP25: Influence

Weaknesses: For weaknesses, identify weak individuals, internal methodologies, and inefficacies by drawing a diagram of your project or organization's workflow. Who carries majority of the responsibility? Which tasks are redundant? Which processes can be centralized or decentralized? Are any of your methods incompatible with those of the larger system?

Draw a shorthand schematic for the workflow:

Program to address them: Write a way to systematically identify them. Creating a work flow diagram is one method. What are some that your team is interested in using?

Program to utilize them: Find a way to use your weaknesses as potential strengths in the future. What may be useless or a weakness in Year One, can be used as a saving resource in Year Five.

Weakness	Program

Program to excise or mitigate them: The natural inclination is to get rid of weaknesses. That requires a program, too. It usually requires a penal or ultra-incentivized program to encourage desired working behavior. This can be applied to either the group as a whole, or to the service or product.

>Penalties: This includes forms of negative reinforcement.
>Incentives: This includes forms of positive reinforcement.
>
>Program to mitigate them: Training and subduing the responsibilities associated with a specific role can accomplish this.

Forces: These are the motivations that push for the existence of the project or organization. You should have a program for all aspects of these motivations. Your strengths, resources, and passion are all driving factors that can create multitudes of group emergent properties. The earlier motivations are identified, the quicker they can be channeled for the benefit of the group and the group's creations.

Program for strengths: What societally agreed upon problem are you solving? What are your core competencies as an organization or project? What are the individual strengths of the group members? How do they motivate each member within the organization? How do those motivations play into the vision of the organization or project?

Problem you are Solving	Relation to Vision:
Strengths of the Team Members	Relation to Vision:
Motivations of the Team Members	Relation to Vision:

Program for resources: How do you plan to grow your resources? How many baskets are you using? Which resources will you need now? Which will you need later? How much will your assets be worth in the future? What are they worth now? How many liabilities do you have? How much do your liabilities total? How will you decrease them?

Your Inventory-

Resource	Year 1	Year 3	Year 5
People and Talent			
Money			
Time			

Your Growth Method. What you own, what you owe, and what you bring in must be considered. Keep in mind that some investments come with liabilities. Your investment arrow should be bigger than the liabilities arrow. Each arrow represents a rate. Of course, the rate can be changed. As your liabilities increase, your assets decrease. If you are making little to nothing in excess of your assets, you are sure to fall into bankruptcy. For the purposes of the simplified diagram, "Investments" encompass profit, seed money, and returns on investments.

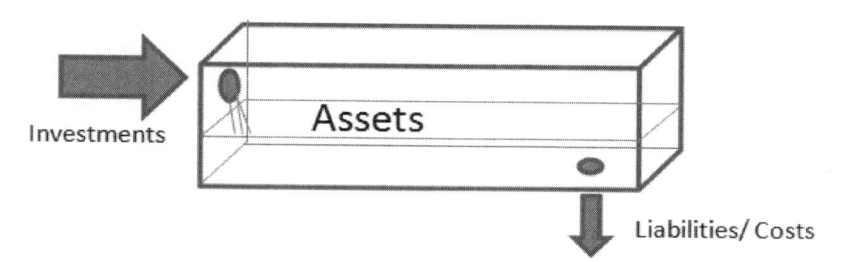

Investment Methods:
- Technology/ Equipment
- Cash Infusions

- Profits, as retained earnings
- Securities and stocks ownership

Liabilities:
- Costs
- Repayments
- Investment losses

Assets:
- Total Equipment
- Savings
- Inventory

Each of these has a monetary value associated with it and over time, a rate can be determined for your project/ organization. You can use these numbers to help your group achieve sustainability and develop the potential to grow. This is just a shortened version of what may be necessary for your project or organization to consider. After reviewing case studies particular to your field and other books that primarily focus on the business constructs within your project, sustainability can become more complicated.

Program for passions: Each person within your group possesses a certain passion for something. You can use these passions to help position your organization or project for success. By assigning and discussing talent-driven, passion filled roles, you allow an individual to "self-actualize" within their role. You should have a program that can help to determine, assign and align, and channel those passions.

Determining passions can be done through discussion, testing, and observation.

Through discussion, situational qualifiers can be made.

With testing, you should pay close attention to the kind of culture you want within your organization or project. IQ, aptitude, personality, leadership, and current events tests can be used to determine the nuances of the individuals within your group. There are also tests which involve the completion of a specific project.

Through observational methods, an individual's ability to work independently and interdependently can be determined.

Assign and align must take place through joint discovery and frequent and clear communication of the overall vision.

The channeling program consists of reiterating the rules of inquiry and engagement within the organization or project, and an influx of new opportunities that challenge the group members.

Focuses: This includes all elements of your project or organization that work together to create a full vision. There are elements that others interact with, some that describe your physical location and industry, others that you specialize in, and the remaining that describe your purpose for existing. Take the time to philosophically determine these elements and envision them. These are your focuses. You can choose to focus on one more than the other.

Program for social: How do people interact with your products, services, and group?

Element	Description
Products	
Services	
Your project/ organization and people	

Program for physical: How do you describe your group?

Element	Description
Products	
Services	
Your project/ organization and people	

Program for mental: How do you describe the inherent capabilities of the group and vision for the group?

Element	Description
Products	
Services	
Your project/ organization and people	

Program for spiritual: What do you believe about the systemic role your groups plays within its system and what emboldens such beliefs? By being honest here, you can determine what some of the inherent fears will be within the group. If you believe that you must sell the best product, yet you do not believe your product is the

LP25: Influence

best, it will limit you when you are trying to describe product capabilities and the way in which people may benefit from them. Know what you truly believe about your group while completing this part.

Element	Description
Products	
Services	
Your project/ organization and people	

    C.   <u>Identify key patrons.</u>

You must determine not just what to do with your resources, but where they are going to come from. Choose from your list of mentors and mentees to begin your search. Then, build those connections to identify your key patrons. To identify the correct person, you should ask several questions.

1. What is the individual likely to offer?
    a. Answers include talent, money, advice, time, in-kind donations, or relationships.
2. Why are they interested?
    a. Answers include that they share the same passions as your group.
3. How do their interests align with those of your group's interests?
    a. Answers include that they understand and perceive the overall vision of the group, and will identify their

best fit role to help accomplish it.
4. How much are they likely to offer?
    a. Answer varies.
5. With what will their offering assist?
    a. Answers are determined by the targets and objectives of the project or organization. Nevertheless, match their offering to one of the measurements you determined in the previous chapter.
6. What are they expecting in return?
    a. Answers may include talent, time, money, in-kind donations, advice, or relationships.

Use the diagram to track your potential key sources:

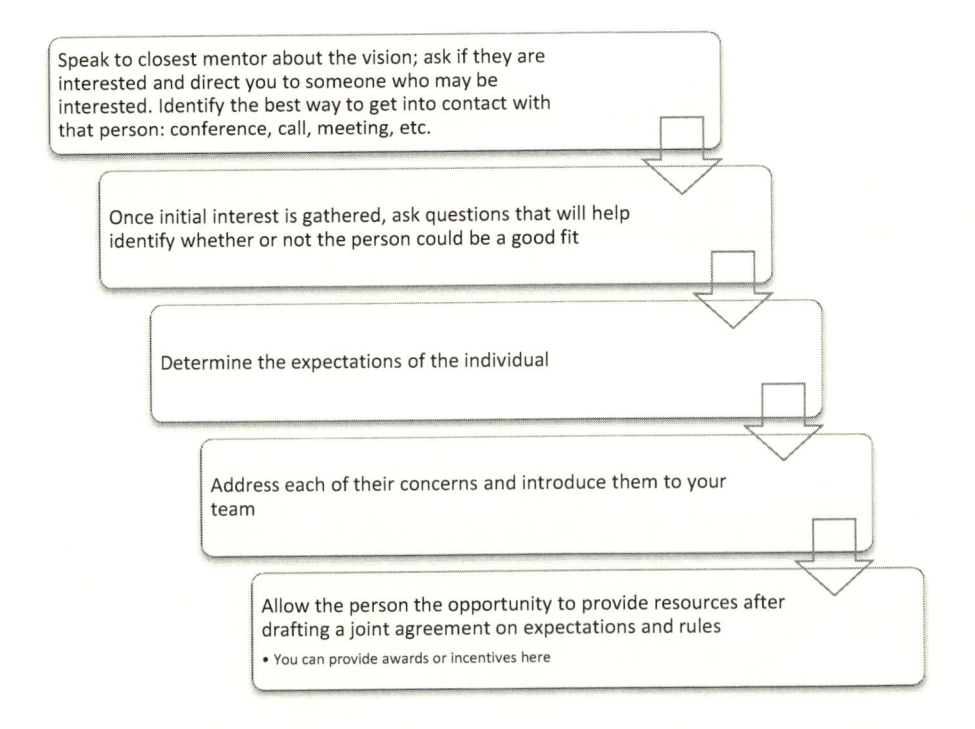

- Speak to closest mentor about the vision; ask if they are interested and direct you to someone who may be interested. Identify the best way to get into contact with that person: conference, call, meeting, etc.
- Once initial interest is gathered, ask questions that will help identify whether or not the person could be a good fit
- Determine the expectations of the individual
- Address each of their concerns and introduce them to your team
- Allow the person the opportunity to provide resources after drafting a joint agreement on expectations and rules
  - You can provide awards or incentives here

D. <u>Operate as a team.</u>

Finally, make sure that you are always operating as a team. When creating a plan maintaining the comfort level of the team is imperative to any success you will realize as an individual and as an organization. As you work to execute each step, remind yourself and your team of all of the steps involved. Make it the culture of the project or the organization, and you will find it very difficult to not be able to adapt and change when new circumstances present themselves.

Your method is important to your success. Create a folder that monitors all of the work you have competed thus far. Identify your problem and vision, plan and specify your targets, and then execute your success using your resources. Remind yourself to revisit your foundation before you grow and when you encounter a problem. For evaluation, which you should perform consistently and especially before growing, use the measurements you selected in the previous chapter.

Category of Measurement	Unit	Result	Change	Reason	Implication

Enjoy the fruits of your labor by translating this into your substantial reality.

Summary

In Summary

Remember the principle of correspondence when encountering problems, and always commit to effective communication. You will find that your community activism will not go without any recognition and your life message will definitely and sincerely impact the systems it partakes in. Use your knowledge about thoughts and manifestation to influence the world around you. Keep in mind the nuances of gatekeepers to gain access to the boundless collection of aggregate resources, and always approach your problems in a win-win manner using the four dimensions of life. Plan your weaknesses, forces, and focuses in accordance with the future, so that you may demonstrate your responsibility as a servant leader and elicit the exact effect of your intention. Pay close attention to the roles you play in order to ultimately achieve your purpose, and concentrate your forces to share with the world your visions and your stories.

Credit is extended to...

7 Habits of Highly Effective People, Stephen Covey

10 Day MBA, Steven Siblinger

33 Strategies of War, Robert Greene

36 Stratagems, Book of Qi, Various Authors

48 Laws of Power, Robert Greene

Abundance, Peter Diamandis and Steven Kotler

The Alchemist, Paulo Coelho

The Arcane Teaching, William Walker Atkinson

Archetypes and the Collective Unconscious, Carl Jung

Arthashastra, Kautilya

Art of Seduction, Robert Greene

Art of War, Sun Tzu

As a Man Thinketh, James Allen

Audacity of Hope, President Barack Obama

Be the Leader You Were Meant to Be, Leroy Eims

The Bible, King James Version, Various Authors

The Black Hole War, Leonard Susskind

Brain Rules, John Medina

CEO Logic, C. Ray Johnson

Decision Points, President George W. Bush

The Elements of Moral Philosophy, James Rachels and Stuart Rachels

The Five Temptations of a CEO, Patrick Lencioni

Game Change, John Heilemann and Mark Halperin

Go Tell it on the Mountain, James Baldwin

How to Win Friends and Influence People, Dale Carnegie

Incidents in the Life of a Slave Girl, Harriet Jacobs

Kabbalah, Various Authors

A Kick in the Seat of the Pants, Roger VonOech

The Kybalion, The Three Initiates, Various Authors

The Masterkey System, Charles F. Haanel

Mind Manipulation, Dr. Haha Lung and Christopher Prowant

Mis-Education of the Negro, Carter G. Woodson

The Neurology of Thinking, D. Frank Benson

Power of the Subconscious Mind, Joseph Murphy

The Prince, Niccolo Machiavelli

The Quran, Various Authors

Rhetoric, Aristotle

The Secret, Rhonda Byrne

A Spiritual Treasury, Kahlil Gibran

Solution Selling, Keith M. Eades

Smart Women Finish Rich, David Bach

To Be Young, Gifted, and Black, Lorraine Hansberry and James Baldwin

Warfighting, U. S. Marine Corps Staff

The Wave, Todd Strasser

The World is Flat, Thomas Friedman

Young Leader, Nick Tarant

These books may or may not have been directly quoted or used, but their considerations were involved in the composition of this book. Some of the content expressed in this book directly contradicts what is within some of the credited books. The materials above were read, some in their entirety and others in piecewise fashion, and then analyzed to devise a way to communicate primary lessons alongside commentary provided by the author. As mentioned in the preface:

> *The philosophy in the book is predicated on the teachings of a broad panoply of literature. Influences from religions, concepts from various philosophers, biographies of the wealthy, and the lessons of the criminalized are all put into perspective in this Library of Philosophy 25 Week Curriculum.*

Bibliography

Carnegie, D. (2009). How to Win Friends and Influence People, Dale Carnegie, Arthur R. Pell, Dorothy Carnegie.

Coelho, P. (2006). The Alchemist, HarperCollins.

Covey, S. (1989). 7 Habits of Highly Effective People.

Covey, S. (1989). 7 Habits of Highly Effective People: Powerful Lessons in Personal Change, Free Press.

Eims, L. (2002). Be the Leader You Were Meant to Be, Chariot Victor Pub.

Gibran, K. (2008). A Spiritual Treasury, Oneworld.

Greene, R. (2000). 48 Laws of Power, Penguin Books.

Greene, R. (2004). "Art of Seduction." 468.

Initiates, T. T. (2008). The Kybalion, Jeremy P. Tarcher/Penguin.

Jung, C. (1981). Archetypes and the Collective Unconscious, Princeton University Press.

Tarant, N. (2005). Young Leader, Inkwater Press.

Woodsen, C. G. Mis-Education of the Negro.